THE RIGHTS OF FREE MEN

The Rights
of Free Men

AN ESSENTIAL GUIDE TO
CIVIL LIBERTIES

---

by Alan Barth

EDITED BY

JAMES E. CLAYTON

ALFRED A. KNOPF

NEW YORK 1984

THIS IS A BORZOI BOOK
PUBLISHED BY ALFRED A. KNOPF, INC.

Copyright © 1983 by The Washington Post Company
All rights reserved under International and Pan-American Copyright Conventions. Published in the United States by Alfred A. Knopf, Inc., New York, and simultaneously in Canada by Random House of Canada Limited, Toronto. Distributed by Random House, Inc., New York.

Library of Congress Cataloging in Publication Data
Barth, Alan. The rights of free men.
Bibliography: p.
1. Civil rights—United States—Addresses, essays, lectures. I. Clayton, James E. II. Title.
KF4749.A2B32 1983   342.73'085   83-47886
ISBN 0-394-52717-8   347.30285

Manufactured in the United States of America
First Edition

CONTENTS

v

Contents

FOREWORD

A few years ago I was watching the finale of a TV "docu-drama" on Senator Joseph McCarthy's nightmarish interregnum in our national life. The young lady interlocutor, gleaming with ex post facto virtue, was saying, "The journalists of those days certainly have a lot of explaining to do." I came as close as I ever have to saluting the little screen with a hard and heaveable object.

Alfred Friendly, colleague of Alan Barth for many rough years on the Washington *Post,* reacted to the program more sensibly, with a *Post* article patiently explaining to the history revisers among the new breed of "advocacy journalists" why the American media in McCarthy's day could not have handled the demagogue and his daily dose of falsehood much differently from the way it was done. I won't recapitulate Friendly's arguments here, though it would be gratifying to set down the long list of journalists in print and broadcasting who stood up to the monster throughout those several neurotic years of slander and threats, of midnight phone calls, lost sleep, lost clients and, for some, lost jobs, savings and health.

Alan Barth was not as prominent as some, because he enjoyed—or suffered—the anonymity of the staff editorial writer. But every sophisticated observer in Washington understood that the unseen author of those graceful, penetrating, relentlessly consistent unsigned essays—reminding us that our civil liberties are their own defense and can be defended, therefore, only as long as we still have them—was a prime mover in the counterattack to McCarthyism. At any rate, many columnists and broadcasters often took their cues from Barth, sometimes without realizing it. And this was true as well through the long years of the struggle for civil rights.

This sweet-natured, tough-minded and elegantly civilized man would be hard to define in the ideological sense. At times he seemed a bit of the political romanticist, a Rousseauan idealizer; at other times, and more so as the years went on, a classical humanist, one who believed as before that order was a means to the great end of liberty, but recognizing that in the America then unfolding, disorder might well be more of a clear and present danger than injustice. That, at least, is how I read him them and read him now in this volume. I would doubt that Barth, during the riotous sixties, ever repeated the left-liberal catch-phrase "Law and order is just a code word for racism." I think he knew that it is a code word for that deepest instinct—social survival.

In any case, he never lost sight of democracy's essential art: the art of balance. The reconciling of order and liberty. The structuring of the political machinery with countervailing forces, to protect man against—himself. Hence the Bill of Rights, which Barth revered and interpreted with an attitude close to absolutism, knowing that absolute absolutism is unreasonable, since truth in the collective affairs of man remains a search.

Washington misses Alan Barth, in person and in print. I miss him, too. Sometimes we argued hard. I like to think I persuaded him that the special governmental restraints on broadcasting, such as the "fairness doctrine," should be held unconstitutional. No one could persuade me that so fundamental a tenet as that of the First Amendment was abridgeable simply because of technological changes in the dissemination of information and ideas.

It would be good to be reading Alan today on this sort of thing. I wonder if he would still feel that America's ethnic diversity is the source of its strength, or merely of its cultural richness, and may end up seriously weakening our national cohesion. I wonder if he would still think that on the world scale freedom is indivisible and peace is indivisible, or if he would be coming regretfully to the conclusion that they are both divisible and will coexist with tyranny and war as they have through so much of human history.

I would love to know what he makes of the current domestic political scene. I never asked him about his party preference, though I presume he voted mostly Democratic. I think he would agree that we can't simply repeat the old New Deal, but that the heirs of that remarkable generation must not lose their humaneness. He would be watching the present torment of the Democrats as they try to think out new definitions of progress and "the American way of life." I have an idea that Alan Barth would be tossing out a notion or two that might give them something to chew on. More—something to grow on.

Eric Sevareid

"Individual freedom is a means, an invaluable means, toward national security and survival. But it is an end as well —— the supreme end which the government of the United States was instituted to secure."

ALAN BARTH
1906–1979

CIVIL RIGHTS

CIVIL LIBERTIES

©1979 HERBLOCK

INTRODUCTION

Alan Barth was a fortunate man who happened to live at the very time the nation needed his mind and his pen. Born in New York City in 1906, he studied at Andover and Yale, apprenticed as a badly miscast contractor in New York, a newspaper reporter in Beaumont, Texas, a newspaper correspondent in New York City and Washington, and a federal civil servant. In the middle of World War II, he found his niche as an editorial writer for the Washington *Post*.

For the next thirty years—through the era of virulent anti-Communism spawned by the Cold War of the 1940s and '50s, the battles over desegregation of the '50s and '60s, and the revolution in the criminal law of the '60s and '70s—Alan Barth preached a simple message of faith in democracy, trust in the American Constitution, and generosity toward all human beings. His work during those years—in the *Post* and elsewhere—brought him national recognition. He was a Nieman Fellow at Harvard (1948) and a visiting professor at Montana State University (1957)—now the University of Montana at Missoula—and the University of California at Berkeley (1958–59). He was honored with awards from the Sidney Hillman Foundation, Sigma Delta Chi, the American Newspaper Guild and the National Capital Area Civil Liberties Union. He was cited for outstanding journalistic contributions by the Education Writers Association, Americans for Democratic Action, the District of Columbia branch of the NAACP and the Washington Area Council of the American Veterans Committee.

What really mattered, however, was that his rhetoric on the subject most basic to free government—freedom of speech—and on the subjects most essential to happiness under any government—equality and fairness—lifted the hearts and pricked the consciences of thousands of Americans. His editorial essays in the *Post,* unsigned as is its practice, reached most of the nation's political leaders daily, delighting or outraging them depending upon their personal predilections. His five books and many speeches and magazine articles spread the same messages to a wider audience. To a generation of college students, his first book, *The Loyalty of Free Men,* provided an antidote to the view that free speech was incompatible with national security and that those who disagreed with prevailing views on national policy were, *ipso facto,* traitors or otherwise un-American.

As the fear of Communist subversion at home waned, Barth turned his efforts in other directions, focusing on desegregation and on the modernization and liberalization of the criminal law accomplished by the Supreme Court under Chief Justice Earl Warren. Barth believed that the protections contained in the Bill of Rights and the Fourteenth Amendment should be rigorously enforced and expanded not only because they are part of the Constitution but because they are essential to the "liberty" which that Constitution was created to provide for all citizens. In editorials, speeches and books, he tried to explain why everyone's rights are endangered if one person's rights are curtailed and why the scales of justice and policy must tip toward individual freedom when that freedom comes into conflict with police procedures or with community sentiment.

Two editorials, written more than two decades apart, summarize Barth's indomitable faith in America and its people:

BILL OF RIGHTS*

The men who drafted the Bill of Rights, adopted 158 years ago today as the first Ten Amendments to the Constitution, subscribed to the political philosophy that governments are voluntarily instituted among men to secure certain "natural rights" and that they derive their just powers from the consent of the governed. Thus the government they created was one of limited powers. The Bill of Rights was designed as an explicit definition of some of the limits imposed. It protects certain areas of human behavior from governmental interference—even if such interference is sanctioned by majority consent of the governed.

Thus, no matter what the wishes of the electorate, Congress may make no law respecting an establishment of religion, or abridging the freedom of speech or of the press or the right of the people peaceably to assemble. The federal government may not conduct unreasonable searches and seizures, nor try any person for a capital or otherwise infamous crime without an indictment by a grand jury, nor deprive him of life, liberty or property without due process of law. These and other prohibitions enumerated in the Bill of Rights were designed to keep the newly created federal government within appropriate bounds.

With the adoption of the Fourteenth Amendment shortly after the Civil War, the most important of these prohibitions became binding upon the states as well. Recent Supreme Court interpretations of the due-process clause of this Amendment have made the federal government, paradoxically, the champion and protector of the people against arbitrary state interference in the very areas from which it was itself barred by the Bill of Rights. . . .

*Editorial, the Washington *Post,* December 15, 1949. *Post* editorials will subsequently be referenced only by date.

Despite these limitations on its powers, the government of the United States has remained for more than a century and a half the strongest and most stable government on earth. Indeed, the limitations have been the wellspring of its strength. For they have made possible the diversity, the conflict of ideas, the realization of individual potentialities, the orderly adoption of political and economic change which are indispensable to the functioning of the democratic process and to the maintenance of a genuine national unity. The individual rights derived from the limitation of governmental power are not, therefore, mere luxuries. They are utilitarian. They have served the American people magnificently well. And those who would diminish them today in the name of national security would do well to remember that they have been the essential sources of security throughout this nation's history.

FAITH IN ONE ANOTHER
October 3, 1971

When the founders of the American Republic dissolved the political bonds that connected them with the British people and signed their names to the Declaration of Independence, they had as yet no country to which they could pledge their allegiance. For the support of this Declaration, they declared instead, "we mutually pledge *to each other* our Lives, our Fortunes, and our sacred Honor." That kind of faith in each other served as the cement of the American society for 175 years.

In the 1950s, however, Senator Joseph McCarthy began to make a cult of distrust among Americans. Fear of Communism, fear of subversion, fear of non-conformity—fear of each other—replaced mutual confidence to a terrifying degree. The superb self-confidence that had been an identifying trait of Americans all but disappeared. Instruments such as the Subversive Activities Control Board and the House Committee on Un-American Activities were forged to keep an official eye on Americans, to search out disloyalty among them, to penalize unpopular opinions and associations, in short, to protect the people from themselves.

It was always a funny thing about the heresy-hunters that they never supposed that they themselves were going to be subverted by Communist propaganda or by other dangerous ideas; it was always and only the loyalty and good sense of their fellow-countrymen that they doubted. They had so little confidence themselves in the gospel according to Thomas Jefferson that they were forever fearful that "ordinary" Americans would easily be won over to the gospel according to V. I. Lenin. They had so little faith in freedom as a way of life that they could never bring themselves to rely upon the free institutions established by the American Constitution.

The bluntest instrument of the heresy-hunters was the Subversive Activities Control Board. A menace to individual liberty at its inception, this clumsy agency collapsed of its own ineptitude as soon as the political health of the American people began to be restored. It was in a state of innocuous, if costly, desuetude when President Nixon, for some unexplained reason, chose this summer to revive it by giving it a thoroughly totalitarian duty to perform—the compilation of lists of officially disapproved organizations which Americans could join only at their own political peril.

That inveterate believer in freedom, Sam Ervin, has taken another swing at the Subversive Activities Control Board and the odious task the President has assigned to it. In a recent speech to the Association of American Publishers the Senator gave a moving expression of his own faith in Americans and in the American dream. "I affirm my faith," he said, "in the sanity and steadfastness of the overwhelming majority of all Americans. I shall not fear for the security of my country as long as love of liberty abides in their hearts, and truth is left free to combat error."

That faith needs to be restored to America. It is time for us to take a new pledge of allegiance *to each other.*

I have attempted in this book to distill, from the seven or eight million words Barth wrote, the philosophy he believed in and its application to contemporary problems. The subjects on which he focused during the half-century ending in 1979 are as vital today as when he first began to write; they will probably still be just as vital after another fifty years. The tactics used by the FBI in its ABSCAM investigation, the limitations proposed on the Supreme Court's power to overturn criminal convictions by state courts, the tuition tax credit suggested by President Reagan, the details of the new charters for the FBI and CIA, the proposed constitutional amendment authorizing prayers in the public schools, the re-establishment of capital punishment, are all today's versions of old and recurring issues. Each generation must debate these issues anew and in resolving the questions that arise must decide how much, if any, personal freedom to sacrifice for the sake of national security and domestic tranquillity. This book owes its existence to my belief that Alan Barth's message is as important to Americans seeking answers to such questions now as it was to other Americans in earlier decades.

Reducing millions of words into one volume has not been easy. Much has been left to sleep in the files, including a host of pieces that might make you laugh or cry. They are superb examples of the editorial writer's art, but focus on myriad day-to-day subjects unrelated to the essence of Barth's philosophy. I have used editorials and signed newspaper articles as much as possible, partly because writing editorials was the core of Alan's professional life and partly because they are the least accessible and most perishable of his writings. The *Post* made this possible by waiving its long-standing rule of anonymity for editorial writers.

Editorials are by nature short and focused on an immediate problem. Their timeliness often makes them period pieces; yet, they are the best examples of the application of philosophy to real, not theoretical, issues. One caution: at the *Post,* at least, an editorial may well reflect a composite view which is not exactly what the author would have written solely for himself. Thus, there are small, and essentially unimportant, conflicts between what Alan

Introduction

wrote when he was speaking for the *Post* and when he was speaking, in books or magazine articles or bylined newspaper columns, strictly for himself. These are the gives he had to make in the daily give-and-take at a newspaper whose editorial policy is vested in a board composed of men and (in his day only a few) women of differing views.

There is no better introduction to Alan's works and to how those who knew him (I was among those who worked beside him for years) regarded his efforts than the editorial published by the *Post* upon his death in 1979:

ALAN BARTH

November 21, 1979

Alan Barth, who died yesterday at the age of 73, was more than just our colleague on this editorial page for over a quarter-century. He was also our friend. That personal entanglement with him, a mixture of admiration and love, makes impossible the cool, objective appraisal we normally try to present here of the lives of people who have been important in the region or the country. Instead, we want to try to tell you why Alan Barth was a very special person to us and why we think the world in which we all live is better because of him.

When Alan joined the staff of the editorial page in 1943, he had a reputation as a staunch supporter of civil rights and civil liberties. . . . When he retired in 1972, his reputation had grown enormously and . . . his views on desegregation, equal rights, freedom of speech and a host of other issues had become, by and large, our views. His insistence on standing up for the constitutional rights of every American, no matter how difficult that might be, had become our insistence. His imprint on editorial policies in those matters is so deep it can never be erased.

We like to think—and you can judge for yourself whether it is true—that these views made a difference not only to this newspaper but to this city and the country. Alan's voice was

xvii

Introduction

the voice of reason, arguing—before it was popular—for peaceful desegregation of the schools, for equal rights for everyone, for protection of the rights of criminal defendants and witnesses before congressional committees, for the widest possible interpretation of that great guarantee of "free speech," and against guilt by association. He stated the case for these positions passionately in hundreds of unsigned editorials and in a stream of books and bylined articles that made his name better known to a generation of college students than it was to our readers. In time, many of the things he argued for came to pass, although some are still a matter of strenuous debate. His professional career, we think, was a remarkable example of the ability of one man to influence the way all men think.

It was not always easy, either for Alan or for this newspaper, to be at the cutting edge of such controversies. The accusations made against us and him, personally, were often quite bitter. Words like "pinko," "pro-Communist" and "nigger-lover"—in the days when those were still part of the debased currency—were thrown at him during the McCarthy days and the original school-desegregation fights. Alan never flinched and his support for the causes in which he believed never wavered. We concede that others on this newspaper were sometimes deeply concerned about the road down which he was taking us. But when it was suggested he had gone too far, that he had defended the rights (as distinct from the deeds) of one too many criminals or political pariahs, he would merely smile that wry smile and start all over again the process of persuading others that the rights of no American are safe unless the rights of all Americans are safe.

Alan never controlled the editorial policies of this newspaper even on those subjects; control rested elsewhere. But he dominated them by persuading his colleagues, through scholarship and force of intellect, that he was right. He was helped, and directed, by his ability to find just the right phrase or just the right quip to bring laughter to a heated internal argument. But it was hard to maintain a disagreement with a man who had distilled so much of the learning of the country's great scholars and judges. There were, however, subjects on which his views did not dominate our policies. When such subjects came up in our daily conferences, he seemed to love the exposure of our differences almost as much as he loved their resolution in his favor. His joy, in other words, was almost as great in intellectual combat as in victory.

That is part of what made Alan so special to us. The rest is strictly personal. He was a man who loved life and people. Those whose personal lives crossed his, as ours did, were enriched by the encounter. He was gentle and kindly, full of wit and humor, always ready to offer help and whatever you might need. He surrounded himself with friends of all kinds. You could find them at his home in the evenings and on weekends—eating, playing softball and, above all, gabbing. You never knew when you went just what to expect or whom you might see, but you did know that when you left you would be glad you had been there.

Oliver Wendell Holmes, Jr., one of those whose writings greatly influenced Alan, once wrote of what he regarded to be the best service one could do for his country or for himself:

"To see so far as one may, and to feel the great forces that are behind every detail—for that makes all the difference between philosophy and gossip—to hammer out as compact and solid a piece of work as one can, to try to make it first rate, and to leave it unadvertised."

We cannot think of a more fitting epitaph for our colleague and friend.

My thanks go to Adrienne Barth, who conceived the idea of reprinting Alan's work; to Donald E. Graham, publisher of the *Post,* and Anthony M. Schulte, executive vice-president of Random House, who made this book possible; and to John P. MacKenzie of the *New York Times,* whose persistence brought us all together. Mark Hannan, librarian of the *Post,* and the staff of the Manuscript and Archives Division of the Yale University Library made their files easily accessible.

Permission to reprint copyrighted material has been graciously granted by Mrs. Barth, the Viking Press, the Beaumont (Tex.) *Enterprise & Journal,* and the University of Colorado.

Alan Barth's words speak for themselves. I have supplied only introductory material and an occasional bit of historical context. Otherwise, what follows is his, changed only to correct obvious errors and to produce a uniform style.

JAMES E. CLAYTON
Arlington, Virginia
August 1983

THE RIGHTS OF FREE MEN

ONE

The Loyalty-Security Cases

It is hard now to remember and reconstruct the mood of America in the decade immediately after World War II. The unconditional surrender of the Axis Powers and the birth of the United Nations had created a hope that friendship and cooperation would replace aggression as the world's way of life. When this hope evaporated as the Cold War began and the Iron Curtain closed off eastern Europe, fear gripped the American people—fear that international Communism would gobble up the United States as it had gobbled up eastern Europe and China, fear that enough Americans would espouse this alien doctrine for it to control the nation, fear that the Soviet Union would steal the secrets of the atomic bomb. Nurtured by the discovery that some Communist agents had infiltrated the government and spurred on by politicians in search of other Communist agents—or of newspaper headlines—the nation indulged in an orgy of Communist-hunting.

This hunt was not conducted by the executive branch of government and its then-renowned Federal Bureau of Investigation, which had quite successfully protected the nation against Axis agents during the war. Instead, it was carried out by the legislative branch; the executive—most particularly the State Department—was portrayed by the new subversion-hunters as a hotbed of Communist agents and American-born Communist-sympathizers. Congressional committees and subcommittees turned their full-time attention to rooting these people out of government.

These investigations might have been highly useful if they had been confined to a search for Communist agents or for those in government whose primary loyalty was not to the United States; there were spies to be found and dislodged. But the investigations were not so confined. The investigators, knowingly or unknowingly, confused dissent from current government policies with disloyalty and defined Communism as encompassing almost every political view that disagreed with their own or was to the left of center. Then they undertook to remove from any position of influence in American society every person, every project, every book that was tinged with Communism as so defined. Thus, the nation's universities, private foundations and libraries, its clergy and its world of entertainment—particularly Hollywood—became prime targets. Persons who had nothing to do with the making or execution of public policy were judged by the same standards of political orthodoxy applied to those who worked at the heart of the national security apparatus.

The names of the chairmen of these investigating committees—McCarthy, Jenner, McCarran, Walter, Dies, Velde—became household words. Newspaper headlines and that new information source, television, reported their investigative exploits daily. Their technique rarely varied: a committee would call as a witness a contrite former Communist, praised by the investigators as a patriot because he had recanted an alien belief. (A few of these witnesses turned out to have invented much of their testimony to please the investigators.) He would testify that he once knew X as a Communist, or that someone had once told him X was a Communist. X was then called as a witness and asked, among other things, if he was then or ever had been a Communist.

Some people admitted having had something to do with Communism—often in the 1930s, when they were students or just out of college. They were then required to detail their Communist activities and tell the investigators the names of everyone they had ever met or heard discussed in Communist circles.

Other witnesses denied that they were or had ever been Com-

4

munists and insisted they had never had anything to do with Communist organizations. Their denials were rarely accepted by the committees, and they were usually threatened with perjury charges because their testimony conflicted with that of the committees' original witnesses. Only occasionally could any person named as a Communist or Communist-sympathizer at one of these hearings ever clear his name—however frail the evidence against him—either before the committee or in the press.

Some witnesses simply refused to answer the questions. Either they claimed their Fifth Amendment right not to answer potentially incriminating questions, or they claimed a nebulous First Amendment right to freedom of speech and association, or they asserted that a congressional committee had no business prying into the personal political beliefs of any American citizen. Those claiming the Fifth Amendment right were dubbed "Fifth Amendment Communists"; those who claimed other reasons for refusing to answer were often prosecuted for contempt of Congress.

As this orgy dragged on, some Communists were flushed out. Many times that number of government officials, professors and entertainers—the favorite targets of investigators—were humiliated and defamed and lost their jobs even though the only thing ever proven about their political beliefs and activities was that somebody said they were once seen at some Communist function or interpreted something they had once written as being "soft on Communism."

The response of the executive branch to this onslaught from Capitol Hill did not do it, or American traditions of fair play and justice, much credit. It adopted an employee loyalty-security program that came to rely heavily on accusations from unidentified informants as evidence and to resolve all doubts about the credibility of evidence or the loyalty of a particular employee in ways that labeled him or her a "security risk." It frequently bowed to pressure from the congressional investigators to oust from any job any employee those investigators wanted ousted. After first resisting the attacks from the committees, the executive branch came, in time, to be so fearful of the investigators and their ability to make the most loyal administrators look disloyal that it joined in the hunt, at least in some departments, with reckless abandon.

Strange and disturbing things happened to American law during those years. Although it had been no crime to be a member of the Communist Party—its candidates for political office had appeared on the ballot in several states—or to sympathize with its platform, the investigators and most citizens regarded those who were or did as "guilty." The presumption of innocence was rejected; persons accused of being Communists or "Com-symps" were presumed guilty unless they could prove otherwise—even though proving a negative is extremely difficult, especially about political views held a decade or two in the past. The Fifth Amendment right not to answer incriminating questions was transformed into a test of guilt or innocence; although its purpose is to make accusers prove their charges by independent evidence, the investigators asserted that only the guilty claimed it. The idea of free speech was emasculated; individuals were condemned as "un-American" not for what they did but for what they said if that happened to differ from the ideological orthodoxy of the investigators.

Throughout this era, Alan Barth was one of the most vocal opponents of those who would curtail civil liberties at home to fight international Communism. He believed that America was not ripe for revolution, that most Americans still believed in democracy and free speech, and that Communism could not survive in America when confronted by the principles of free government in an open marketplace of ideas. He stoutly opposed Communism as a philosophy or a principle of government. But he feared that America was on its way to adopting the tactics of Communism—guilt by association, denial of free speech, controlled education, punishment by executive act or legislative decree—in its effort to repulse the philosophy itself. He fought, in the editorial columns of the *Post* and elsewhere, against denigration of civil liberties by the investigators and for re-establishment of the traditional values contained in the Bill of Rights.

From the dozens of investigations and individual "loyalty" cases Barth wrote about, six may reveal the extent to which this effort to root out Communism had permeated the nation. Two of these concern institutions—one which was a part of government (American libraries overseas) and one which had been separated traditionally from government (American universities at home). The others concern individuals. One of these involved a man with no connection at all with the government or with national security—Maurice Chevalier, the French entertainer. Another involved a man whose only connection was musical—Albert Sprague Coolidge, a math teacher and oboe player. A third involved an obscure disabled veteran—James Kutcher. Their only common ties were that each had done something someone else regarded as disloyal and suffered for it. Yet each was representative of a class of individuals whose private lives and past actions were brought into question in the name of improving national security. The fourth case is different.

Of all those ensnared in the loyalty investigations, Professor Owen J. Lattimore, then on the faculty of Johns Hopkins University, stood alone. He was regarded as one of the nation's leading experts on China and central Asia when he was singled out by Senator Joseph McCarthy in 1950 as "one of the top Communist agents in the country." Lattimore denied the charge vigorously and bitterly. During the next five years, he was brought before one investigating group after another. His denials never wavered, and not one shred of solid evidence was ever produced that he was a Communist agent or a Communist or even sympathized with the Communists in their desire to control the world. The most that could fairly be said against him was that he had underestimated or misunderstood the Communists who gained control of China. Perhaps he was pursued so long and so diligently because he had the audacity to challenge the patriotism as well as the intelligence of the Communist-hunters themselves.

NOT A SECURITY RISK

MAY 3, 1951

The renowned French comedian Maurice Chevalier appears to be a man somewhat unstable in his political judgments and unsettled as to principle. He prefers, as do many men, to hunt with the hounds. The French underground charged him with having collaborated with the Nazis during the war. And since the war, he has, it seems, been far from unfriendly to the Communists. Nevertheless, he has virtues as an entertainer, and some people would like to hear him sing. It is hard to see how his presence in the United States would endanger the national security.

He has been denied a visa to come here as a visitor, however, in part, according to Secretary [of State Dean] Acheson, because his name has been constantly mentioned with favor in Communist newspapers. The reason strikes us as a very unsatisfactory—and, indeed, a very dangerous—one. It puts into the hands of the Communist press a formidable weapon, enabling it to damn with praise anyone whom it wishes to destroy. Communist condemnation is not necessarily proof of virtue, and Communist approbation is not an infallible test of vice.

Mr. Chevalier has been charged additionally with having signed the Stockholm peace petition, with having sung for an organization which later handed its profits to a Communist affiliate and with having taken part in meetings organized by pro-Communists. Such actions afford good grounds for individual unwillingness to attend his performances. But they do not afford good grounds for denying him freedom of movement. Only considerations of national security should bar from the United States persons otherwise eligible for admission. If we exclude aliens simply because we do not like their opinions, we shall be imitating one of the worst of Communist characteristics.

8

BOOK-BURNING

JANUARY 7, 1953

The investigation of American colleges and universities projected by Senator McCarthy and Representative Velde presents those institutions with a magnificent opportunity to accomplish some most important adult education. We hope the opportunity will be grasped—affirmatively and forcefully—to explain to the American public the real nature and the real social utility of academic freedom. If the faculties and officials of colleges and universities grasp this opportunity effectively, they can do much to check the current onrush of know-nothingism symbolized by Messrs. McCarthy and Velde.

The effort of these legislators to purge American institutions of non-conformist teachers and to lay down standards of political purity operates, and is no doubt intended to operate, as a powerful form of intimidation; it limits the freedom of teachers to set ideas before their students and thus limits the ability of teachers to discharge their vital function. Academic freedom—that is, security of tenure and protection against outside censorship or coercion—is no mere luxury or privilege conferred upon the teaching profession. It is a form of assurance to society that the teaching profession will be able to do its job conscientiously. . . .

The educators had better recognize the McCarthy and Velde investigations for what they are—attacks upon intellectualism and upon freedom of the mind. And they had better join hands in meeting those attacks. . . .

Neither Senator McCarthy nor Representative Velde, nor any other member of Congress for that matter, has any special qualifications for investigating American colleges. These investigations amount, in substance, to a species of book-burning. They ought to be resisted on principle—as fiercely as the burning of books would be resisted, and with as little reference to the merits of the individual teachers to be purged as would be given to the merits

9

of the individual books to be burned. Educators are peculiarly the trustees of intellectual freedom. It is this freedom itself that is now imperiled and this trusteeship that they are now called upon to vindicate.

FREEDOM TO READ

JULY 2, 1953

What has happened in libraries flying the flag of the United States in foreign lands casts an ominous shadow upon libraries flying that flag in its homeland. No kind of fire spreads with more terrible rapidity than a fire kindled by the dry, inflammable pages of books and fueled by the heady, explosive stuff of ideas. No kind of fire is so dangerous to matters of the mind. No kind of fire so grimly threatens the whole structure of freedom. . . .

The democratic process by which we live, and which it is the function of American information activities overseas to extol, is a process of intellectual conflict—rooted in a confidence that when ideas are put in competition before free minds, the fitter will survive. It is perhaps no great cause for astonishment, in a time of national anxiety and confusion, with a new administration just taking over the reins of office, that subordinate employees of the State Department should have forgotten or ignored these principles. If this were all that happened, the banning of a few hundred "controversial" books in overseas information libraries might be dismissed as an unfortunate bureaucratic error.

Much worse than the banning of the books, however, has been the complacency with which the administration has treated this bureaucratic error. The Secretary of State has found little more to say on the subject than that only a very few books were actually burned. The President, having spoken at Dartmouth with electrifying fervor about the horrors of book-burning in the abstract, gave the impression at a press conference a few days later that he condoned the concrete instances of book-banning in the State

Department's overseas libraries. At his conference yesterday, Mr. Eisenhower recovered some of the lost ground; he indicated at least a concern about the situation—but without the sense of moral outrage that is to be expected of an American President.

It is this apathy—this failure of indignation and protest—which confuses and confounds the civilized world. A lynching is always an ugly and an evil thing in itself; but if it were to be condoned by responsible authorities, the very foundation of society would be corrupted. It is time—indeed it is past time—to let the world know unequivocally that the United States of America does not condone intellectual lynching.

MAJESTY OF THE LAW

DECEMBER 24, 1955

Few Americans, we think, can read the story of James Kutcher . . . and not weep for their own country. James Kutcher lost both his legs fighting for the United States in a battle at San Pietro, Italy, in 1943; he had previously gone through the campaigns at Kasserine Pass and Bizerte, at Turino and at Volturno. But because he was, and continues to be, a member of the Socialist Workers Party, an anti-Soviet, Marxist organization which the Attorney General of the United States listed as subversive in 1947 without any notice or hearing, Kutcher was thrown out of his job as a postal clerk. And then the Veterans Administration notified him that he was to be stripped of his veteran's pension, the sole means of livelihood for himself and his aged parents. . . .

The charge against him, in addition to membership in the Socialist Workers Party, is that, according to an unidentified informant, Kutcher at some time in 1950 or 1951 made what someone considered disloyal remarks about the United States government. What has freedom of speech come to in this land if men are to be deprived of rights on such a charge and on such evidence as this! What has the majesty of the United States descended to when a crippled veteran can be so hounded and harassed in the name of national security! Perhaps the only words fit for this folly are words peculiarly appropriate to the season: "Forgive them, Father; for they know not what they do."

ANTISEPTIC CHAMBER MUSIC

FEBRUARY 2, 1956

The pinnacle of patriotism has now been achieved by the Library of Congress. Albert Sprague Coolidge has disclosed that the library recently asked him to withdraw his acceptance of an invitation it extended to him two years ago to serve as an adviser of the Coolidge Foundation established by his mother, the late Elizabeth Sprague Coolidge, in 1926. The foundation . . . has made the Library of Congress pre-eminent in chamber music and has brought the work of great musicians to all parts of the country.

The reason the invitation was withdrawn, apparently, was that the FBI report on Mr. Coolidge produced "derogatory information" to the effect that he belonged to so-called "front" organizations. Mr. Coolidge, who is an amateur oboist and viola player and a lecturer on chemistry at Harvard University, says that one organization to which he belonged that is on the Attorney General's list was the North American Committee to Aid Spanish Democracy. There has been no Spanish democracy to aid for about eighteen years.

It is not easy to see how the security of the United States could be much imperiled by letting this amateur oboist—even if he was politically unsophisticated—serve as an adviser to the Library of Congress on chamber music. The injury done to the prestige of the United States by denying him the position is readily apparent, however. And it is made the more ludicrous and the more damaging because the action comes from the Library of Congress, which is supposed to be the repository of America's intellectual heritage and best traditions.

What are we doing in the United States with this sort of sick silliness? The FBI is a very good police force; but it is not a very good judge of viola players. Disqualification of a man as an adviser on chamber music on the grounds of political unorthodoxy was standard operating procedure among the Nazis and is still in vogue among the Communists. But it has never until now been accepted in the United States. Let's go back where we came from.

McCARTHY'S EVIDENCE

APRIL 2, 1950

The "evidence" furnished by Senator McCarthy in support of his accusations boils down on examination to additional accusations. How does he know that Owen Lattimore is a Soviet agent? Somebody, unidentified of course, told him so—or told him, at least, that he had information to this effect from someone else, also unidentified. The whole of his long harangue to the Senate on Thursday is so fuzzy, so founded on imputation of guilt by association and so dependent on undisclosed affidavits by anonymous sources of unknown reliability that there is nothing for one to take hold of.

The Senator said, for example, "I also have the name of a witness which I am turning over to the Federal Bureau of Investigation. This witness has been used by the Justice Department as a Government witness in another matter. . . . He will testify that Owen Lattimore was known to him to be a member of the Communist Party, a member over whom they had disciplinary powers." It would seem a fair presumption that the FBI already has the testimony of this witness, has investigated it and has found it to be erroneous. It is precisely because of the danger that disproved allegations would be misused in this way that the director of the FBI has been unwilling to make the raw material in his files available to congressional investigators.

Mr. McCarthy has another document from an anonymous source

asserting that Mr. Lattimore was "very obviously receiving instructions from the Soviet government concerning the line which the Institute of Pacific Relations ought to follow." This informant, said the Senator, "gave his consent to his name and this statement being given to the FBI. . . . We had to promise him, however, that his name would not be given to the committee." But Mr. McCarthy wants to force the FBI, by subpoena, to turn over to the committee its entire confidential file on Mr. Lattimore in which the name of this informant would, of course, be included!

Without knowledge of the sources of the Senator's information, without anything more, indeed, than his own vague paraphrasing of the nature of the information, how can reasonable men accord it any weight against the tremendous mass of candid testimony by known persons of the highest repute in support of Mr. Lattimore's integrity and loyalty? What the Senator has offered is a very far cry from the promise he had made to the Foreign Relations Subcommittee that he would "check all the information, document it, and give it to you." The information remains unchecked, undocumented and unavailable. If Attorney General McGrath is our guide, the Senator's "documents" "have fizzled so far as producing any spies" is concerned.

A MAN STANDS UP

APRIL 7, 1950

Owen Lattimore, an American fighting like an American in the open, came before the Tydings Subcommittee yesterday and defended himself against slander. There was not a point in the allegations made against him by Senator McCarthy from the protection of the Senate floor that he failed to rebut with vigor and evidentiary detail. There was not a single poisonous slur by hidden, anonymous defamers that he did not expose and ridicule. His performance was not so much a defense as an attack. The position of United States Senator, he said, "carries with it a responsibility which this man Joseph McCarthy has flagrantly violated." And he enumerated the violations:

He has violated it by impairing the effectiveness of the United States Government in its relations with its friends and allies. . . . He has violated it by instituting a reign of terror among officials and employees in the United States Government. . . . He has without authorization used secret documents obtained from official Government files. He has vilified citizens of the United States and accused them of high crime, without giving them opportunity to defend themselves. . . . He has invited disrespect to himself and his high office by refusing to live up to his word. Twice on the floor of the Senate he stated that any charges that he made under the cloak of immunity, he would repeat in another place so that their falseness could be tested in a court of the United States. He said that if he should fail to do this he would resign. He has been called to repeat his charges so that they could be tested in a court action. He has failed to do so. And he has not resigned.

Dr. Lattimore revealed the sordid operations of the "China Lobby" back of Senator McCarthy which the Department of State has been too timorous or too circumspect to lay bare, even in answer to newspaper inquiry. He showed the striking parallelism between Senator McCarthy's charges and the propaganda of this lobby. He disclosed the planned campaign to destroy anyone who challenged this propaganda. He made plain how the Senator was "being used as the simple dupe of a group of fanatical persons who have been thoroughly discredited." And he unmasked the motives of this band of paid and unpaid propagandists and stooges, a band that is a cabal, with influence not only on Capitol Hill but also in key posts of government.

But the most important part of what Dr. Lattimore said to the Senate subcommittee yesterday was not said in his own defense.

It was said in defense of the ancient right of Americans to speak their minds on public issues without having their patriotism impugned. This is a right that is something more than a personal privilege. Its preservation is a matter of the highest utility to the nation. It is an indispensable factor in a system of government by the consent of the governed. Dr. Lattimore's concluding words on this subject deserve restatement:

> I say to you, gentlemen, that the sure way to destroy freedom of speech and the free expression of ideas and views is to attach to that freedom the penalty of abuse and vilification. If the people of this country can differ with the so-called China lobby or with Senator McCarthy only at the risk of the abuse to which I have been subjected, freedom will not long survive. If officials of our government cannot consult people of diverse views without exposing themselves to the kind of attack that Senator McCarthy has visited upon officers of the State Department, our governmental policy will necessarily be sterile. It is only from a diversity of views freely expressed and strongly advocated that sound policy is distilled. He who contributes to the destruction of this process is either a fool or an enemy of his country. Let Senator McCarthy take note of this.

Senator Tydings' decision to hold future hearings in executive session is a wise one. It is time for the Senate of the United States to cease giving the protection of its immunity to contemptible personal abuse of the kind Senator McCarthy has launched. It is time for the Senate to put an end to a corruption of the democratic process undertaken in its name.

THE McCARTHY RECORD

MAY 2, 1950

Dr. Owen Lattimore's clearly deserved rebuttal appearance before the Tydings Subcommittee today should bring an end to the public, or circus, phase of the inquiry into Senator McCarthy's charges. Thereafter, we hope, the subcommittee will retire into the closed sessions with which it should have undertaken its task from the beginning. Perhaps, then, this is a suitable juncture to recall the original McCarthy charges, although the Senator seems anxious to have them forgotten.

The initial charge came in a speech at Wheeling, West Virginia, on February 9. "I have here in my hand," Mr. McCarthy was quoted as saying, "a list of 205 that were known to the Secretary of State as being members of the Communist Party and who nevertheless are still working and shaping the policy of the State Department." This was followed by a telegram to President Truman asserting, "I have in my possession the names of 57 Communists who are in the State Department at present." Then, in a four-hour speech to the Senate, February 20, Senator McCarthy declared: "I have approximately 81 cases . . . the names are here." On that occasion, he outlined the cases without disclosing the names, insisting that he had all the data necessary to support his charges. "I shall be willing, happy, and eager," he said, "to go before any committee and give the names and all the information available. I shall refuse to give the source of the information, however."

It can scarcely be recalled too frequently, moreover, that in the same Senate speech Mr. McCarthy made the following categorical statement: "I will not say anything on the Senate floor which I will not say off the floor. On the day when I take advantage of the security we have on the Senate floor, on that day I will resign from the Senate. Anything I say on the floor of the Senate at any time will be repeated off the floor." Since then, he has named individuals and accused them of atrocious crimes, taking advantage of the security of the Senate. But he has conspicuously failed to repeat the accusations outside the Senate's immunity. And he has not yet resigned.

In his appearances before the Tydings Subcommittee, Senator McCarthy did not provide the information to support his indictment of the 205 or the 57 or the 81. He pleaded that he could not prove his charges unless the FBI would prove them for him by surrendering the confidential investigative records which the President had previously forbidden the agency to surrender. And at last he said he would let his whole case stand or fall on the validity of his accusations concerning Dr. Lattimore, whom he called at first the "top espionage agent" in this country and ended by describing as a "bad policy risk."

Dr. Lattimore, it should be remembered, is not and never has been an employee of the State Department. He is a private citizen, recognized throughout the academic profession as one of the foremost authorities on the Far East, who has occasionally submitted memoranda, in response to State Department requests, concerning policy in the area of his experience. Senator McCarthy's case against him rests primarily on the opinions Dr. Lattimore expressed—opinions with which the Senator happens to disagree, although many of them have been abundantly vindicated by events.

Two facts appear to be plain concerning the Lattimore case. One is that it can prove nothing whatever about the validity of Senator McCarthy's charges that there are 205 or 57 or 81 Communists in the State Department. The other is that the Senate of the United States has no business conducting a trial and passing judgment on the "loyalty" of a private citizen. Of course, if this involves the crime of espionage, then such a case should be referred to a grand jury. However, Senator McCarthy has apparently abandoned this charge.

In view of the misrepresentation of Dr. Lattimore as a State Department employee and the extravagance of the charges made against him under the Senate's immunity, the Tydings Subcommittee was under an obvious obligation to allow him the opportunity to reply in public. It is now under obligation, as a matter of elementary justice, we think, to give Dr. Lattimore a speedy and unequivocal vindication, and in view of the wide mischief and alarm that have been caused, to make a ringing declaration in behalf of the freedom of inquiry which has been gravely threatened by the Lattimore case.

DAY IN COURT

FEBRUARY 27, 1952

For eight months Owen Lattimore has waited for a chance to refute in public charges made concerning him before the Mc-Carran Subcommittee. That chance, which seemed at last to have been accorded him yesterday afternoon, was systematically frustrated by subcommittee members. Mr. Lattimore had prepared a statement fifty pages in length, refuting point by point the attacks on his conduct and character. The hearing began at 2:30 p.m. By 3:40 he had managed, in face of innumerable interruptions, to read two paragraphs of what he had come to say. When the hearing recessed at five o'clock he had completed no more than four and a half paragraphs.

The reason for this hostility appears to be that Mr. Lattimore has had the hardihood to stand up to the committee like a man—to stand up to it in an old-fashioned and thoroughly American way. He refused to cringe; he refused to placate; he felt deeply aggrieved by the injuries inflicted on him as a result of the committee's hospitality to former Communists and professional informers, and he said so in his prepared statement with more vigor than diplomacy.

Surely, having borne so much, he is now entitled to be heard in his own defense. But a drumfire of questions, coming without any semblance of order or pattern from half a dozen subcommittee members as well as from the Judiciary Committee's counsel, made any coherent spoken statement from Mr. Lattimore impossible. These questions seemed to have no other purpose than to impede his testimony. They left the impression that the subcommittee was much more interested in heckling and embarrassing this witness than in discovering the truth about his role in the Institute of Pacific Relations.

Virtually all the accusations about him made before the McCarran Subcommittee had been made two years ago by Senator McCarthy and by witnesses before the Tydings Subcommittee. The Tydings Subcommittee, after exhaustive investigation, vindicated him as completely as any congressional body could. Small wonder that he is now doubtful of the McCarran Subcommittee's impartiality and indignant at its whole procedure.

Mr. Lattimore's prepared statement—let us hope that eventually he will be permitted to read it all to the committee—is less a defense of himself than a defense of the right of students and scholars—of free men in general—to think, to write, to report to their government in conformity with the dictates of their own judgments and consciences. This is not only a basic American right; it is the basis of American security. As Mr. Lattimore hopes to be allowed to say for the record, "We must be ever alert to encourage, and not to destroy, freedom for the vigorous expression of views, even of wrong views; and freedom for our private institutions, as well as our official personnel, to make their contributions to the formation of policy and the determination of our destiny. This is the essence of democracy, and it is democracy's strength. It must not be destroyed."

ORDEAL BY EXHAUSTION

MARCH 8, 1952

In the nine consecutive days during which Owen Lattimore has been in its power, the McCarran Subcommittee has revealed a clear and deliberate pattern of procedure. It is not, in our judgment, a pattern designed to get at the truth; it is not a pattern which conforms to American standards of fair play; and it is not a pattern which reflects credit upon any congressional committee. We submit four observations concerning it.

1. The subcommittee has given to Mr. Lattimore, and to other witnesses before it, the semblance but not the substance of the right to counsel. Mr. Lattimore has been accompanied at the hearings by an able and highly esteemed member of the local bar. But this lawyer has been allowed to do little more than remain in the room. He has been forbidden to cross-examine the witness or even to suggest questions to be asked by committee members. He has been forbidden to advise the witness on his own initiative, or to object to questions which he may consider improper. The most he has been able to do is to whisper an opinion when his client turns and publicly asks his advice on a point of law. This is a procedure which makes a mockery of the right to counsel.

2. The subcommittee appears to be bent upon entrapment of the witness. Its studied method is to ask him to recall events, conversations and correspondence a decade or more in the past; and then, when he suffers the slightest lapse or inaccuracy of recollection, the subcommittee counsel comes up triumphantly with something from the files which, in the interest of getting at the facts, should have been shown to the witness before the question was asked. This kind of stacking of the evidence is exacerbated by a bullying insistence on the part of committee members that questions involving subtle shades of meaning be answered with a flat yes or no.

3. The subcommittee persists in viewing opinions, actions and associations of a decade or more ago as though they had taken place in the context, and with the full knowledge, of the contemporary situation. It wholly ignores the fact that a man might conscientiously have been less suspicious of possible Communist sympathies on the part of an associate in 1938 than he would be in 1952; that a man might reasonably have viewed the Chinese Communists in one light in 1945 and in quite another later on, after their enmity to the United States had been demonstrated. There is much merit to the old maxim that "circumstances alter cases."

4. The subcommittee seems determined to beat Owen Latti-

more into sheer physical exhaustion, to make fatigue and despair extort admissions which he would not make of his own free will. When Mr. Lattimore pleaded fatigue and asked for a respite the other day, Senator McCarran said the members of the subcommittee were tired, too. The subcommittee with half a dozen members and two staff lawyers, all acting as prosecutors, has been able to question this lone witness in relays. For nine days it has subjected him to an incessant drumfire of interrogation—in a process uncomfortably like that which the Russians so commonly employ to break down innocent men. He has stood up to it well enough and will go back on Monday for more. But it is a frightening spectacle, as one foreign journalist put it, to see a committee of the United States Senate bully and torment a witness in this fashion— as though he were in an arena, at bay, providing sport for the public. Perhaps the subcommittee chairman, Senator McCarran, needs to be reminded that bullfighting, so popular in Spain, has never had much appeal in the United States.

TARDY JUSTICE

JUNE 30, 1955

Attorney General Brownell's decision to drop the long-standing perjury charges against Owen Lattimore is decidedly welcome and praiseworthy even though it is tragically belated. The decision brings to a clear conclusion a case that should never have been brought into the courts—a case that will remain for a long time a black mark on the record of the Department of Justice. The courts, recognizing its emptiness, were obliged repeatedly to rebuke the department and its prosecutors. The dropping of the charges represents, therefore, not only a final acknowledgment of error by the department but a real victory for the principles of justice under law which Judge Luther Youngdahl and the Court of Appeals expounded.

"No man has ever been more relentlessly persecuted by a congressional committee," said Elmer Davis,* "than Owen Lattimore by the Internal Security Committee under Senator McCarran." For twelve days on end, members of the committee and their counsel grilled him in turn about incidents which occurred ten or twelve years earlier, checking his recollection against documents which they had seized and refused to let him see, until at last they led him into trivial errors which the Department of Justice made the basis of a perjury indictment. No charge of perjury was lodged against Mr. Lattimore for his categorical denial that he had ever been a Soviet agent or a Communist. Instead, the department devised charges so vague that Judge Youngdahl and the Court of Appeals called them invalid, together with some subsidiary charges so frivolous that Mr. Brownell has now acknowledged that they afforded "no reasonable likelihood of a successful prosecution."

Mr. Lattimore is now lecturing in Europe, where a number of universities have honored him with invitations. The treatment accorded him by universities at home, and particularly by his own university, Johns Hopkins, has been less fortunate. For five years his professional career has been interrupted and his reputation as a scholar has been impugned. . . . The only amends that can be made to him must lie in an end to the kind of persecution for opinion of which he was an unhappy victim.

THE INVESTIGATING POWER
OF CONGRESS†

. . . I think that no one ought to talk critically of congressional investigations . . . without a clear recognition at the outset that

*Elmer Davis was the most distinguished of the early radio newsmen.
†From a speech on December 4, 1954, at Mount Holyoke College, South Hadley, Massachusetts. It was published in mimeograph form as part of an Intercollegiate

they have a vital and tremendously useful role to play in the work of the United States Congress. The power to investigate is an indispensable companion of the power to legislate. No legislature could operate as an effective law-making body without this power; it would be not much more than a forum for the adoption of resounding resolutions. I think, too, that the power to investigate must be given a broad definition—that it must be viewed as something more than a mere incident to law-making. It serves two different, though related, functions. First, it gives Congress a means of studying the matters about which it wishes to adopt laws; it provides the legislature, as Senator Fulbright put it, "with eyes and ears and a thinking mechanism." Since the function of law is to correct inequities and to control anti-social actions, Congress could scarcely legislate at all without first obtaining knowledge of the conditions it aimed to correct and control.

Second, the power to investigate gives Congress a means of imposing an effective check on the power of the executive branch of the government. The law-making power of Congress would be a nearly empty one if it did not imply also a right to call the executive to account for the administration of the laws. . . .

Congressional use of the investigating power . . . [however] has sometimes been frivolous and sometimes mischievous. It has produced excesses and is now, I think, threatening to undermine the nature of the American political system. But it has also produced great benefits and been responsible for valuable reforms. It would be as foolish to condemn the investigating power because it is now and then abused as it would be to condemn, say, the idea of freedom of the press because some newspapers sometimes behave irresponsibly. The proper limits of the investigating power are hard to define—and still harder to enforce. But the power remains an indispensable one.

Let us look now at some of the current uses of the investigating

Symposium on Freedom vs. Security by the Lecture Committee of Mount Holyoke College. Barth delivered essentially the same speech on March 5, 1954, at Sweet Briar College, Sweet Briar, Virginia, and on March 11, 1954, at the University of Nebraska, Lincoln, Nebraska.

power. The thesis that I want to set before you . . . is that the power is being employed today by certain committees of Congress in such a way as to threaten a congressional tyranny. Under the guise of investigation, certain committees are undertaking to perform functions that are obviously administrative—and obviously in the jurisdiction of the executive branch of the government. And they are undertaking also, at times, to perform functions that are obviously judicial—such as placing individuals on trial, judging and punishing them. . . .

Let me offer a specific example of congressional intrusion into the domain of the executive branch. About a year and a half ago—on March 28, 1953, to be accurate—the chairman of the Senate's permanent investigating subcommittee announced that he had negotiated an agreement with the Greek owners of 242 merchant ships to stop trade with North Korea, Communist China and Russia's Far Eastern ports. The announcement produced headlines of which the chairman was indubitably the hero.

"Negotiation" and "agreement" were the words he used. Furthermore, he stressed the point that the "agreement" had been concluded with no collaboration whatever from executive agencies of the government, the State Department included. "I didn't want any interference by anyone," the chairman said. At the same time, he accused the State Department of "dismal failure" in its efforts to reduce shipping to Communist ports.

Well, obviously, if business of this kind is to be transacted by a congressional committee, there is really no need to maintain a large bureaucratic establishment such as the Department of State. But there are two considerations which argue against congressional discharge of so characteristically executive a function.

One is that the congressional committee simply does not have the detailed knowledge, the trained personnel, the detachment from immediate political pressures required for this sort of business.

The other consideration is that if policy were to be carried out by the same branch of the government that authorized it, there would be no check upon performance, no counter-balancing of power. The concentration of executive and legislative powers in a single set of hands would lead inescapably to uncontrolled—which is to say, tyrannical—authority. It was against this danger that the authors of the Constitution tried to protect the American people by divorcing legislative from executive power.

Yet more and more in recent years congressional committees, on the pretext of investigation, have been taking over the active management of executive affairs. They have, for example, virtually dictated the operation of the Voice of America abroad. They have, for all practical purposes, undertaken to decide what books shall be on the shelves of overseas information libraries.

Through "investigation"—I am using the word now in quotation marks—congressional committees have purged the Far Eastern Division of the Foreign Service of almost everybody who ever incurred the displeasure of the China Lobby—which is to say, of almost everybody who had any knowledge of the Far East. . . .

Legislative invasion of the judicial domain, through abuses of the power of investigation, is even more flagrant than the legislative invasion of the executive domain—and even more menacing. It takes the form of legislative trials—trials conducted, as Abe Fortas, a distinguished Washington attorney, said of them, with "no standards of judgment, no rules, no traditions of procedure or judicial demeanor, no statute of limitations, no appeals, no boundaries of relevance, and no finality. In short, anything goes; and everything frequently does—and often on television."

The job of a congressional investigating committee is to look into broad general problems. This is a job for which rather rough and ready, informal procedures are entirely suitable. It is a radically different job from the job entrusted to courts of law—determination of whether an individual is guilty or innocent of a specific crime with which he has been precisely charged. The job entrusted to a court of law—the judgment of an individual—can be properly and fairly carried out only by strict observance of the procedural safeguards contrived by civilized men for the administration of justice and summed up in the phrase "due process of law."

Congressional committees are well adapted to judge general questions and badly adapted for the judgment of individual cases. . . .

But the plain fact is that the whole trend of congressional investigation, ever since the House Committee on Un-American Activities was first established in 1938, has been in the direction of trying individuals. And the fact is, also, that the trend has been to try them for offenses which are not criminal—and which Congress could not constitutionally declare criminal. In short, the investigating power has been used—consciously and cynically—to punish men by publicity for conduct which is not punishable by law.

The investigating power has been used to punish men for thinking "dangerous" thoughts, for having "dangerous" associations, for expressing "dangerous" ideas.

Consider, for example, a statement made just the other day by Representative Francis E. Walter, who is to become the chairman of the House Committee on Un-American Activities in the next Congress. He plans, he said, to hold large public hearings in industrial communities and to subject suspected Communists to the full glare of publicity.

"We will force these people we know to be Communists to appear by the power of subpoena," Representative Walter declared, "and will demonstrate to their fellow workers that they are part of a foreign conspiracy." And he added this observation: "I have every confidence that the loyal Americans who work with them will do the rest of the job."

Think about this for a moment. It is nothing less than an incitement to riot and an encouragement of lynch law.

The use that Mr. Walter plans to make of the investigating power has nothing to do with gaining information to help the lawmaking function of Congress. It has nothing to do with supervising or checking the executive branch of government. Its purpose is to punish men by publicity—to subject them to a kind of trial without any semblance of due process, without any of the protections to which they would be entitled in a court of law, and to expose them to mob violence.

This is not investigation. And it is not justice, either, in any sense in which Americans have understood the term. It is, in fact, a subversion of the Constitution more dangerous than anything within the power of Mr. Walter's victims. It is a negation of the concept of a government of laws.

There has been no impartiality, no judicial detachment, in this process. The prosecutors have been the judges and the jury.

There has been no semblance of due process. Former Communists and professional informers have been encouraged to spew hearsay and opinion under the protection of congressional immunity. Mere association has been taken as evidence of guilt and mere accusation as positive proof.

There has not even been respect for the role of the courts. Men have been deliberately goaded into behavior which could be prosecuted as contempt of Congress or entrapped into denials which could be prosecuted as perjury. And they have been subjected to so much publicity that it is no longer possible for any court to accord them a fair trial in the old-fashioned sense of the term. . . .

[The power of investigation] has been used, in addition, it seems to me, in a still more dangerous fashion to invade an area traditionally reserved in the United States for non-governmental management. . . .

It has taken . . . [governmental authority] into the conduct of the great philanthropic foundations—and has had a chilling influence on their willingness to encourage unorthodox experimentation or research. Yet the special function of these foundations is to foster new ideas, new approaches, new ways of doing things— to make unorthodoxy possible because it is the only avenue to progress.

The power of investigation has been used to intrude governmental authority into American churches—a domain from which the founders of the nation sternly barred it. A congressional committee has presumed to hale ministers of religion before it and question them concerning matters of belief which involved no violation of law and concerning which they were accountable only to their parishioners, their ecclesiastical colleagues and their God. . . .

On the pretext of investigation, a congressional committee has summoned the editor of a newspaper and questioned him about his editorial policies. The First Amendment to the Constitution guaranteed freedom of the press because the authors of the Constitution desired the press to serve as one of the elements in the system of checks and balances they contrived to keep governmental authority within proper bounds. But of course if newspaper editors are to be haled before a congressional committee and interrogated every time they criticize the government, the guarantee of press freedom will come to mean very little. . . .

Finally, committees of Congress have undertaken to investigate our institutions of higher learning. They have, to be sure, merely presumed to purge college faculties of professors they considered undesirable. But it is of the very essence of academic freedom that the selection and qualification of faculty members be in the hands of their professional colleagues. . . .

What I am trying to tell you is very simple: I believe that abuse and distortion of the investigating power is threatening to establish in this country a legislative tyranny. It is threatening to overthrow the American form of government by upsetting its tripartite balance of powers and usurping the powers reserved to the people.

This is not a novel notion of mine. The men who founded the American Republic feared the development of a legislative tyranny and endeavored to guard against it. Madison warned in *The Federalist* that "The accumulation of all powers, legislative, executive, and judiciary, in the same hands, whether of one, a few, or many, and whether hereditary, self-appointed, or elective, may justly be pronounced the very definition of tyranny."

Madison and his associates in the Constitutional Convention of 1787 understood well enough that tyranny need not necessarily come from a single dictator on horseback. Madison pointed out "the danger from legislative usurpers, which, by assembling of power in the same hands, must lead to the same tyranny as is threatened by executive usurpations."

And he declared, indeed, that "it is against the enterprising ambition of this department [the legislative department, that is to say] that the people ought to indulge all their jealousy and exhaust all their precautions." . . .

"Tyranny," I acknowledge, is a large and loaded word. Perhaps you think me extravagant and alarmist in resorting to it. Perhaps you are right about it.

But tyranny is best averted by attention to its early symptoms. Free men need to take alarm when arrogance manifests itself among their elected officials—when men of intellect are ridiculed and disparaged, when ministers of religion are denounced and derided, when even heroes wearing the uniform of their country are humiliated and vilified by an individual wearing the cloak of legislative authority.

It would be folly to ignore such symptoms. Complacency is the mother of servitude. . . .

TWO

The Loyalty of Free Men

During the winter of 1950–51, with the hunt for Communists approaching its zenith, Alan Barth's first book was published. Widely hailed in book reviews, *The Loyalty of Free Men* became a source of inspiration for those who shared Barth's belief that investigators who equated dissent from government policies with disloyalty were threatening to destroy the diversity of political opinion which lies near the soul of America. It also became standard reading in many universities and colleges, where it was regarded as the most forceful statement in print of the civil-libertarian viewpoint. Of course, the book was bitterly denounced by those who believed that the threats of international Communism and internal subversion were so serious that traditional American values of free speech and fair play had to be compromised to save American democracy.

The Loyalty of Free Men has two elements. The first is a persuasive argument for maintaining freedom of speech and of thought in a free country. The second is a careful and comprehensive report on what the Communist-hunters had been doing and how they had swept through the government. This stands, thirty years later, among the best accounts of how the investigators worked. It owes its lasting impact, however, to the interplay between particular contemporary events and the philosophy of free government set out in Barth's first chapter. That philosophy, drawn from Milton and Mill, Madison and Jefferson, Holmes and Brandeis, is timeless because every generation, or so it seems, must learn for itself the values of liberty and freedom.

The book catapulted Barth onto the lecture circuit. Two subjects on which he often focused were loyalty oaths and academic freedom. The loyalty oath was a curious invention. Most government workers had long been required to take an oath in which they swore (or affirmed) they "will bear true faith and allegiance to the United States of America and will support and defend the Constitution and laws of the United States of America against all its enemies, foreign and domestic." Although no member of the Communist Party could truthfully make that declaration, this oath was regarded by the Communist-hunters as insufficient evidence of loyalty to the United States. To it they added a second oath, required of many government workers and used by some private employers, under which individuals had to swear "that I do not believe in, and am not a member of and do not support any organization that believes in or teaches the overthrow of the United States Government by force or violence or by any illegal or unconstitutional methods." Nobody ever explained why those who swore both oaths were deemed more loyal than those who swore only the first, or why any member of the Communist Party who perjured himself by taking the first oath would hesitate to take the second one. Yet, there seemed to be some magic about the new oath that assured the Communist-hunters of the oath-taker's loyalty. In a speech before the national convention of the American Association of University Professors in 1951, Barth detailed the absurdity, uselessness and offensiveness of these new, as he called them, "non-disloyalty oaths."

Two years later Barth was back before the professors with an even more somber message. In the summer of 1953, the Senate Internal Security Subcommittee, headed by Senator William Jenner, had set out to expose the "Soviet conspiracy hidden in our schools and colleges." Several universities and colleges responded by disciplining, through suspension or dismissal, any faculty member who did not fully cooperate with the subcommittee. A few, with Harvard and Sarah Lawrence leading the way, refused to respond so unthinkingly to the committee's charges, and considered independently and individually any accusations it or its witnesses made against their faculty members.

Barth saw the episodes as an attempt by the congressional Communist-hunters not only to drive out of the colleges teachers who preached Communism to their students but also to assume the power of determining who was fit to teach. He made the case before the professors, and before many other groups, that academic freedom only exists when the academic community, not the government, decides who shall teach.

There were other issues. Among the most important were the denial of passports to would-be travelers and the use of anonymous informers in the government's loyalty-security program. The former was used to keep distrusted citizens at home and to keep all citizens from visiting certain countries; at one time in the mid-'50s, passports were stamped as invalid for travel to China, Albania, Bulgaria, North Korea, North Vietnam, Israel, Jordan, Egypt and Syria. The latter had become commonplace in security cases. Individuals were denied clearances, and thus jobs, on the basis of information supplied by persons unknown not only to them but often to the officials charged with evaluating the information; sometimes even the information itself was undisclosed, so no rebuttal was possible. Barth believed that both these practices violated basic concepts of American liberty and, indeed, the Constitution itself.

THE CULT OF LOYALTY*

The relation of the individual to the State—or of individual liberty to national security—is the crucial issue of our time. The emphasis in this relation marks the essential distinction between a total-

*Chapter I, *The Loyalty of Free Men*, Viking Press (1951), copyright, 1951, by Alan Barth. (Footnotes omitted.)

itarian society and a free society. A totalitarian society emphasizes the supremacy of the State, seeking national security through
rigid governmental control of individual activity and expression.
A free society emphasizes the supremacy of the individual, relying for its national security upon a democratic adjustment of diverse
views and interests and upon the freely accorded devotion of its
constituents.

The function of national security in a totalitarian society is to
preserve the State, while the function of national security in a free
society is to preserve freedom. Those who established the American Republic counted freedom among man's "unalienable" or
"natural" rights and believed that it was in order to secure these
rights that governments are instituted among men. But there is a
looseness about freedom that makes it seem hazardous to security.
It involves an inescapable element of risk. There have always been
men everywhere who viewed it skeptically as a luxury to be
enjoyed only within prescribed limits and when the nation is not
subject to any external threat. It is commonly in the name of
national security that individual liberty is lost.

· · ·

This is by no means to suggest that national security can be
neglected. The institutions of liberty are under attack. They are
threatened by an aggressive totalitarianism abroad, and they need
the protection of a strong and resolute government. If that government should fall, the institutions of liberty would fall with it. In
some measure, too, the institutions are threatened in novel ways
by agents of that totalitarianism at home. They are threatened
most of all, however, by well-meaning and patriotic but frightened
Americans who have come to think of liberty as a liability rather
than an asset.

The error of these men is that they confuse loyalty with orthodoxy. Acting upon this confusion, they tend to suppress diversity
and to insist upon a rigid conformity. But loyalty may take as
many forms as religious worship. This much about it seems indisputable: like love, it must be freely given. It can be evoked, but it
cannot be commanded or coerced. Members of a family are loyal

to one another, not through any oath or compulsion, but as a result of shared experiences, community of interest and long mutual dependence. A great aggregation of individuals and families becomes and remains a nation, not through geographical propinquity alone, but rather through much this same process of shared experiences—which is to say, a common history—and, above all, through common acceptance of certain fundamental values. The national loyalty of free men is not so much to their government as to the purposes for which their government was created.

The United States, which is the supreme example of national union by voluntary compact, is peculiarly illustrative of the point. Founded by men committed to the idea that the just powers of government are derived from the consent of the governed, it began as an experiment. The vast American wilderness was populated by men and women who came to it voluntarily from a more settled world, desiring to participate in the experiment. Thus, a pledge of allegiance to the United States was essentially a pledge of allegiance to a political ideal. This ideal is, to be sure, very difficult of expression and susceptible of varying interpretations. But its kernel may fairly be said to lie in the concept of a society affording the widest possible scope for the realization of individual potentialities.

"The American compact," Walt Whitman wrote, "is altogether with individuals." Certainly respect for the individual personality is among the most settled and generally extolled of American principles. This is a respect necessarily rooted in the recognition, tolerance and even encouragement of diversity. This country has grown to greatness on the premise that wide diversity of interest and opinion is not only consistent with loyalty but essential to the generation of it. The only genuine loyalty is the loyalty of free men.

The United States was established as a nation by men whose national loyalty was rooted elsewhere. Most of them had been born and bred in allegiance to the English crown. They were divorced from this allegiance and from divisive sectional loyalties only by common adherence to certain overriding ideas and values. There were no national traditions, no national heroes, no national history to unite them. When they dissolved the political bonds that connected them with the British people and affixed their names to the Declaration of Independence, there was no nation to which they could pledge devotion; for the support of this Declaration, they said, "We mutually pledge *to each other* our Lives, our Fortunes, and our sacred Honor."

The new nation they created became an embodiment of the ideas they shared. It drew devotion not because of its past but because of its promise. The Constitution which made it a Federal Union guaranteed freedom of expression and of conscience. The constitutions of its constituent states had already provided similar guarantees. Freedom and opportunity were its dynamic elements. They were the elements that evoked loyalty and cemented union and afforded the matrix of growth.

The tolerance on which freedom and opportunity must rest was a necessity of early life in America. Conquest of a continental wilderness fostered a tradition of individualism. The opening of successive frontiers widely different in physical conditions and in the problems of settlement encouraged a variety of political forms. Differences of religion, of social background, of economic interest among the settlers required tolerance of diversity. Out of this necessity the early Americans made a virtue. The idea that they had raised a standard to which the lovers of liberty could repair became a source of tremendous pride to them. "This new world," Thomas Paine boasted in *Common Sense,* "hath been the asylum for the persecuted lovers of civil and religious liberty from *every part* of Europe."

It was tolerance of diversity that made possible the union of thirteen disparate colonies. It was tolerance of wide differences in religious faith and cultural background that enabled America to absorb and gain enrichment from the great variety of immigrants seeking opportunity and freedom here. Opportunity and freedom were sufficient to make loyal Americans of the newcomers. There was never, until very recently, much fear that those who came to this country, let alone those who were its native sons, could grow up in American homes, attend American schools, play American games, join in the robust rivalry of American life and turn out disloyal to America. "It was nothing to us," Congressman Page of Virginia contended in 1790 in support of a liberal naturalization policy, "whether Jews or Roman Catholics settle among us; whether subjects of Kings, or citizens of free States wish to reside in the United States, they will find it in their interest to be good citizens, and neither their religious nor political opinion can injure us, if we have good laws, well executed." Whatever may have been the vices and weaknesses of this country in the past, want of confidence in itself was not among them. The nation knew that the American dream would inspire all who had a chance to dream it.

But that sublime self-confidence has now disappeared. Aliens are suspect; there is no longer the old certainty that they will be swept into the mainstream of American life. Prospective immigrants must prove that they are not the bearers of contagious opinions, and even transient visitors are feared. In 1950 the State Department denied visas to the Dean of Canterbury and later to twelve members of the Communist-sponsored World Congress of Partisans for Peace, Pablo Picasso among them, because of their political and economic views. The faith of Americans in their own institutions is apparently no longer considered strong enough to withstand Communist propaganda. Eminent artists have been barred merely because their political sympathies were suspect. The German conductor Wilhelm Furtwängler was kept out because he had collaborated with the Nazis. Later Josef Krips, the conductor of the Vienna State Opera, was forbidden to fill a summer engagement with the Chicago Symphony Orchestra because he had previously conducted performances at Moscow and Leningrad. Tolerance of diversity and faith in the democratic process are giving way to reliance on the quarantine of hostile doctrines.

Indeed, even those born into the American heritage are now only tentatively trusted; they are obligated to affirm and reaffirm their allegiance. And beyond this ritual of affirmation, in the potency of which there is no longer any confidence, they are commonly required before entering upon any post affecting the national interest to deny disloyalty. Anyone who goes to work for the government of the United States today must swear that he does not advocate its overthrow. In point of fact, Congress thought it necessary in 1940 to make it a penal offense for any citizen to teach or advocate the duty or necessity of overthrowing "any government in the United States by force or violence."

A terrible distrust lies behind this shift to negativism. The country's doubts about the loyalty of its citizens are not unlike the doubts of a husband about the fidelity of his wife. The protestations that answer his doubts are never convincing and are likely to dissipate the mutual confidence that is the essence of a marriage. When men lose faith in one another, they lose the substance of what constitutes a community among them. Thus, to a national community, there is nothing that so dangerously corrupts its integrity as such a loss of faith. As in the case of the suspicious husband, this distrust is the expression of a neurotic insecurity.

Such insecurity is perhaps the most pervasive characteristic of our time. The fear of freedom and the difficulties of realizing its potentialities have been illuminatingly treated by the psychiatrists and the social psychologists. They have contributed invaluable insights of which political theorists have as yet made too little use. The forces that have led great numbers of Europeans and Asiatics to seek the fellowship of disciplined submission to authority as an escape from the responsibilities and isolation of freedom are at work here too. They exhibit themselves in the exertion of powerful pressures, cultural as well as political, toward conformity and in an attitude novel among Americans that they can neither comprehend nor change the awful tides in which they feel themselves engulfed. The consequence is a stultifying tendency to seek unity through uniformity.

"Loyalty" has become a cult, an obsession, in the United States. But even loyalty itself is now defined negatively. It is thought of not so much in terms of an affirmative faith in the great purposes for which the American nation was created as in terms of stereotypes the mere questioning of which is deemed "disloyal." The whole post-war accent is on something called "un-Americanism"—a hyphenated synonym for unorthodoxy. Deviations to the Left are regarded as more suspicious or criminal than deviations to the Right; but the tendency is to question all deviations. "Loyalty" consists today in not being un-American, which is to say, in not being different or individualistic. The very diversity which was the wellspring of loyalty in the past is now distrusted.

The term "disloyalty" as it is commonly used today is nothing more or less than a circumlocution for treason. The authors of the Constitution went to a great deal of trouble in dealing with the subject of treason because they knew from experience how readily the term can be twisted to make discontent or dissent, or mere criticism of the government, a major crime. They took care, therefore, to define treason in the narrowest terms. "Treason against the United States," they declared in Article III, Section 3, of the Constitution, "shall consist only in levying war against them or in adhering to their enemies, giving them aid and comfort." No acts other than those specified in the Constitution can be made treasonable by legislation. Congress can neither extend, nor restrict, nor define the crime. Its power over the subject is limited to prescribing the punishment.

The Constitution is no less exacting as to the means by which conviction of treason may be obtained. "No person shall be convicted of treason," Section 3 continues, "unless on the testimony of two witnesses to the same overt act, or on confession in open court."

James Madison explained in Number 43 of *The Federalist*—that brilliant exegesis of the Constitution characterized by Thomas Jefferson as "the best commentary on the principles of government which ever was written"—the reasons that prompted the Constitutional Convention to define treason so narrowly and to make conviction of it so difficult:

> As treason may be committed against the United States, the authority of the United States ought to be enabled to punish it. But as new-fangled and artificial treasons have been the great engines by which violent factions, the natural offspring of free government, have usually wreaked their alternate malignity on each other, the convention have, with great judgment, opposed a barrier to this particular danger,

by inserting a constitutional definition of the crime, fixing the proof necessary for conviction of it, and restraining the Congress, even in punishing it, from extending the consequences of guilt beyond the person of its author.

There is a whole lesson in political science in this paragraph—a lesson peculiarly applicable today. The use of "disloyalty" as a "new-fangled and artificial" form of treason has indeed promoted the rise of violent factions and led to a wreaking of "their alternate malignity on each other." There is no way to measure the impairment of national security that has resulted from this disruption of the sense of national community.

Disloyalty, to be sure, has not officially been held to constitute treason. But when a congressional committee or a quasi-judicial government board says that an individual is disloyal—or that he is un-American, or subversive, or a security risk, or ineligible for employment by the United States, or any of the other circumlocutions of the circumlocution—it is saying in not very euphemistic terms, or at least is encouraging the public to believe, that he is a traitor. The difference is that disloyalty is nowhere to be found detailed as a crime upon the statute books, that nowhere has it been defined, that nowhere has a punishment been prescribed for it by law. This ambiguity merely makes the charge more difficult to avoid and a condemnation less difficult to obtain.

Real disloyalty presents a threat to national security. It might find expression in betrayal of the nation—even in espionage or sabotage. Of course these are statutory crimes, clearly defined and punishable through the normal processes of indictment and trial by jury. The law can easily be used to punish any actual spy or saboteur. But the law can no more be used to punish a potential spy or a potential saboteur than it can be used to punish a potential pickpocket or a potential embezzler. The law punishes specifically prohibited anti-social acts. It does not prohibit and cannot punish anti-social ideas or intentions. The distinction has always been considered basic to a free society.

In a period of international tension, however, a potential spy or saboteur is likely to seem very dangerous—so dangerous that there is enormous temptation to deal with him outside the law. The United States, engaged in a world-wide struggle that has led to armed conflict in Asia,* has yielded to this temptation to an alarming degree. It has devised an elaborate system and ritual for punishing men—and punishing them most cruelly—for crimes they have not committed but are suspected of desiring to commit. It punishes them by stigmatizing them as disloyal.

Anyone so stigmatized becomes to some degree an outcast. If he retains any friends, he knows himself to be a menace to them. Any association with them may result in their stigmatization too. Wherever he goes he is marked as a man who would be willing to betray his country. He remains at large but is regarded as a menace to society. He is expatriated without being exiled and denied the opportunity to gain a livelihood without the compensation of being maintained in prison at the community's expense. He and his fellows might come, in time, to constitute something new in American life—a caste of untouchables.

The punishment in such cases is something like that in the old story about the Quaker and his dog Tray. " 'Go to,' said the Quaker to poor Tray. 'I will not kill thee, but I give thee a bad name,' as he turned him into the streets with the cry of 'mad dog,' and somebody else did kill Tray."

Perhaps the punishments meted out on the ground of disloyalty are not too severe for anyone who clearly and demonstrably intends to serve the interest of a foreign government to the detriment of his own countrymen. The fact is, however, that these penalties are meted out without any of the safeguards embodied in the Anglo-American system of justice for the protection of innocent persons against unjust conviction. They are inflicted on the loyal and the disloyal almost without discrimination.

By the simple stratagem of charging a man with disloyalty, instead of with treason or espionage or sabotage, it is possible to evade the constitutional requirements that he be indicted by a grand jury, that he enjoy a speedy and public trial by an impartial petit jury, that he be informed of the nature and cause of the

*Korea—Ed. note.

accusation and confronted with the witnesses against him, that he be accorded the benefit of compulsory process to obtain witnesses in his favor. He is indicted and tried and sentenced by congressional committee or administrative tribunal, with the same men acting as prosecutors, judges and jury. The presumption of innocence supposed to surround him is ignored. The mere charge of disloyalty is treated as evidence of guilt. . . .

[I]t is the press which executes, so to speak, the sentences passed by congressional committees or by mere individuals speaking under the immunity from suits for slander or libel afforded by Congress. Newspapers especially tend to make headlines out of accusations and to treat denials less prominently. This stems in large measure from the concept of news as sensation and is scarcely less true of those newspapers that strive for objectivity than of those that deliberately use their news pages to serve editorial biases.

The tradition of objectivity, which is the great virtue of the American press, has operated in this context to make the press an instrument of those seeking to inflict punishment by publicity. Allegations which would otherwise be ignored because they would be recognized as groundless and libelous are blown up on front pages and given a significance out of all relation to their intrinsic merit after they have been made before a committee of Congress. Thus, what is one day properly regarded as unpublishable gossip is treated the next day as news of great moment because it has been uttered under official auspices. Refutation, no matter how compelling, never catches up with charges of disloyalty and never erases their imprint. In addition, of course, many newspapers welcome such charges and inflate them for political reasons or for their commercial value in stimulating street sales.

The cost of this system of punishment by publicity is worth reckoning. It entails sacrifices not only for the individuals who become involved in it, but also, on a wider scale, for the society as a whole. If all the elements of due process can be thus evaded, the personal security of individuals in the United States from arbitrary and summary punishment becomes a fiction. One result is to heighten the general insecurity of which this evasion of constitutional safeguards is a symptom.

The short-cut to punishment has an effect on society in other ways as well. The knowledge that men may be accused and found guilty of disloyalty in so summary a manner becomes a restraint on the exercise of constitutional rights. It is no longer safe to talk recklessly or foolishly. If the effect of this were no more than to silence recklessness and folly, perhaps the loss would not be great. But the discouragement of reckless and foolish talk tends inescapably to suppress sound and sensible dissent which may seem unpatriotic because it happens to be unpopular.

The trouble with putting any halter upon individual freedom to talk nonsense—even subversive or seditious nonsense—is that it tends to frustrate the democratic process. That process is one in which nonsense cannot be silenced by authority; it can be silenced, or overcome, only by sense. Since it is often not altogether easy to distinguish between the two, silencing of the one cannot help but result in silencing of the other. What happens, of course, is that unorthodox ideas, whether sensible or not, are suppressed in favor of orthodoxy. And consequently the attention of the society is diverted from its real problems, which call for adaptation and change, and focused instead upon a preservation of things as they are.

The situation should not be overstated. There has been, as yet, no formal or statutory suppression of speech in the United States beyond the prohibition of advocacy of violent overthrow of the government and the punitive restrictions of the McCarran Act. Men may, and fortunately a number of them still do, express nonconformist views liable to be termed treasonable. But, as Senator Margaret Chase Smith observed in a speech expressing her revulsion against the name-calling tactics of Senator Joseph McCarthy, "Freedom of speech is not what it used to be in America. It has been so abused by some that it is not exercised by others." Freedom of speech does not mean, to be sure, that a man who says what is unpopular should be protected from the penalties of unpopularity. Heretics and reformers must expect denunciation. The alarming characteristic about what is happening today lies partly in the official source of the denunciation, partly in the easy identification of dissent with disloyalty, partly in the punishment of it by the government itself through extra-legal mechanisms.

The cult of loyalty, and its attendant hunt for heresy as a symptom of disloyalty, has generated an intellectually shackled feeling for which terror is too strong a term, but which is marked nevertheless by widespread anxiety. The feeling is most acute, naturally, in Washington, and among government employees. . . . But outside the capital, the pressures for conformity are mounting to a degree never before experienced by the American people. The Committee on Un-American Activities in the national House of Representatives has spawned imitators in state legislatures; some of them, such as the Tenney Committee in California, the Canwell Committee in Washington, the Broyles Commission in Illinois, have rivaled the tactics of the congressional body. In their role of investigators and with the stated object of protecting national security, they have had the effect of penalizing Americans for exercising the fundamental rights of advocacy and association.

Similarly, the Federal Employee-Loyalty Program has been aped and embellished in states and municipalities—where there is far less warrant for such restrictions. Protective measures designed to keep disloyal persons out of jobs that directly affect the national security become merely punitive when applied indiscriminately to all forms of public employment. In many states extremely repressive legislation, of doubtful constitutionality, has been adopted. These laws are aimed at Communists, but their result is to penalize all forms of heterodoxy. Some of the laws deny a place on the ballot to Communists, thereby revealing a distrust of the democratic process. Some, like the Ober Law in Maryland, drastically restrict the right of citizens to join in voluntary associations if the purpose of these associations is officially regarded as subversive. A number of municipalities, especially in the South, have adopted ordinances banning Communists and Communist-*sympathizers* from the city limits. Birmingham, Alabama, for instance, announced that it would jail anyone found guilty of "voluntary association" with a Communist. Other cities have undertaken to require the registration of all Communists. The patent invalidity of such edicts from a constitutional point of view has given no apparent pause to local legislative and law-enforcement bodies. In a number of places, police chiefs have intimated that they mean to apply virtual lynch law to political undesirables. Behind all these measures is a fear of freedom and a panicky willingness to disregard the great procedural safeguards that distinguish a free from a totalitarian society.

The hounding of heterodoxy in the name of loyalty takes an especially ugly and mischievous form in connection with schools and universities. The proliferation of loyalty tests and oaths required of teachers inhibits discussion precisely where it should be most free. But perhaps the gravest consequence of the official cult of loyalty is the inflammation of public opinion to a sometimes hysterical pitch. When political disagreement is branded as disloyalty, when neighbor is invited to look with suspicion on neighbor, the bonds of national unity are strained in a way that is directly injurious to national security. Tragic incidents such as the Peekskill riots in the summer of 1949—when war veterans expressed their devotion to American ideals by behaving like Nazi stormtroopers—flow inevitably from official stimulation of intolerance. No matter how wrong-headed Paul Robeson may be, nothing that he might have said or sung at Peekskill could have injured the credit and the peace of the United States as grievously as the silencing of his voice by violence.

The war in Korea gave a tremendous impetus to this intolerance. In the grip of its excitement, many normally rational and gentle people tended to look upon any association with Communism, no matter how remote or tenuous, as evidence of disloyalty and to regard a mere charge of such association as incontrovertible proof of guilt. A pathetic instance of this tendency occurred in connection with the cancellation of a talk scheduled to be given at a New Hampshire resort hotel by Professor Owen Lattimore in the summer of 1950. A woman who had been active in having Professor Lattimore's appearance canceled gave this explanation of her attitude: "Just now with the critical conditions of this country, anyone about whom there is any question should not be allowed to speak.'' This extraordinary patriotism came well after the Senate subcommittee appointed to investigate Senator Mc-Carthy's charges had given Professor Lattimore the most complete exoneration of which it was capable and had called the charges ''a fraud and a hoax'' perpetrated on the United States Senate.

Apparently exoneration is impossible today for anyone who has ever expressed unorthodox opinions, unless he is willing to profess the most extreme anti-Communism and denounce everyone who shared his past beliefs. One is reminded a little bit of a letter written about A.D. 112 by the younger Pliny to the Emperor Trajan:

> I am very uncertain . . . whether repentance should earn a pardon or if, when a man has once been a Christian, he gains nothing by leaving the sect; whether nominal Christianity without crime deserves punishment or only when crime is coupled with it. In the meantime this is the procedure I have adopted when any so-called Christians have been brought before me. I asked them if they were Christians. If they admitted it, I asked them a second and again a third time, adding threats of death. If they still claimed to be Christians, I gave orders for their execution. . . . Soon in the usual way the investigation itself led to further accusations, covering several types of charge. An anonymous accusation appeared, containing many names. Some of those named denied that they were Christians or ever had been. As they joined with me in invocations to the gods and offered supplications with incense and wine to your Majesty's ikon, which I had brought in with the divine images for this purpose, and finally cursed Christ, I thought they could be discharged, as it is said that genuine Christians cannot be forced into these acts. Others whose names were quoted by the informer said they were Christians but soon withdrew their plea; to be sure, they had once been Christians but they had ceased, some three years before, some for a longer time and a few even for twenty-five years. All these worshipped your Majesty's ikon and the images of the gods; and cursed Christ.

The Emperor commended Pliny's conduct but added this warning:

> There should be no search made for Christians; though, if they are summoned and convicted, they must be punished. But the method should be that anyone who denies that he is a Christian and proves it by his actions, namely by worshipping our gods, whatever suspicion he may previously have incurred, should earn pardon by repentance. Public accusations by anonymous persons should have no place in criminal practice. Such a procedure would be thoroughly bad and out of keeping with the spirit of our age.

Intolerance has taken its most extravagant form in relation to entertainment and the arts. Self-appointed censors have aimed, like Soviet commissars, to dictate the forms and observances of what they consider patriotism and to purge from the stage, screen and radio any performer whose private associations or opinions cross the frontiers of conformity they have delineated. Paul Draper and Larry Adler were their most notable victims in 1949; their procedure has since been put on a mass-production basis. A formal index for their purge of radio and television was published in June 1950 under the title *Red Channels;* this interesting brochure, issued under the auspices of *Counterattack,* a newsletter founded in May 1947 by a group of former FBI men, contains the names of writers, actors, dancers and directors, together with a listing of the committees and organizations with which they are alleged to have had some affiliation. The listing is based in most instances on statements made by or before the House Committee on Un-American Activities or its California counterpart, or on newspaper references, generally from the *Daily Worker;* in some cases it is based on nothing more than information contained in *Counterattack* itself, and often the alleged affiliation is so tenuous as to involve no more than an appearance as an entertainer before some group supposed to be subversive. *Red Channels* makes no charges; its technique is accusation by innuendo. It could perhaps be considered as negligible as Elizabeth Dilling's *Red Network* of a decade ago were it not for the fact that it has been made effective by an organized program of pressure and intimidation brought to bear upon the advertisers and broadcasters who employ the performers it blacklists.

Advertisers appealing to a mass market are obviously vulnerable to this kind of pressure. *Red Channels* scored its outstanding triumph shortly after its publication in the dismissal of Miss Jean Muir, a television actress, from the leading role in a network program. Her name appeared in the book, and a few telephone protests led the sponsor of the program to drop her from the program as a "controversial personality." It is clear that, if this sort of vigilantism is permitted to flourish, the American public will be able to see and hear only those entertainers who can pass the censorship of the vigilantes.

Censorship in the name of patriotism occurs on an unorganized basis too. Perhaps the most sensitive example of it was provided by a Hollywood motion-picture studio which, after six months of work, shelved plans to produce a film dealing with the life and exploits of Hiawatha, the Onondaga Indian chief immortalized by Longfellow. Hiawatha had succeeded in establishing peace among the warring Five Nations; and it was felt, according to a studio spokesman, that this might cause the film to be regarded as a message for peace and thus as Communist propaganda.

Political discussion has been debased to a species of fishwifery by shrill and redundant accusations of disloyalty. The immunity from suit for slander afforded by the floor of Congress has been abused over and over again to launch extravagant attacks on the good faith of opponents in every issue of policy. Demagogic exploitation of popular anxiety, such as Senator McCarthy's blanket indictment of the State Department early in 1950, can have no other than a shattering effect on the confidence of the American people in their government. The prestige of the United States abroad suffers incalculably from such attacks. And the formulation of foreign policy is paralyzed at home by the fear that restraint and reason will be characterized as traitorous. In such an atmosphere only the most extreme chauvinism can pass for patriotism.

The point is patently illustrated in connection with events in the Far East. The readiness of the China Lobby to impute disloyalty to every realistic appraisal of the collapse of the Chinese Nationalist government has made a rational China policy impossible. The State Department has been forced to cling to a transparent fiction. In other areas as well, mere anti-Communism has taken the place of a reasoned evaluation of American interests, allying this country with discredited regimes abroad. Those who dared to protest or dissent were liable to vilification as Communist-sympathizers.

George Kennan, the former counselor of the State Department, expressed the nature of the danger:

> The atmosphere of public life in Washington does not have to deteriorate much further to produce a situation in which very few of our more quiet and sensitive and gifted people will be able to continue in government. . . . The margin of safety with which our country moves in the world today is not great enough to permit us to be reckless and wasteful with the talents and the idealism of those people we depend on for the generalship of our peacetime battles.

This is not an atmosphere conducive to national security. The men responsible for creating it may be credited with good intentions. They will be referred to . . . for the sake of convenience, and to avoid imputing to them any impropriety of motive, as Americanists. But they are guilty nonetheless of the gravest and most dangerous form of disloyalty to the United States. They are disloyal to the principles and purposes that are the genius of the American society.

In the aftermath of World War I, when there was a similar fear that America might be subverted by enemies from within, the late Senator William E. Borah observed:

> The safeguards of our liberty are not so much in danger from those who openly oppose them as from those who, professing to believe in them, are willing to ignore them

49

when found inconvenient for their purposes; the former we can deal with, but the latter, professing loyalty, either by precept or example undermine the very first principles of our government and are far the more dangerous.

The disloyalty of the Americanists impairs national security more seriously than the comparable disloyalty of the Communists. . . . It is more deeply subversive, strikes more injuriously at the real roots of loyalty and of American strength. It would, in fact, meet the threat of Communism by the substitution of Communist techniques for the techniques of freedom. If the relatively impotent Communists aim at overthrowing the government of the United States, the Americanists, whether they are aware of it or not, aim at overthrowing the essential values which that government was instituted to secure.

THE LOYALTY OF FREE MEN*

. . . I do not mean to talk to you this evening about the problem of academic freedom as though it were an isolated problem. I want to talk about academic freedom not from your special point of view as professors but from my point of view as a layman—not in terms of its importance to you as teachers but in terms of its importance to the society as a whole.

It would be presumptuous on my part, I think, to speak about the present threat to academic freedom in its relation to your professional responsibilities. In the first place, you are more intimately familiar with the problem than I am. In the second place, this association has already demonstrated its awareness of the problem in a way that is unique among educational organizations.

*Extracted from an address on March 16, 1951, at the annual dinner of the American Association of University Professors in Cincinnati, Ohio. The text was published in the *Bulletin* of the American Association of University Professors, Spring 1951.

It has stood resolutely for the maintenance of academic freedom against the assaults of those who would qualify teachers on the basis of political purity and standards of orthodoxy. . . .

I want to talk particularly about loyalty oaths—not because I suppose them to be any more baleful in respect to teachers than in respect to any other trade or calling, but because they have become the most pervasive symptom of the neurotic anxiety which I presume to be the real root of our present troubles.

One can only guess at the judgment of posterity. My own guess is that historians sufficiently removed from the present to look at it with detachment may very well refer to it as the era of the oath. Oath-taking is not new, of course. It has served a ritual function throughout the whole history of Western civilization. The peculiarity of contemporary oath-taking, however, is, first of all, its prevalence and, second, its negative nature. It is a mistake to call the kind of oath so commonly required of men today a "loyalty oath." A loyalty oath, by definition, would have to be an affirmation. But the kind of declaration to which more and more Americans are now being asked to subscribe is a disclaimer. Instead of calling it a "loyalty oath," we ought, in the interest of accuracy, to refer to it as a "non-disloyalty oath."

Oaths of affirmation have long been familiar to us. There can scarcely be a man, woman or child in America who has not pledged "allegiance to the flag of the United States of America and to the Republic for which it stands—one nation indivisible with liberty and justice for all." The meaning of this pledge, recited in unison by millions of schoolchildren every weekday morning, is perhaps vague and uncertain. Undoubtedly it has had many meanings for many individuals. The flag itself is a symbol; liberty and justice are abstractions with different connotations, it may be presumed, for a Negro child in a southern community and for one of the well-born. Nevertheless, participation in this ritual has certainly had a unifying influence. The very act of recitation has served to charge the flag with emotional significance and thus to evoke devotion to it. And it has drawn young Americans closer together through a sense of common devotion.

No one has ever supposed, however—and certainly no one

supposes today—that the taking of this oath is an effective guarantee against disloyalty. No real reliance is placed upon it. The best that can be said for it in this respect is that, like any incantation, it gives solidarity to the participating group and a comforting sense that it has warded off evil spirits. And certainly this is a utility not lightly to be dismissed.

Something of the same ritualistic quality lies behind the oath we have always required of our public officials. We insist that upon assuming office they swear solemnly to support and defend the Constitution of the United States against all enemies, to bear true faith and allegiance to the same, and to discharge their duties well and faithfully—or some such form of words. We do not feel any great confidence that this will protect us against simony, graft, or even treason. But it is useful as a reminder to government servants of the responsibility with which they have been entrusted.

Similarly, we exact of everyone who testifies in a court of law a sworn promise that he will tell the truth, the whole truth and nothing but the truth. We are not so naïve as to suppose that this will infallibly keep him from bearing false witness; and judges often instruct juries that they must choose between conflicting testimony. But the ritual helps to bring home the solemnity of the occasion and to impose caution, at least upon the conscientious.

There is a vast difference between oaths of this kind and the negative swearing which has lately come so much into vogue. The pledge of allegiance to the flag has been debased by insistence that men swear in addition that they are not disloyal to the United States. It is no longer sufficient that a man swear to uphold the Constitution when he undertakes to work for the government; he must now swear, besides, that he does not advocate the overthrow of that government.

Our total lack of confidence in oaths is measured by this redundant insistence on them. If we do not believe a man when he swears to uphold the Constitution, why, in the name of common sense, should we be any more disposed to take his word when he swears that he will not attempt to destroy the Constitution? The answer, of course, is that we have lost all faith in what he says in either case. But we insist on his saying it over and over again in the blind, unreasoning way that primitive tribes insisted upon rites of purification and blood sacrifices that had no relation to reality.

The non-disloyalty oath has become as fashionable as public-opinion polls or canasta. The exaction of it has spread from the federal government to state governments. It has, as you know, permeated our schools and our institutions of higher learning. And now it is spreading into professional associations and even into private industry.

Just a couple of weeks ago a special committee of the American Bar Association—an organization which might reasonably have been expected to show a somewhat greater regard for the spirit of American institutions—recommended not only that all Communists be disbarred but also that every member of the bar be required to file an affidavit stating whether he is now *or has ever at any time in the past been* a member of the Communist Party or of any organization on the Attorney General's list. And it urged investigation of all persons suspected of subscribing to the affidavit falsely. The protests of such distinguished lawyers as John W. Davis and Robert P. Patterson and Owen J. Roberts were ignored.

A month or two earlier, the Columbia Broadcasting System—in an apparent attempt to prove that it could wave the American flag more dizzily than any other network—demanded that all of its employees file an affidavit of the same sort telling whether they had ever at any time belonged to one of the Attorney General's proscribed groups. And behind the inquiry there was implicit, of course, the threat of dismissal for failure to answer, or for an answer that proved displeasing to the officials of the company. Whatever justification there may be for this sort of inquisition into the lawful past affiliations of an employee of the government, there is no justification for it, I think, on the part of a private employer. Employees—whether teachers or radio broadcasters or hod-carriers—deserve to be judged on the basis of their performance in their jobs, not the basis of private beliefs and associations, so long as these do not affect the quality of their work.

Now, I do not propose to dwell on the objections to this sort of inquiry and oath-taking from the point of view of the individual affected by them. My principal concern is with their effect upon society. But before I launch upon this main thesis, let me say briefly why I think that any American has good cause to resent and resist demands of this sort that he profess his innocence of sympathies and intentions of which there are no good reasons to suspect him.

First of all, the protestations extorted by loyalty oaths and inquiries are humiliating—senselessly humiliating. Professor Zechariah Chafee has made this point, it seems to me, in an extraordinarily illuminating way. "Let us," he said, "picture the parallel situation of a loyal wife whose chastity is similarly doubted by a suspicious husband. He too demands a public assertion—at a dinner party in their home. He insists that his wife tell all their guests that she has never been unfaithful to him, and particularly not with a person he names. It is all true—why not say so?" It seems to me that even if loyalty oaths were not demanded discriminatorily, they would be an abomination. It is never comfortable to wear one's heart on one's sleeve.

Second, these oaths and inquiries invade long-recognized rights of privacy. If a man may be held accountable to society for what he believes, as distinguished from what he does, he becomes subject to something very like the thought control which we so derided when it was practiced by the Japanese. And thought control is, I think, the real purpose back of this kind of inquisition. You need only translate the questions now asked so commonly about political belief and affiliation into questions about religious belief and affiliation to see how mischievous and offensive they are. Perhaps men ought to be courageous enough always to say what they think—to proclaim their religious or political faith (or their lack of it). But they do not always have this kind of courage when what they believe is unpopular. And their right to privacy and silence on this score is of the essence of liberty.

Third, these oaths and inquiries imply a presumption of guilt instead of the presumption of innocence that has traditionally protected individuals under American law. And they shift the whole burden of proof from the accuser to the accused. It is enormously difficult for a man to prove that he was not, in some indefinite time in the past, a member of the Communist Party or, say, of the League for Peace and Democracy. For one thing, the attributes of membership—as distinguished from "sympathetic association" or informal affiliation or ideological support—have never been precisely defined. For another, it is impossible to get corroborative testimony. If you are accused of having robbed a bank on the night of March 16, 1951, you may be able to produce a number of university professors who will swear that you were here at the Sinton Hotel at that particular time. But if you are accused of being a secret member of some group or conspiracy, no one can provide any conclusive support of your denial. Your friends can do no more than affirm their faith in you—a weak form of assistance, since it has been amply demonstrated that friends may be mistaken in their faith. And your own denial will seem, of course, manifestly self-serving. Given the present tendency to use perjury prosecutions as a means of punishing people for past affiliations which are not in themselves unlawful and the present overheated atmosphere in which juries reach their verdicts, any denial of such a charge may be dangerous. And even the most honest subscription to a non-disloyalty affidavit may lead a man into serious trouble. It is a slightly wonderful paradox that these oaths and inquiries present far graver perils to those who deny Communist affiliations than to those who acknowledge them.

I have said nothing about the futility of these oaths and inquiries from the point of view of the national security which they are supposed to protect. It is generally taken for granted that Communists have no moral scruples about false swearing. Yet it seems to be assumed, by those who place reliance on non-disloyalty oaths, that a Communist can somehow be counted upon to answer truthfully when asked about his party affiliation. I have no doubt that there are dangerous Soviet agents in the United States plotting espionage and sabotage and the overthrow of the government. But I have a great deal of doubt that they will step forward to register with the Attorney General or proclaim their intentions when confronted with an affidavit. The dangerous people are carefully disguised, I suspect, as vociferous anti-Communists. No oath or inquiry is likely to cause them the smallest qualm. So far as catching real enemies of the country is concerned, this ritual procedure is about as effectual as a requirement that all criminals register with their local police departments—or a requirement that all citizens take an oath they will do nothing unjust, unethical or unpatriotic.

Let me now turn to the aspect of the oath obsession that seems to me most serious because it affects the fabric of our society as well as the rights of individuals. It can be argued that injuries, or even injustices, to individuals ought to be endured in a time of crisis if they serve real social purposes. But the impact of the present craze to extirpate heresy, or disloyalty—call it what you will—is, I think, socially disastrous—disastrous to the national security itself no less than to the great values which it is the function of the nation to make secure.

Behind the shift to negativism implicit in the non-disloyalty oaths, there lies a terrible distrust. A nation, in many ways, is like a family. The cement that holds its members together is compounded of mutual dependence, mutual confidence and common acceptance of certain basic values or purposes. Under the corroding influence of a spreading distrust, that cement is seeping away dangerously in America.

We are not a national family today. We are losing the solidarity that has always been our primary source of strength. We are tending more and more to look at one another with suspicion—to question the motives that lie behind dissent or disagreement—to abandon the tolerance of diversity that has been the genius of American life.

We are succumbing to fear—to a fear that is, in large part, groundless and neurotic. I have no wish to gloss over the real dangers that confront us today. The Soviet Union is an aggressive totalitarianism. Like every other totalitarian society, it is made inescapably aggressive by its inner tensions and compulsions; and it is, therefore, necessarily menacing to free societies. It can be checked only through resolute action and mobilized armed strength on the part of the United States.

It is equally plain, of course, that the Soviet Union has agents in this country striving to injure us and impair our strength. Members of the Communist Party are no doubt among those agents, just as the party itself is manifestly an instrument of Soviet policy. But the most dangerous agents may not be party members at all. Their activities must be checked by rational security measures and by vigilant counter-intelligence. And they *can* be checked in this way—just as the activities of German and Japanese agents were checked; and so effectively that J. Edgar Hoover was able to report that not a single enemy-directed act of sabotage occurred during the whole course of the Second World War.

Espionage and sabotage are real threats to security. But fear that the Communists can overthrow the government of the United States by force and violence is an absurd nightmare. Fear of subversion—that is, of the influence of Communist propaganda and doctrine—is equally a bugbear. The United States is not ripe for revolution. And democratic ideas are quite healthy enough to withstand Communist ideas. The democratic system is not only superior to the Communist system, but it is superior also in its appeal to men who have been privileged to live under it. We need not be afraid that our fellow-Americans will choose submission and servitude in preference to responsibility and liberty.

Nevertheless, neurotic fear, like an infectious disease, has taken a strong grip upon the American people. And this fear is being aggravated and exploited by reckless demagogues. I think it safe to say that the mad-dog barkings of Senator McCarthy would have been recognized for what they were and laughed off by the American people a few years ago. But in the atmosphere of anxiety and distrust that prevails today, they have a deadly impact. When panic takes hold of a community, even the most far-fetched rumors and accusations find credence. And, finding it, they exacerbate the panic. . . .

The result is that the United States is being deprived of its most stabilizing influence—the resolution of policy through challenge and criticism and debate. This is the real secret weapon of a democracy. The lack of it is the fatal defect of a dictatorship. Dictators may carry policy into practice more swiftly than governments dependent upon the consent of the governed; but this may mean no more than that they can more swiftly translate errors into national disaster. Free men—if they exercise their freedom—have a means of correcting their mistakes. But if they suppress dissent by calling it disloyal, they rob themselves of their greatest asset.

"Like the course of the heavenly bodies," Mr. Justice Brandeis once observed, "harmony in national life is a resultant of the struggle between contending forces. In frank expression of conflicting opinion lies the greatest promise of wisdom in governmental action; and in suppression lies ordinarily the greatest peril."

Unity, in short, does not grow out of uniformity; it grows out of resolved conflict. The present short-circuiting of this kind of democratic conflict presents a deadly peril to national security.

The democratic process depends, above all else, on a broad and generous tolerance of diversity—tolerance of opinions we despise and even of opinions that we deem disloyal. It is always easy to find a rationalization for the suppression of opinion; and the temptation to do so is very great when men are frightened and angry. They are prone then to call the opinions they detest treasonable and to characterize the holders of such opinions as conspirators. And once the labels have been applied, it is but a short step to the conclusion that freedom of speech was never meant to protect treason and conspiracy. . . .

It is no accident that non-disloyalty oaths and inquiry into political opinions are directed in large part at our schools and universities. They are devices for compelling conformity. And the men responsible for them are men who distrust diversity and fear ideas. They are in revolt against rationality. Their attack is directed in the first instance at schools and universities precisely because these are centers of ideas.

Professor Chafee has called this attack, aptly, "a barbarian invasion." It is just that. It is another manifestation of the age-old assault of ignorance upon learning, of bigotry upon reason. It is the thrust of the lowered brow upon what it cannot understand. The men who launch it here are one with their spiritual kinfolk in Germany and Russia who prefer to think with the blood and who despise everything that concerns the intellect. If we do not ward off their attack, we shall descend into a new dark age.

Universities are the citadels of intellectual freedom. And it is against these citadels that the attack is launched because its aim is nothing less than the extinction of intellectual freedom. You of the academic profession are, therefore, its first targets—and the first defenders of the whole great tradition of diversity. In a period of profound anxiety, when fear can be exploited and unreason flourishes, the danger of this attack must not be underestimated. The attackers will have their way, as their counterparts had it in Germany and Italy before the war and have it today behind the Iron Curtain, unless you, as men of learning, close your ranks, recognize the deadly peril to your independence and fight resolutely, with every resource at your command, to repel the barbarians. You have a responsibility in this that goes beyond your own interest as teachers. You are the trustees of a cultural heritage.

If you defend freedom for your profession, you defend the whole of human freedom. And it is to this, more than to any other value, that Americans owe allegiance. The loyalty of free men is, above all, a loyalty to the illimitable freedom of the human mind.

UNIVERSITIES AND
POLITICAL AUTHORITY*

. . . It seems to me that in the academic world today there is a widespread failure to face and to assess realistically the forces in American life which are now mobilized to extinguish academic freedom. Specifically, I think that many university professors and presidents are failing to recognize the real peril presented—to themselves and to the society they serve—by the current congressional investigations of their institutions.

*From an address on March 27, 1953, at the annual meeting of the American Association of University Professors in Chicago, Illinois. The text was published in the *Bulletin* of the American Association of University Professors, Spring 1953, and in the *Education Digest*, November 1953, and abridged in *The Nation*, April 18, 1953.

There seems to be a widespread tendency to treat these investigations as minor irritations to be borne philosophically or as bridges to be crossed when reached with a little caution and circumspection. Not very long ago, for example, the Association of American Colleges adopted a resolution in which it expressly declared that "the colleges should welcome any free and impartial inquiry" as a means of promoting popular understanding of the accomplishments of higher education. . . .

I should like to lay before you as earnestly as I can the reasons why I am convinced that this attitude of "welcome" toward legislative investigations of universities is an utterly disastrous folly. It reflects—at least, so it seems to me—a total misconception of the problem. In the first place, only the most absent-minded of college professors could suppose that in any serious sense the investigations would prove to be "free and impartial." The men conducting them have no intellectual competence for the undertaking; they neither understand nor care about the meaning of academic freedom. In the second place, the manner in which the investigations have been conducted makes it plain that their purpose is coercion; they are aimed at forcing the dismissal of individuals who have earned the committee's displeasure. It seems to me that they menace academic freedom, therefore, in the most direct and destructive way.

I have heard the policy of "welcome" toward these investigations of colleges and universities defended on the ground of the old adage that a soft answer turneth away wrath; and I have heard this defense buttressed by the argument that the great philanthropic foundations escaped censure by just this technique of meeting their congressional critics with open arms.

But I submit to you that it is a mistake to suppose that the philanthropic foundations emerged from their investigation unscathed because they emerged uncensured. It is true enough that at the conclusion of the investigation they were given a pat on the back by their inquisitors. But this affords no real measure of how much they will have to pay for this pat on the back in terms of submission and intimidation. They know now that if they want to be patted again when a congressional committee chooses to investigate them another time, they had better not give any more fellowships to Aaron Copland—or to any musician whose political opinions may be tinged with unorthodoxy. They know now that they had better not make any grants to colleges that keep "questionable" teachers on their faculties; a "questionable" teacher, you understand, is any teacher whom an investigating committee wants to question. They know now that they had better not appropriate any of their funds for research into political experimentation or social innovation of any sort.

The business of the foundations is to support unorthodoxy, to promote the discovery of new ideas, new talents, new challenges to authority and to accepted ways of doing things. And the test of how largely they escaped injury in their recent ordeal by investigation will be the vigor that they display in the years ahead. It will be a great loss to society if they are chastened and timorous. . . .

I am convinced that the attitude of hospitality and welcome toward congressional investigations is a mistaken one, both in terms of expediency and in terms of principle. So far as expediency is concerned, it pitches the inevitable battle on the worst possible ground from the universities' point of view; and so far as principle is concerned, it gives away the essential moral basis of resistance to what is, really, a barbarian invasion of American intellectual life.

Let me set before you a few of the considerations which make me think that a congressional hearing—at any rate, a hearing conducted under the prevailing know-nothing auspices—is a disadvantageous ground on which to fight the battle for academic freedom. It provides, to begin with, an atmosphere entirely unfriendly and unfamiliar to men of learning. It is an atmosphere in which the presentation of a considered and reasoned argument is virtually impossible. The presentation is bound to be incessantly interrupted by the explosion of photographic flashbulbs, by the movement of newspapermen and curious spectators, by the gavel-pounding of a chairman determined to exclude rationality from the hearing room, and by impertinent questions from members of the committee.

The notion that under such auspices it will be feasible to promote public understanding of what universities are doing and why they need academic freedom to fulfill their vital function seems to me to be completely naïve. Such understanding could be promoted only if there were a disposition on the part of Congressmen conducting the hearing to promote it. There is no such disposition.

It is perfectly clear that the discussion in such a hearing is not going to be about academic freedom. It is not going to concern itself with the accomplishments of universities or with the problems of promoting intellectual maturity among students. It will concern itself, as the investigating-committee chairmen have made quite clear, with individuals. It will be a discussion not of principles but of personalities.

Thus these hearings will revolve around such questions as whether Professor A is a Communist because Louis Budenz says that someone told him that Professor A was believed to be a Communist a quarter of a century ago. It will revolve around such questions as whether Professor B is subversive because he belongs or once belonged to organizations which have incurred the disapproval of the Attorney General or the House Committee on Un-American Activities. It will revolve around such questions as whether a particular college is Communist-dominated because it allowed on its campus a visiting lecturer who denounced the Un-American Activities Committee. It will revolve around such questions as whether a university is Red because Allen Zoll doesn't like its textbooks or some of its teachers.

Out of this kind of inquiry and discussion can come only divisive controversy and confusion. No doubt some of the academic witnesses will respond to questions which seem to them impertinent and offensive with dignity and coolness and clarity. But some others, no doubt, will lose their tempers and talk foolishly. The committee, presumably, will be able to discover a few present members of the Communist Party on college campuses. They will doubtless also be able to discover a number of teachers who joined the party years ago for respectable reasons, who got out of it years ago for respectable reasons and who do not now choose—for equally respectable reasons—to make witnessing a career. Some of the professors in this category will seek the protection of the Fifth Amendment—mistakenly, in my judgment—in order to avoid possible prosecution or in order to avoid being required to give the names of persons who, like themselves, joined the party innocently and got out of it long ago. Some will refuse to answer the questions of the committee on abstract grounds of conscience, pleading the protection of the First Amendment, and may find themselves cited for contempt of Congress.

This is a point at which I should like to say something about the use of the Fifth Amendment as a means of avoiding acknowledgment of past membership in the Communist Party. I do not mean to attempt here any exhaustive discussion of its scope and protection in ordinary circumstances. I mean merely to consider its application to teachers in the special context of the current inquiries into colleges and universities.

When a committee of Congress hales a man before it and asks him if he has ever been a Communist, it impales him on one or another of the prongs of a trident. If the witness answers "yes" to this question, the committee is all too likely to insist that he identify individuals who were in the party with him—a kind of degradation which any sensitive man might understandably desire to escape. If he answers "no" to the question, then the committee may hold over his head the threat of a prosecution for perjury based upon testimony calling him a former Communist by one or another of the committee's former—and professedly reformed—Communists. And if he refuses to answer the question at all, pleading the constitutional privilege against self-incrimination, the committee hopes to have his university discipline him by dismissal.

I submit to you that it is outright folly for any university to lend itself to this stratagem. I submit to you that it is an abdication of academic independence for any university to serve indiscriminately as the executor of punishments arbitrarily imposed by a congressional committee.

There is much force, I think, to the statement made by Dr. Barrows Dunham of Temple University, who, with frank defiance, recently refused to tell the House Committee on Un-American Activities anything beyond his name, age and place of birth. The committee, in response, moved to have him prosecuted for contempt of Congress—an offense of which he may well be guilty. But this is a judicial question, involving nice points of constitutional law which Dr. Dunham is entitled to have tried in a court of law. If convicted there, he will be subject, of course, to punishment. Temple University, I think, should not have prejudged him; and it should not in the absence of compelling evidence have imputed disloyalty to conduct which was apparently undertaken conscientiously on grounds of principle. Dr. Dunham stated the principle in these words:

> There is no question that Congress has the right, as it has the power, to investigate for legislative purposes. What I encountered last week, however, was not genuine inquiry but public defamation intended to extirpate from the colleges not disloyalty but dissent. I conceive that no act of mine could have better displayed my loyalty to this country and its traditions than the course I followed last Friday.

Whatever Dr. Dunham's past may have been, whatever the merits and motives of his individual position—and without more knowledge I have no wish either to condone or to condemn what he has done—it seems to me that he is quite right in the essential point that he has made: that the committee has been conducting not an investigation of universities but a purge of university professors.

The committee has devised a powerful instrument for this purge. The action taken by Temple University is not novel. Not long ago Rutgers University dismissed two members of its faculty because they had invoked the protection of the Fifth Amendment in refusing to answer questions before the Senate Internal Security Subcommittee. Lesser institutions have cooperated with this committee or with the House Committee on Un-American Activities in the same way. Indeed, the latter was able to announce proudly not long ago that of thirty-nine professors who had availed themselves of their constitutional privilege against self-incrimination thirty-seven had already been dismissed by their institutions.

For my own part, I think that teachers who plead this privilege are neither admirable nor astute. But if they are to be automatically disciplined for doing so, the committee will have developed a formidable method for determining the membership of university faculties—something which ought to be determined by the faculties themselves in a free society. If the colleges and universities of the United States allow this system of selection to go on, they will have effectively shifted the fulcrum of control from their own hands to the hands of the United States government.

Universities, and the individual members of the faculties, have, of course, a duty of respectful cooperation with any duly constituted congressional body. But this duty does not require of them blind obedience. They have a duty also to their own values which obliges them to judge each case individually on its individual merits.

Now this brings me around to the second basis on which I believe a college "welcome" for these investigations to be tragically mistaken. It is mistaken, I am convinced, in terms of principle, as well as in terms of expediency. It is mistaken because it does violence to the fundamental principle that institutions of higher learning ought to be independent of the government in the same way, and for much the same reasons, that the church and the press are independent of the government. They cannot make their vital contribution to a free society if they are subject to political control.

Of course, I am not questioning the legal authority of Congress to investigate institutions of higher learning. I do not, for that matter, question the authority of Congress to investigate the church or the press, despite the constitutional limitations on legislation in these spheres. Congress has plenary power—and must have such power—to look into any area of American life. But to say that Congress has power to investigate is not necessarily to say that this power ought to be exercised. In my own view, it ought resolutely to be eschewed in regard to universities—at least when the aim and tendency of the investigation is coercive.

One function of institutions of higher learning in a free society is the propagation of unorthodoxy. Their business is to produce men and women who will question inherited values and challenge constituted authority.

Professor John L. Mothershead, Jr., of Stanford University, was quite right, I believe, when he said in a recent issue of *Educational Record:*

> . . . there are persons in this country who speak as if they wanted to produce American robots who could safely be granted civil liberties because their minds would be limited to ideas certified as safe by various investigative committees and censors at the Federal, State, county and community levels. These persons do not seem to understand that what they advocate is really a complete spiritual capitulation to communism.

The notion that religion, the press and the universities should serve the State is essentially a Communist notion. Government control of these institutions is a distinguishing characteristic of every totalitarian system. In a free society, these institutions must be wholly free—which is to say that their function is to serve as checks upon the State, as devices for keeping governmental authority within appropriate bounds.

A free society differs from a totalitarian society in that its government is one of limited powers—and limited jurisdiction. There have always been important areas of American life which have been left to private regulation—higher education among them. The administration of state universities has generally been delegated to boards of regents, responsible ultimately to state legislatures but never to the federal government. The administration of America's great privately endowed universities has always been in the hands of boards of trustees, self-perpetuating or elected by the institution's graduates.

And these have been, on the whole, sober, conscientious and capable governing bodies—in no need whatever of congressional supervision. Generally speaking, these boards can be confidently relied upon for patriotism and sound judgment. . . .

If American universities are to remain free, they must also remain independent. They cannot afford to compromise their independence.

If they "welcome" congressional investigation today, they will end by embracing congressional control tomorrow. If they let a congressional committee purge professors now, they will eventually let it control curricula. The seeds of ultimate surrender are sown inexorably in seemingly trivial and innocent concessions. Let me quote to you the solemn warning on this score expressed in a leader in *The Times* of London more than a century ago:

> The greatest tyranny has the smallest beginning. From precedents overlooked, from remonstrances despised, from grievances treated with ridicule, from powerless men oppressed with impunity, and overbearing men tolerated with complacence, springs the tyrannical usage which generations of wise and good men may hereafter perceive and lament and resist in vain. At present, common minds no more see a crushing tyranny in trivial unfairness or ludicrous indignity, than the eye uninformed by reason can discern the sap in the acorn, or the utter desolation of winter in the first autumnal fall. Hence the necessity of denouncing with unwearied and even troublesome perseverance a single act of oppression. Let it alone and it stands on record. The country has allowed it, and when it is at last provoked to a late indignation, it finds itself gagged with the record of its own ill compulsion.

The record of the current investigations into colleges and universities has been a record of "powerless men oppressed with impunity, and overbearing men tolerated with complacence." It is a record which we can review only with a sense of shame.

But it is not too late, I believe, to reverse it and to make an effective defense of intellectual freedom and academic independence. Let us begin now to mobilize the great, untapped reserves of devotion and good will which the universities possess. Let us carry the battle outside the rigged hearing rooms of the congressional committees and appeal to the alumni associations in every city and town throughout the United States. Let us appeal to the pride of the American people generally in the great, free institutions of learning which they have built and maintained.

Let us tell the alumni groups that alma mater is imperiled today by men who wish to make her in their own image and to set upon her the stamp of their own limited and warped mentalities. Let us appeal to them to defend their own loved college—and to defend at the same time the whole great American heritage of intellectual liberty.

Let us turn to the trustees of our institutions of learning and remind them what it is they hold in trust. They are trustees of something more than a collection of buildings and football stadia and other physical assets. They are trustees of a tradition. And now is the time for them to redeem their trusteeship.

Let us seek the support of the American people by explaining boldly and clearly the meaning—and the social utilty—of academic freedom, by making them understand that academic freedom is not a privilege or indulgence extended to teachers for their idle enjoyment but an indispensable means of assuring society that teachers will be able to fulfill their vital function conscientiously.

The battle is joined; and none who chooses to call himself a teacher may now be laggard. From our ivory towers, we can see this battle—and see what it portends. Our obligation is to warn our countrymen of the danger that confronts them and then to close ranks and fight as toughly, as resourcefully, as resolutely as we can. We shall be fighting for much more than freedom for ourselves. We shall be fighting for the whole of human freedom.

RESTRAINTS ON TRAVEL

MAY 12, 1957

. . . Although passports were not required for travel prior to the First World War, they have become in recent years a kind of exit permit without which no one can leave the country; and although even today they are, in fact, somewhat like birth certificates, mere documents of identity and nationality, the State Department uses them as instruments of policy, withholding them whenever it deems it to be in the national interest to do so. A serious question exists as to whether these restraints on freedom of movement—whether applied indiscriminately to certain areas or discriminatorily in regard to all travel abroad by suspected individuals—do not violate a basic American constitutional right.

There is, to be sure, no explicit guarantee in the Constitution; but freedom of movement has been recognized ever since Magna Carta in the common law of England and in the traditions of the United States as a right of free men. In 1948 the United States was among the signatories to a Universal Declaration of Human Rights adopted unanimously by the General Assembly of the United Nations providing in Article 13: "Everyone has the right to leave any country, including his own, and to return to his country." In recent decisions the Court of Appeals for the District of Columbia Circuit has referred to the right to leave the country as "an attribute of personal liberty" and as "a natural right subject to the rights of others and to reasonable regulation under law."

Nevertheless, it has been a crime since 1918 to leave or enter the United States without a passport in time of war; and in 1941 Congress gave the President authority to make the restriction applicable during periods of national emergency. An executive order forbids citizens to go abroad except in conformity with rules prescribed by the Secretary of State. Under this order the State Department denies passports on two grounds—one, that travel by ordinary American tourists might affect foreign relations and, two, that travel by persons suspected of Communist sympathies might impair national security.

Leaving out of consideration the vital constitutional issue involved, it is questionable whether, as a matter of national policy, the freedom of Americans ought to be limited so drastically at the mere discretion of a public official. The power to conduct foreign relations can hardly be held to imply a power to control all the acts of Americans which may affect foreign relations. . . . American citizens in this country may, by acts or utterances, affect foreign relations more significantly than by routine tourist travel, yet the State Department has no power to regulate such acts or utterances. The department may properly warn against travel into countries where danger exists, as in China, for example; but to prohibit such travel at the tourist's own risk seems a kind of paternalism wholly alien to the American tradition. The department may refuse protection to such tourists; it ought not to refuse exit.

So far as suspected "security risks" are concerned, one cannot help wondering whether the power to deny passports is not more dangerous to liberty than the travel itself. It is true, of course, that disloyal persons might serve as Communist couriers or might do things abroad disadvantageous to the United States. But the danger is hardly so great as to justify reposing in the Passport Office an arbitrary authority to keep Americans at home.

Since freedom to travel is a basic human right, it ought to be denied, we believe, only when the exercise of it would facilitate a violation of law—that is, in the case of fugitives from justice, draft-evaders or others seeking to escape lawful responsibilities. Perhaps it would be best to return the passport to its earlier status, that of a letter of introduction, which the Secretary of State could issue in his discretion to those of whose travel he approves and to whom he wishes to promise the protection of the American government; but others wishing to go abroad should be able, as a matter of right, to obtain some lesser form of identification—a kind of *laissez passer*—which would enable them to travel at their own risk where and when they pleased.

SECURITY: TIME FOR REAPPRAISAL

MARCH 27, 1955

. . . The fundamental vice of the security program, in our judgment, is its reliance on information from unidentified sources.
This is the defect which gives rise to the constitutional question
. . . , it is the defect on which most of the testimony before the
Humphrey Subcommittee [which is evaluating the program] has
centered, it is the defect which is inevitably underscored by the
discovery that Harvey Matusow and other informants have been
brazen liars.

The argument against reliance on anonymous informers is generally based . . . on a concern for the rights of accused individuals; and the argument in support of using such information is
generally to the effect . . . that national security requires this
disregard of rights an individual would have, as a matter of course,
under a judicial procedure. Both arguments, we think, ignore the
most vital point of the problem: the consideration of anonymous
charges puts an impossible burden on a security board.

When a security board is asked to pass upon the trustworthiness
of a federal employee in the light of information from an unidentified source, it is asked to engage in a species of divination or
clairvoyance. It has no independent means of knowing whether
the source is a sage or a fool, a patriot or a concealed Communist,
a reputable citizen or a Harvey Matusow. Yet this lies at the very
heart of the judgment which the board must make. The reliability
of the informant is the crux of the question which the board must
decide. Without any means of weighing the credibility of informants, the decision of the board becomes not a judgment but a
guess.

This newspaper believes it is possible to let security boards and
employees know the identity of informants in most cases without
impairing the efficacy of the Federal Bureau of Investigation or

injuring national security. The FBI uses two distinct types of informant in its security investigations. One type consists of genuine undercover agents of the bureau—operatives who have gained access to strategic positions and whose anonymity must be jealously guarded. Informants of this type are very rarely used, however, in personnel security cases. In the extraordinary instances when they are used a real question arises whether concealment of the informant's identity may be warranted in the interest of national security. We think this question ought to be answered in each case not by the FBI but by an independent board or committee made up of citizens of the highest repute. Manifestly, protection of this sort ought not to be extended to informants who are no longer undercover—that is, whose service to the FBI has already been disclosed.

Most of the information in FBI personnel reports comes from casual informants—neighbors, office associates, domestic servants, random acquaintances, etc.—who understandably find it more comfortable and convenient to talk to investigators in confidence. But their comfort and convenience is not the same thing as the national security. To require them to come forward and confront those they accuse would not impair the FBI's secret operations. It is said that they would talk less freely if they were required to do this. Perhaps so. Perhaps this would put a damper on careless babbling and malicious allegations. But it does an injustice to the patriotism of Americans generally to suppose that they would fail to tell what they really know and face the rigors of cross-examination in any situation genuinely affecting the nation's security.

If the identity of informants were concealed only in those exceptional cases in which an independent board considered the concealment necessary to national security, decisions about accused employees could be made by real judgment instead of by guesswork. The danger of mistaken or malicious accusations would be minimized. Employees could feel confident that they were not being victimized by concealed Communists or personal enemies. National security and individual rights would both be strengthened by such a reform.

INFILTRATING MOTHERHOOD

APRIL 19, 1953

Congressman Velde having always befriended this newspaper, we are happy to pass on to him *gratis* a suggestion which will enable him to put Messrs. Jenner and McCarthy in the shade. If he can just get his mind off the colleges and the clergy for a few minutes, we think it's high time for him to take a good hard look at American motherhood. The Communists have been looking at it, you may be sure of that, for some time. Only the most romantic and abandoned liberals could believe that the Kremlin would ignore so influential an institution as the American mother.

Mr. Velde will not want, we quite understand, to investigate motherhood as an institution. He is extremely fastidious about investigating any institution; as he has taken great pains to point out on more than one occasion, he has never had the slightest interest in education or religion, as such, but only in individual teachers and individual ministers. Naturally, he will want to approach motherhood on the same high plane. If he were to investigate mothers in general, there would be, of course, aweeping and awailing among the liberals, who persist in regarding motherhood as somehow sacrosanct and beyond any regulation by Congress. But to investigate individual mothers would be, obviously, a quite different thing.

The situation is becoming, to be blunt about it, parlous. Quietly and unobtrusively, a number of undercover Communists—we cannot say how many—have become mothers in the last few years since the party has been driven more or less underground. Very few mothers, however, have become Communists, we are happy to say—perhaps because washing the baby's diapers, fixing the formula and other maternal chores make it difficult, as Mr. Malenkov can readily understand, to attend cell meetings or read the requisite literature. It may not be easy to ferret out all the concealed Communist mothers—or, rather, all the concealed mother

Communists, but we are sure Mr. Velde is the man for the job. If any mother tries to hide behind the protection of the Fifth Amendment when confronted with her shame, we are confident that the committee can count upon every red-blooded American husband to divorce her forthwith.

The danger of the situation can scarcely be over-estimated. Mothers sometimes exercise a considerable influence upon children, especially while the children are still impressionable, which seems to be approximately between the ages of four. The investigation cannot begin too soon. We hope Mr. Velde will get to this surefire, three-ring opportunity with its built-in headlines before the Jenner crowd can grab it away from him. We'll do everything we can to help. Remember, Harold, M-O-T-H-E-R spells mother.

THREE

The Law and the FBI

In the end, the worst abuses of the heresy-hunters vanished. Senator McCarthy was censured by the Senate in 1954 for contumacious conduct toward committees investigating his own activities. His credibility and with it his power quickly waned, and so did the influence of the other investigating-committee chairmen; most were out of the public eye by 1960. Congress itself reined in the activities of these committees by installing rules of procedure for investigations which ended the harassment of witnesses; these rules conformed largely to the ideas presented by Alan Barth in his second book, *Government by Investigation*. The Supreme Court, in a long series of decisions, clipped the power of the other two branches of government to punish government employees or other citizens without providing them with the full protection of due process of law. The executive branch finally listened to what the court was saying and amended the loyalty-security program so that it complied somewhat more faithfully with traditional American values. More importantly, perhaps, the nation and many of its politicians seemed to have learned a lesson about the value of dissent. In the late 1960s and early 1970s, as dissent from the government's policy in Vietnam grew stronger and turned toward violence, the widespread assumption of the McCarthy era that all dissenters were traitors or fellow-travelers did not return. And in the early 1980s efforts by some politicians to label those who opposed the government's nuclear-weapons policy as dupes of the Communists were promptly met by charges from other politicians that this was guilt by association and "McCarthyism" at its worst.

But many of the issues raised during the decade of legislative Communist-hunting did not disappear; they simply moved off Capitol Hill and up Pennsylvania Avenue to the Department of Justice and its investigative arm, the Federal Bureau of Investigation.

At the end of World War II, no agency of the federal government stood in higher repute than the FBI. No one outside the bureau really knew what it did, but its record in attacking crime and in protecting the nation against sabotage and espionage was beyond reproach.

Then, in 1949 and 1950, during the two trials of Judith Coplon, a Justice Department employee charged with espionage, unsettling information surfaced about the FBI's investigative techniques and the quality and quantity of the files it maintained on the activities of American citizens. Questions that paralleled some of those being asked about the legislative investigation were quickly raised, by Alan Barth and others, about the FBI's activities. Should it be investigating the political affairs of private citizens and accumulating that sort of information? Was it capable of distinguishing between legitimate political dissent and dangerous subversive activities? Does the government have any business at all building dossiers that consist in large part of unverified and unevaluated allegations from unidentified sources?

After the Coplon trial, Barth became one of the FBI's sharpest critics. He argued again and again that its wiretapping activities were illegal and that the dossiers it collected were a serious threat to individual liberty. He pursued these arguments for the rest of his life, even though the full extent of the bureau's surveillance activities did not become known until after Barth's retirement, the death of J. Edgar Hoover and the investigations of the executive branch triggered by the Watergate affair—if then. The issues he raised still figure in discussions of what the FBI's job should be and what legislative limitations should be placed on its activities.

Even in 1983 the curtain has not been fully lifted on the FBI's role in the legislative Communist-hunts of the 1940s and '50s. But disclosures of the way it pursued citizens who opposed racial segregation, or the government's policy in Vietnam during the 1960s and early '70s, suggest that it easily and quickly occupied the space vacated by legislative committees as the self-appointed enemy of dissent—if it was not the unseen instigator of the congressional investigators in the first place.

BACK TO AMERICA

MAY 3, 1962

The Atomic Energy Commission has announced that it will henceforth give its employees and job applicants the right to confront accusers in security cases. How could this right ever have been denied in the United States? What right is more fundamental to the discovery of truth and the administration of justice? What right is more characteristically American?

Speaking some years ago about the code of the American frontier, President Eisenhower said: "In this country, if someone dislikes you or accuses you, he must come up in front. He cannot assassinate you or your character from behind without suffering the penalty an outraged citizenry will impose. . . . If we are going to continue to be proud that we are Americans, there must be no weakening of the code by which we have lived."

But the stark truth is that there was a terrible weakening of that code. Fifteen years ago, in a sudden panic over internal security, the country adopted a clearance program for federal employees which did violence not only to its traditions but to its common sense as well. It chose to rely, in determining the trustworthiness of federal employees, on unverified and unverifiable allegations from unidentified informers.

In some cases not even those who had to decide whether an accused employee was loyal or disloyal were permitted to know the source of the accusations against him.

Denial of the ancient right of confrontation and cross-examination meant not only that accused employees were at a loss to defend themselves and were punished by dismissal and disgrace without any semblance of due process; it meant, in addition, that the government could not apply reason or intelligence in the selection of its personnel. The government, as well as the individuals involved, was denied the benefits of cross-examination which Dean John H. Wigmore characterized as "beyond doubt the greatest legal engine ever invented for the discovery of truth."

The Supreme Court has never categorically ruled that the denial of the right of confrontation and cross-examination in the government security program is unconstitutional. But in 1959 it struck down the industrial security program covering employees of defense contractors on the ground that neither Congress nor the President had authorized a denial of that right. And the Chief Justice [Earl Warren] in his opinion for the court characterized the right as among those principles which "have remained relatively immutable in our jurisprudence." He wrote:

. . . Where governmental action seriously injures an individual, and the reasonableness of the action depends on fact findings, the evidence used to prove the Government's case must be disclosed to the individual so that he has an opportunity to show that it is untrue. While this is important in the case of documentary evidence, it is even more important where the evidence consists of the testimony of individuals whose memory might be faulty or who, in fact, might be perjurers or persons motivated by malice, vindictiveness, intolerance, prejudice or jealousy. We have formalized these protections in the requirements of confrontation and cross-examination. They have ancient roots.

The Atomic Energy Commission has set an example which every agency of the federal government ought to follow. It will be stronger, not weaker, for dealing with its employees justly. It has pointed the way back to America.

THE GROWTH OF THE FBI*

The FBI fixed its eye on espionage and sabotage with admirable precision in the war against the Axis dictatorships. It did not make the mistake of supposing that everyone who spoke with a German accent or who was anti-Semitic or who hailed Adolf Hitler's "regeneration" of the Fatherland was a potential spy or saboteur. It should be set down as a matter of everlasting credit to the FBI that it had no part in the tragic stupidity which led the Army to drive eighty thousand American citizens from the West Coast of the United States on the sole ground that they were of Japanese ancestry. Promptly after Pearl Harbor, the FBI rounded up the small number of actual enemy agents who endangered the security of the United States—and did it so discriminatingly that enemy espionage and sabotage were forestalled without violence to the rights of great numbers of aliens and citizens who might otherwise have fallen under suspicion. The FBI accomplished this because it knew what to look for. . . .

There are disturbing signs that the FBI does not now know what to look for and that it is looking in erroneous directions. The signs are that it is looking for disloyalty—even among law-abiding citizens who have no connection with the Federal Employee-Loyalty Program—and that this search is leading it down innumerable blind alleys and into areas which are not a proper part of any police agency's business. To see these signs, one does not need to give credence to the myriad stories that FBI agents ask whether subjects under investigation read *The Nation* or the *New Republic* or oppose racial segregation; these anecdotes are probably often exaggerated and are, in any case, unverifiable. The signs are to be seen indisputably enough, however, in the official reports of

*From Chapter VII, "The Growth of the FBI," in *The Loyalty of Free Men*, pp. 155–60, 162–7.

FBI agents which were made public in the course of the trial of Judith Coplon for espionage in the summer of 1949.

Miss Coplon was charged with having tried to transmit to a Russian agent abstracts culled from certain classified documents vital to the security of the United States—confidential files of the FBI. One of the shocking aspects of her trial was the attempt by the Department of Justice to secure her conviction without disclosing the character of these documents. They were essential evidence, since one of the significant questions to be determined by the jury was whether they were, in fact, vital to the national security. Federal Judge Albert Reeves, who presided at the first trial of Miss Coplon in Washington, ruled, over the vehement protests of Justice Department attorneys, that if the government wished to prosecute Miss Coplon, it would have to produce in court the evidence on which its prosecution was based. "I regretfully have to state," said Judge Reeves, "that a judge is charged with a responsibility—to see that justice is done. If it turns out that the government has come into court exposing itself, then it will have to take the peril. If it embarrasses the government to disclose relevant material, then the government ought not to be here."

In sober truth, it embarrassed the government greatly. It embarrassed the government, in the first place, because publication of the FBI files may have revealed the identity of certain confidential and strategically placed informants—a high price to pay for the punishment of a young woman who had ceased to be a danger as soon as her espionage activities had been discovered and she had been removed from her job. Publication of the FBI files was embarrassing in another way as well. It disclosed that the FBI had been collecting much "information" of dubious value and that it had been investigating the private lives of citizens who were neither criminals nor threats to the security of the State.

The published files contained, for example, an assertion that one of the assistants to the President of the United States had given some help in obtaining a passport for a trip to Mexico to a friend with whose wife, according to an informant, the presidential aide had once been in love. The files contained a statement by an informant that his next-door neighbors entertained Army and Navy officers up to the rank of colonel "under suspicious circumstances"; that those neighbors "engaged in parties which lasted throughout the night and sometimes into the following morning"; that "approximately once a month an unknown individual in civilian clothes, appearing to be a foreigner, attended the gatherings," and that "when this individual appeared, great secrecy was maintained at the house, and all curtains were drawn"; that, according to the informant, on different occasions the neighbors were observed "moving around the house in a nude state"; that the informant's eleven-year-old boy said he saw one of these interesting neighbors go out on the porch, undressed, to get the newspaper. The identity of the newspaper was not disclosed.

It seems legitimate to ask what an agency of the United States government is doing with gossip of this sort as part of a permanent record. One answer customarily given by law-enforcement officers is that information which may seem valueless today has a possible future utility when considered in the light of additional data which may be uncovered at some later date. Perhaps so. But it also has a possible future danger which it would be folly to ignore. Records are the blood plasma of every modern police system. When they are confined to criminals, they are undoubtedly an effective means of suppressing crime. When, as in the case of the Gestapo and the Italian OSNA and the Russian NKVD and MVD, they involve persons innocent of crime, they may be an effective means of suppressing political dissent or unorthodoxy. They invite misuse. Indeed, the likelihood that they will be misused is far greater than the possibility that they will at some time, as the saying goes, come in handy. It cannot be taken for granted that all future directors of the FBI will have Mr. Hoover's integrity. The possession of great numbers of dossiers on individual citizens could put into the hands of some future police chief a malevolent power.

The FBI makes no pretense that its files contain only tested, reliable material. On the contrary, it has declared candidly on innumerable occasions that they are made up of unchecked and what it calls "unevaluated" information. "The files," Mr. Hoover said in testimony before a Senate Foreign Relations subcommittee, protesting against that body's demand for confidential investigative reports, "do not consist of proved information alone. The files must be viewed as a whole. One report may allege crimes of a most despicable sort, and the truth or falsity of these charges may not emerge until several reports are studied, further investigations made, and the wheat separated from the chaff. Should a given file be disclosed, the issue would be far broader than concerns the subject of the investigation. Names of persons who by force of circumstance entered into the investigation might well be innocent of any wrong. To publicize their names without the explanation of their associations would be a grave injustice." . . .

These reports are supposed, then, to be inviolably secret. If they are kept secret, the argument runs, they cannot do any damage. The first fallacy in this has already been made apparent: they are not necessarily kept secret. Secrecy is an elastic term. The files of the FBI are available to a number of the employees in the Department of Justice. Judith Coplon, for example, evidently had access to them. She conveyed a knowledge of their contents outside the department. The department itself, when it undertook the prosecution of Miss Coplon, decided that the confidential character of the FBI files was not so inviolable as to forbid their disclosure for the sake of convicting Miss Coplon. President Truman, after protesting that he would never, never, never make FBI loyalty reports available to the Senate subcommittee investigating Senator McCarthy's charges, nevertheless allowed subcommittee members to inspect them. . . .

Even if knowledge of the contents of these files never passed beyond the portals of the Department of Justice, they would have a cancerous influence upon American life. The most serious danger in these compilations of random hearsay on the private lives of private citizens is the anxiety and inhibitions they inspire. One thing is quite clear: the files are kept secret from their subjects. No man knows, therefore, whether the FBI has a dossier on him, culled perhaps from unfriendly sources and full of unevaluated untruths. No man can gauge the hidden mischief that may be wrought by such a dossier. Who can tell what avenues of public employment have been closed to him because an administrator has discovered that there is derogatory information concerning him buried in the vaults of the FBI and has not taken the trouble to determine whether this unevaluated information is true or false? It is only in the rare instances when FBI reports are actually disclosed, as in the Coplon case, that subjects can discover, and perhaps repair, the injury done to them. . . .

One of the most shocking documents that came to light in the course of the Coplon trial was an FBI report that an informant, unidentified, was "satisfied" that a number of Hollywood actors or writers were members of the Communist Party. A seven-page single-spaced report on Fredric March and his wife, Florence Eldridge March, was read to the jury and a jammed courtroom after the prosecutor had pleaded with Judge Reeves not to divulge the top-secret FBI files lest the nation's security be imperiled. It is difficult to understand how this particular report could have imperiled anything but the FBI's own reputation. A few excerpts should serve to show its character:

Confidential Informant T-6 advised in December 1947 that Fredric March and Canada Lee were two outstanding Communist Party fellow-travelers connected with the Institute for Democratic Education, Inc., 415 Lexington Avenue, New York City, along with Daniel L. Marsh, president of Boston University; Clyde R. Miller, a professor in the Teachers College at Columbia University; and Norman Corwin of the Columbia Broadcasting System. . . .

On November 27, 1945, Confidential Informant ED-324 advised that he had observed a throw-away advertising a meeting to be held in Madison Square Garden on December 4, 1945 at 8 p.m. This circular was headed "Crisis Coming, Atom Bomb—for Peace or War?" The program was set forth and listed Fredric March thereunder as a speaker, along with Dr. Harlow Shapley, chairman; Julian Huxley, F.R.S.; Senator Charles W. Tobey; R. J. Thomas; Colonel Evans Carlson; Dr. Harold C. Urey; Helen Keller; Danny Kaye; Jo Davidson; and Henry A. Wallace. . . .

Confidential Informant ND-305 advised December 25, 1945, that the subject partook in the entertainment program at a meeting sponsored by the American Society for Russian Relief held at Madison Square Garden, New York City, December 8, 1945. The informant, who was one of about 13,000 attending the meeting, stated that Helen Hayes, noted actress, and the subject portrayed a Russian schoolteacher and a Soviet soldier, respectively, in a skit, whereby they described the devastation of Russia by the Nazis at the battles of Stalingrad and Leningrad. . . .

The question that springs most immediately to mind in connection with these "unevaluated facts" is why the FBI was spending the energy of its agents and the money provided by taxpayers to uncover the private lives of a famous actor and actress. Neither Fredric March nor Florence Eldridge was an applicant for a government job. There is not the slightest indication in the material collected by the FBI that either of them was engaged in any violation of a federal law. There is no activity in the reports quoted above which was not candid and lawful and readily ascertainable from public records—except the evaluation by Confidential Informant T-6 that the subject was "an outstanding Communist Party fellow-traveler." . . .

Prior to the disclosure of this FBI file, Mr. and Mrs. March had been the targets of abusive stories in *Counterattack*. The publication had stated or plainly implied that they were Communists, apparently on the basis of information strikingly similar to that contained in the FBI file. As a result of the allegations, film studios closed their doors to the Marches. They brought a libel suit against *Counterattack* for half a million dollars. The suit was settled out of court, and the newsletter published a statement that it "withdraws and retracts its previously published statements that Fredric March and Florence Eldridge are Communists." Mr. and Mrs. March cannot, of course, get such satisfaction from the FBI.

The second trial of Judith Coplon . . . shed an even more disturbing light upon the FBI's activities. Miss Coplon's counsel had made a charge in the first trial that the government's case was based upon evidence secured through wiretapping—evidence not admissible in a federal court. This charge had been indignantly denounced by the United States Attorney prosecuting the case as a "fishing expedition"; and Judge Reeves, accepting the government's word, had declined to hold a pre-trial hearing to determine whether wiretapping had played any substantial part in the preparation of the government's case.

Judge Sylvester Ryan, who presided over the second trial in New York, did hold such a hearing. The testimony made it clear that the FBI had tapped the telephones of Miss Coplon and Mr. Gubitchev extensively, and the Judge granted a request on the part of defense counsel to compel the government to produce in court thirty FBI agents who had monitored tapped wires leading to the home of Miss Coplon's parents and ten agents who had tapped the wires in Gubitchev's residence. He required the government to produce also about 150 double-faced discs on which were recorded conversations intercepted by tapping the wires of Miss Coplon's apartment in Washington and by planting a microphone in her desk in the Department of Justice. Additional records of monitored conversations which the defense sought to have brought into court could not be produced by the FBI because they had been destroyed. . . .

Several agents testified under oath that these records had been destroyed "as a matter of routine." Subsequently it was disclosed that they had been ordered to destroy the records "in view of the imminency of her trial." . . .

What the FBI agents had done in the course of the Washington trial amounted to nothing less than a deliberate hoodwinking of Judge Reeves. They had sat silent while the prosecutor expressed indignation at the defense suggestion that wiretapping had been employed; several agents had said they "had no knowledge of wiretapping." . . . One agent even asserted that he had had "no personal knowledge" of wiretapping in the Coplon case, although it was subsequently established that summaries of wiretaps had been routed to him for months before the Washington trial and that he, personally, by his own admission, had destroyed "quite a number" of them. In short, the FBI had resorted to wiretapping, which Judge Ryan said was illegal, in the surveillance of Miss Coplon, and had resorted to something very like perjury in an attempt to conceal this illegality from a United States court.

All this was done, it may be readily acknowledged, with a sincere intent to protect the national security. But the government has an imperative obligation to observe restraints imposed upon it by law, and an affirmative duty, when it prosecutes its citizens, to lay before a court all the relevant and significant facts. The government has vast resources and tremendous power, against which individuals may be helpless and the courts impotent to protect them unless the government itself considers the protection of individual rights as much its responsibility as the protection of national security. It is, after all, precisely against the threat of totalitarian rule that we seek to be secure. . . .

THE LAW AND THE FBI

MAY 24, 1958

When FBI Director J. Edgar Hoover acknowledged in a filmed television interview on Sunday that his bureau was operating ninety telephone wiretaps across the country, he in effect pleaded guilty to ninety violations of federal law. The tapping of telephone wires is a crime. It is a crime whether done by private detectives for purposes of blackmail or by the FBI for purposes, as Mr. Hoover put it, of keeping tabs on "internal security cases." Congress, in 1934, adopted the Federal Communications Act with a section, 605, providing that

. . . no person not being authorized by the sender shall intercept any communication and divulge or publish the existence, contents, substance, purport, effect, or meaning of such intercepted communication to any person. . . .

86

And when the Department of Justice argued that this statute applied only to private persons, not to government officers, the Supreme Court ruled unequivocally in 1937 that

> the plain words of 605 forbid anyone, unless authorized by the sender, to intercept a telephone message, and direct in equally clear language that *no person* shall divulge or publish the message or its substance to *any person*.

The pretext on which the FBI has violated the Federal Communications Act ever since its adoption is that President Franklin Roosevelt, in 1941, when the country was on the brink of war, advocated legislation which would authorize wiretapping in cases involving espionage or sabotage against the United States. Such legislation has been advocated in session after session of Congress. But Congress has never adopted it. Unless or until Congress in its wisdom decides to change the clear stipulations of the Federal Communications Act, every wiretap will be a federal crime; and it will remain a crime whether authorized by the director of the FBI, by the Attorney General or even by the President of the United States. This is a government of laws; and laws can be made only by legislatures.

CONTROLLED WIRETAPS

MARCH 3, 1962

Attorney General Kennedy has submitted to Congress a new wiretap bill more carefully drawn than past proposals and containing some reassuring procedural safeguards. It is designed to put an end to the widespread wiretapping which now takes place in violation of the laxly drawn and even more laxly enforced existing wiretap legislation. But there is no blinking the fact that it would authorize a great deal of wiretapping by law-enforcement agencies.

The bill begins with some incontestable legislative findings— that existing law "has not been effective to preserve the integrity of the Nation's wire communications systems"; that "modern criminals make extensive use of the telephone and telegraph"; that "the privilege of wiretapping should be limited to certain major offenses and accompanied by safeguards to ensure that the interception is justified and that the information obtained thereby is not misused."

With this conscientious recognition of the importance of privacy, the bill proposes to permit wiretapping by appropriate federal agencies in cases presenting "a serious threat to the security of the United States." Normally, the tapping would be done only in conformity with a Justice Department application to a federal judge demonstrating that facts concerning a national-security threat could be obtained by the tap and that "no other means are readily available for obtaining such information." If, however, the Attorney General should be convinced that application to a federal judge "would be prejudicial to the national interest," he could himself authorize wiretapping on the basis of a determination "in his sole discretion" that a crime involving treason, espionage, sabotage, subversion or breach of the Atomic Energy Act seriously threatening the national security "has been, is being or is about to be committed."

This newspaper believes, as it has said many times, that wiretapping may be justified when the security of the country is genuinely and seriously imperiled. But to let the justification be determined by a single appointed official is to confer an arbitrary power susceptible of dangerous abuse. The magnitude of this danger can be measured by recalling the character of some past Attorneys General—A. Mitchell Palmer or Harry Daugherty, for example.

We believe strongly that if an Attorney General is to be allowed to tap telephones in cases seriously affecting the national security, he should be required in every case, without exception, to satisfy an impartial judicial authority respecting the need for such action and respecting the probable cause to believe that the particular wiretap will produce information of real value. In short, he should be required to get something in the nature of a warrant, just as he is required to do now if he wants to conduct a search of a suspect's home. And we believe, considering the dragnet nature of a wiretap search, that such a warrant should be obtainable only from a senior judicial officer, say the chief judge of a Federal District Court or a judge of a Circuit Court of Appeals.

The Justice Department bill would permit wiretapping by federal authorities, in conformity with a judicial authorization, in connection with certain other specified crimes—murder, kidnapping, extortion, narcotics violations, interstate racketeering. And it would permit wiretapping by state law-enforcement agencies in the investigation of these crimes on the application of a state Attorney General or a District Attorney to a state judge.

This is much more sensibly limited than the wholly indiscriminate state wiretapping authorized under previous proposals. Nevertheless, it would, we believe, open a Pandora's box, introducing evils far graver than those it would prevent. Wiretapping by such diverse state authorities under varying state standards and without centralized control would make abuses and excesses inescapable; it would mean no Americans anywhere could use the telephone with any confidence that they were talking on a private line.

In considering this bill, Congress needs to weigh competing values. The bill is conscientiously designed, as its painstaking procedural provisions attest, to impede the use of the telephone for criminal purposes. It would at the same time, however, seriously impede the use of the telephone for completely lawful and proper purposes—the exchange of business information, of special confidences, of conversations supposedly privileged between husband and wife, between lawyer and client, between doctor and patient, between priest and parishioner. In curbing freedom of communication for criminals, it would also curb freedom of communication for the law-abiding.

This is a high price to pay. Men who are not free to say what they please without fear of being overheard by official eavesdroppers have lost a vital element of freedom. If combating crime is important, so is the protection of privacy. We believe the price should be paid only in cases vitally affecting national security. . . .*

ELECTRONIC SEARCHES

DECEMBER 23, 1967

The great significance of the Supreme Court's decision of Monday in the *Katz* case is that it brings electronic eavesdropping within the rule of reason. It recognizes that such eavesdropping, when undertaken by police officers for the purpose of obtaining evidence, constitutes a search subject to the restraints of the Fourth Amendment to the Constitution. And, by implication, it invites legislatures to try, if they can, to authorize "reasonable" searches by this means.

It is no more than a recognition of simple reality that the court has now, at long last, overruled its *Olmstead* decision of 1928 holding that wiretapping did not constitute a search in Fourth Amendment terms. In one of the great dissents of legal literature, Justice Louis Brandeis argued brilliantly for a construction of the Fourth Amendment not in literal terms but in its larger design, which, as he conceived it, "conferred, as against the Government, the right to be let alone—the most comprehensive of rights and the right most valued by civilized men." And he warned prophetically that "The progress of science in furnishing the Government with means of espionage is not likely to stop with wiretapping. Ways may someday be developed by which the Government, without removing papers from secret drawers, can reproduce them in court, and by which it will be enabled to expose to a jury the most intimate occurrences of the home."

The view that prevailed in 1928 and that was rather bewilder-

*When Congress passed a wiretap bill six years after the Kennedy proposal, it contained many of the limitations suggested in this editorial.—Ed. note.

ingly echoed in dissent on Monday by Justice Black was that the electronic surveillance entailed no search because it entailed no physical invasion of private premises and seized no material things. It is hard to see how such surveillance can be deemed anything other than a search since its plain purpose is to seek evidence. And the test of the reasonableness of this surveillance must be determined not by the nature of the premises invaded but by the nature of the intrusion of privacy. "For the Fourth Amendment," as Justice Stewart said for the court on Monday "protects people, not places."

The electronic eavesdropping in the case before the court involved the bugging of a public telephone booth. Justice Stewart's opinion contains an observation of great importance for the determination of policy in this delicate area. "No less than an individual in a business office, in a friend's apartment, or in a taxicab," he wrote, "a person in a telephone booth may rely upon the protection of the Fourth Amendment. One who occupies it, shuts the door behind him, and pays the toll that permits him to place a call, is surely entitled to assume that the words he utters into the mouthpiece will not be broadcast to the world. To read the Constitution more narrowly is to ignore the vital role that the public telephone has come to play in private communication."

Since electronic eavesdropping is a form of search, it is constitutionally permissible, if circumscribed in ways that have been held to make other forms of search "reasonable." Justice Stewart even says that the telephone bugging in the *Katz* case would have been permissible had it been authorized in advance by a magistrate, "with appropriate safeguards." So legislatures, including Congress, may now try, if they consider it wise, to write "appropriate" safeguards into a statute permitting electronic eavesdropping. We continue to think that they will find it extremely difficult, and probably impossible, to do so because of the inescapably dragnet character of the device. It is bound to overhear more than is authorized. And we continue to think also that the burden which such eavesdropping will put upon lawful communication between law-abiding citizens will far outweigh the benefits it may confer upon law enforcement.

OUTSIDE THE LAW

JUNE 19, 1969

The Department of Justice has come forward with an appalling paradox: entrusted with enforcement of the federal laws, it holds itself to lie outside the ambit of those laws; committed to the championship of the United States Constitution, it holds itself to be free from the restraints of that fundamental charter. Expressly, the department declared on Friday that it possesses legal power— despite a clause of the Constitution and an Act of Congress to the contrary, and without bothering to obtain judicial authorization in advance—to carry on electronic surveillance of any members of organizations who, in its opinion, may be seeking to "attack and subvert the Government by unlawful means."

No more pernicious notion has ever been propounded by an agency of the United States government. What this comes down to is a bald assertion that the department can take the law into its own hands whenever it thinks the national security is threatened— from within or from without. Last week, in a Federal District Court in Chicago, the department disclosed that it had employed wiretapping or bugging devices to monitor conversations of the anti-war activists who were indicted for inciting riots at the Democratic National Convention last August. What is the department's justification? "Any President who takes seriously his oath to 'preserve, protect and defend the Constitution,' " the department asserts, "will no doubt determine that it is not 'unreasonable' to utilize electronic surveillance to gather intelligence information concerning those organizations which are committed to the use of illegal methods to bring about changes in our form of government and which may be seeking to foment violent disorders."

Of course, the Constitution which any President has taken an oath to "preserve" specifically forbids unwarranted searches. And the Supreme Court has plainly said that electronic surveillance constitutes a search permissible under the Fourth Amendment only when properly circumscribed and authorized in advance by a judge. Congress only last year, wishing to regularize and control electronic eavesdropping, stipulated precisely in the Crime Control Act the conditions under which bugging and wiretapping could be authorized.

Yet the Department of Justice appears to be saying that both the Constitution and the Crime Control Act can be ignored whenever the President thinks that certain groups are "committed to the use of illegal methods to bring about changes in our form of government." What could better illustrate the absurdity of this standard than its application in regard to the tatterdemalion crew of New Leftists who stirred up disorder in the streets of Chicago? If the President or the Department of Justice can see a threat to the nation's security in that tawdry, loose-lipped cabal, it can see a threat in anything.

And if a supposed threat to national security can justify setting aside the Constitution and the law respecting electronic eavesdropping, why can it not be used to justify setting them aside for any other purpose the President and the Department of Justice may deem expedient or convenient in the protection of national security? Will they someday think it not "unreasonable" to set aside the prohibitions against arbitrary arrest or against random physical searches of citizens' homes or against imprisonment without trial or against suppression of speech deemed dangerous? What the Department of Justice has so blandly enunciated is the rationale of dictatorship. It is the justification of every despot from Caligula to Adolf Hitler.

It has been disclosed recently that the Federal Bureau of Investigation systematically, over a period of years, tapped telephones in flagrant violation of the law and in cases having nothing whatever to do with national security. It bugged and tapped the homes and hotel rooms of the Rev. Dr. Martin Luther King and of Elijah Muhammad, the Black Muslim leader, for example. It is beside the point if, as the FBI now asserts, the Attorney General, at that time Robert F. Kennedy, authorized the eavesdropping; no Attorney General had any authority to do so. The FBI also bugged and tapped numerous persons alleged to be part of that undefined group called the "Mafia." This eavesdropping was done in violation of the Constitution, in violation of the law, in violation of a presidential order and in violation of repeated assurances by the director of the FBI that it was not being done. J. Edgar Hoover has forfeited the confidence of the American people. He ought to resign or be removed from office.

A Federal Bureau of Investigation which eavesdrops on citizens is a peril to privacy and a menace to freedom in any circumstances. But a Federal Bureau of Investigation which does this in direct defiance of Congress is intolerable. Congress, in its wisdom, decreed last year that bugging and tapping could be done under court order. For the Department of Justice to assert now that it may bug and tap at its own discretion is to undermine the whole concept of a government of laws.

SHOULD MITCHELL EAVESDROP WITHOUT COURT APPROVAL?*

Attorney General John Mitchell has come forward with a proposition which, for sheer audacity in the assertion of executive power, may well be unsurpassed by anything since the late Oliver Cromwell installed himself as Protector of England in 1653. The general purport of the proposition can be summarized in a slight variant of a currently popular slogan: All power to the President.

The proposition is set forth in a memorandum filed a few days ago by the Department of Justice with the Sixth U.S. Circuit Court of Appeals, asking that court to set aside a ruling by U.S. District Judge Damon J. Keith in Michigan that the Attorney General has no authority to conduct electronic surveillance in domestic national-security cases without prior court approval. The

*Article, the Washington *Post,* February 18, 1971.

department has asked the Ninth Circuit Court to overturn a similar ruling by another U.S. District Judge in California.

In order to appreciate the peril from which the Attorney General was seeking to save the country by electronic eavesdropping, it is necessary to know a little bit about the facts of the Michigan case. It involved three defendants who call themselves White Panthers and who are accused of bombing the Ann Arbor offices of the CIA in 1968, presumably because they disapprove of U.S. government policies.

Bombing is a very serious crime, of course, and no one suggests that it should not be investigated and prosecuted. Whether or not it threatens the security of the United States, it undoubtedly violates the laws of Michigan. Judge Keith did not even suggest that he had any objection to the use of electronic surveillance in investigating the crime—provided a warrant, or court order, had been obtained in advance—something which the Omnibus Crime Control and Safe Streets Act of 1968 specifically authorizes.

Judge Keith even went so far as to say that the obligation to get a warrant for electronic surveillance could be waived in an investigation of subversive activities carried out by foreign agents, a debatable position. He asserted, however, that the "executive branch of our government cannot be given the power or the opportunity to investigate and prosecute criminal violations under two different standards simply because the accused espouses views which are inconsistent with our present form of government."

The proposition put forward by the Attorney General, in his own language, is as follows: "The President, acting through the Attorney General, may constitutionally authorize the use of electronic surveillance in cases where he has determined that, in order to preserve the national security, the use of such surveillance is reasonable." And he contends that it makes no difference whether the threat to the national security comes from foreign subversives or from domestic subversives.

The reasoning behind this proposition is the reasoning behind every form of totalitarianism. The first duty of a sovereign is to protect his sovereignty; the first responsibility of any government is its own perpetuation. Therefore the Presidency carries with it "inherent" power to do whatever the President thinks he needs to do to protect the government of the United States from overthrow by force and violence. The Constitution which the President has sworn to preserve would, argues the Attorney General, "hardly render him powerless to do so."

Setting aside the question whether an inability to tap telephones without a warrant would actually render the President "power-less"—getting a warrant has never proved very difficult—and setting aside also the question whether the White Panthers seri-ously threaten to overthrow the government of the United States by force and violence, the scope and reach of Mr. Mitchell's proposition remains altogether staggering.

The doctrine of inherent power is a doctrine of limitless author-ity. It is the very antithesis of a government of laws—and espe-cially the antithesis of a government of limited powers specifically delegated to it by the people through a written constitution.

In 1967 the Supreme Court ruled that electronic surveillance entails a search of the sort circumscribed by the Fourth Amend-ment. "Over and again this Court has emphasized that the man-date of the [Fourth] Amendment requires adherence to judicial processes," wrote Mr. Justice Stewart, "and that searches con-ducted outside the judicial process, without prior approval by judge or magistrate, are *per se* unreasonable under the Fourth Amendment. . . ."

If Mr. Mitchell argues that the inherent powers of the President entitle him to tap a citizen's telephone or bug his bedroom without a warrant, why should he not also argue that these powers entitle him to ransack a man's home and seize his private papers without a warrant whenever he suspects him of subversion?

One cannot help wondering, indeed, if Mr. Mitchell's logic will not carry him one day into contending that the President, act-ing through his Attorney General, may, when he deems the na-tional security to be in peril, clap a suspect in jail or have him exe-cuted without any of the inconvenient formalities of due process.

Could the President, acting through his Attorney General in the name of national security, order a telescreen—in the manner of George Orwell's *1984*—placed in every American home, in order to save the country from subversion? It is no answer to this anxiety to say that the Attorney General has no intention of committing such excesses.

In his memorandum to the Court of Appeals, the Attorney General advances another ingenious but essentially disingenuous argument. "The government merely contends," he says, "that when the President, through the Attorney General, determines that the use of electronic surveillance is necessary to gather intelligence information needed to protect the national security, the resulting search and infringement of constitutional rights is not 'unreasonable.' "

But this is a patent begging of the essential question to be decided. The purpose of the Fourth Amendment was to interpose between the citizen and his government the detached and impartial judgment of a judicial officer. The determination of the reasonableness of a search cannot fairly be made by the executive official who wants to prosecute the suspect; it can fairly be made only by a judge. That distinction is a foundation of American jurisprudence.

Mr. Mitchell is a conscientious as well as a zealous and patriotic Attorney General. But there is very little in the past record of official electronic surveillance—or at least in what little has been disclosed of that record—to indicate that if left to unchecked administrative authority it would be applied discriminatingly or exclusively against real threats to national security. When one remembers the names of persons reportedly bugged or tapped by the FBI in recent years—the late Dr. Martin Luther King, for example, or Muhammad Ali or Bobby Baker or the gambling czars of Las Vegas, to cite but a few—one cannot help concluding that the Justice Department fishes for subversives as one fishes for sardines, with a very large net.

Electronic surveillance may be an effective device for catching subversives. There have been Attorneys General who say it is and Attorneys General who say it is not. But whatever its virtues, it has vices, too. And Mr. Mitchell seems to have given these vices scant consideration.

In a recent article on the prevalence of FBI wiretapping, Washington *Post* staff writer Ronald Kessler reported: "About a quarter of the senators, congressmen, lawyers, businessmen and journalists responding to a Washington *Post* questionnaire said they have suspected or believed that their telephones were tapped or their offices bugged."

Such fears may be, as Mr. Mitchell termed them, symptomatic of paranoia. But they are also symptomatic of an anxiety altogether out of place in a free society.

There is a terrible and exorbitant cost in such anxiety. Law-abiding men and women are kept from communicating with each other freely. The very essence, the core, of what makes Americans believe that life in this country is better than life in the Soviet Union is not so much the prevalence of affluence as the absence of constraint. To feel secure against officious intrusion, against the fear of that ominous rap upon the door at night which is the symbol of the police state, is to enjoy the reality of what is meant by "the blessings of liberty."

It was, according to the authors of the American Declaration of Independence, precisely for the purpose of securing to individuals certain "unalienable rights" that "governments are instituted among men." What a travesty it would be if, in the name of protecting national security, Americans were to forfeit the individual security for the protection of which their government was established! Perhaps the Attorney General has his priorities reversed.

THE CITIZENS' FEAR
OF THE FBI IS REAL*

How nice it is for Congressmen to have the Attorney General's categorical assurance that their telephones have never, never, never been tapped by the Federal Bureau of Investigation! Some of

*Article, the Washington *Post*, April 11, 1971.

them, being notoriously cynical and remembering that there have been Attorneys General whom the director of the FBI didn't even speak to, let alone confide in, may be a little skeptical that the incumbent AG, a relative newcomer in the Department of Justice, is fully qualified to go bail for Mr. Hoover. But at least it must be a comfort to them to know that Mr. Mitchell regards them as belonging to a special category of untouchables.

Mr. Hoover himself looks upon members of Congress as sacred. The office of the Senate Minority Leader quoted the FBI director as saying: "I want to make a positive assertion that there has never been a wiretap of a senator's phone or the phone of a member of Congress since I became director in 1925, nor has any member of Congress or the Senate been under surveillance by the FBI."

But what, when you come to think about it—if you'll forgive the *chutzpah* in asking—is so special about Congressmen? What about newsmen? Generally speaking, they are, as everybody acknowledges, a wonderful collection of fellows, engaged in a vital form of public service so important to the operation of the democratic process that the Constitution of the United States itself guarantees them a special grant of immunity from government intimidation or interference.

What about butchers and bakers, teachers and tailors? What about doctors, lawyers, merchant chiefs? Are they less entitled to be free from FBI surveillance than the men and women they hire to represent them in the national legislature?

It cannot be said that Senators and Representatives are an invariably law-abiding lot. At least one member of Congress, Representative John Dowdy of Texas, is at this very moment under indictment for the acceptance of a bribe. Daniel Brewster of Maryland is charged with criminal conduct while he was a sitting Senator. A former Congressman from New Jersey, J. Parnell Thomas, spent more time than he meant to in the federal penitentiary at Danbury, Connecticut, because he had taken "kickbacks" in violation of the law. The list is long and unlovely and there is no sense in itemizing it here. The point is simply that members of Congress, like ordinary mortals, sometimes misbehave; and to suggest that the FBI never takes a look at their behavior is to suggest that the FBI is playing some sort of footsie with the people who have the power of the purse. That is an insult to every Congressman.

The trouble with the FBI is that it has become a sovereignty. It is, in a true sense of the term, irresponsible. It reports to no one, except, perhaps, in a formal way to a succession of Attorneys General who have had no power to choose its director; in the course of his forty-seven years in the directorship, Mr. Hoover has seen no fewer than sixteen Attorneys General come and go, and it is safe to say that he is not much awed by them. No committee of Congress has presumed in all those years to demand a look at his dossiers in order to determine if they are really any good and if they really serve the public interest. Nobody really knows—on a basis that would qualify him to testify under oath—whom the FBI currently has under surveillance and whom it bugs and taps.

The truth—the appalling and terrible truth about J. Edgar Hoover and the FBI today—is that they are widely feared by honorable, patriotic and law-abiding citizens. Say that the fear is unjustified, say, as Mr. Mitchell has done, that it is paranoiac, say that it is altogether undeserved. Nevertheless, the fear is real. And it is altogether inconsonant with the idea of a free country.

The fear grows in part out of Mr. Hoover's overlong tenure and unchecked power. What a personal tragedy it is for Mr. Hoover that he did not avert that fear by relinquishing his office voluntarily when he was at the pinnacle of his prestige.

The fear grows in part also out of the development of electronic eavesdropping techniques and computerized record storage.

It grows in no small part out of the Attorney General's arrogant assertion that he possesses power, acting in the name of the President, to tap or bug anyone, any time he regards it as "reasonable" to do so for the protection of internal security—and without bothering to pay deference to the Constitution by obtaining a judicial authorization in advance.

But most of all, fear of the FBI and its director grows out of a widening realization that the bureau has under surveillance great numbers of Americans (outside of Congress) who have violated no law but whose political opinions and associations it deems dangerous.

This realization is based on FBI records which have lately come to light. It is true that they are stolen records. It is equally true that they were selected and distributed by enemies of the bureau. It may well be true, too, that they are not typical. But they are the only FBI records available to the public on which to base a judgment of the bureau's performance. And they indicate unmistakably that the bureau, in the name of protecting internal security, is hounding heterodoxy.

You can measure the prevalence and the virulence of this fear by the appalling fact that the House of Representatives of the U.S. Congress has retained an independent electronics firm to make periodic checks to discover hidden microphones in congressional office suites.

The fear itself is a disease more dangerous than "subversion." It paralyzes the interplay of political forces and ideas that makes the American system work.

WHAT IS IT THAT SECURITY
IS SUPPOSED TO SECURE?*

Pollution of the political atmosphere is as dangerous—and as difficult to reverse—as pollution of the physical environment. Once the healthy balance of a polity has been upset, reason is not easily restored to it. The virus of panic stays latent in the political system, continuously liable to be fanned into fever by demagogy.

Obsessed by the notion that it alone possessed the "secret" of atomic energy and could somehow maintain a monopoly of

*Article, the Washington *Post*, February 9, 1970.

knowledge in this field, the United States made a shibboleth of secrecy in the years immediately after World War II, as though secrecy afforded a magic key to national security. The atom bomb was a guilty secret because it entailed a responsibility for having been the first to unleash upon the world this new and terrifying force. And it was an inevitably corrupting secret because it made Americans look with suspicion on everyone who might discover and disclose it—first upon outsiders and then upon one another.

The anxieties and the mutual mistrust of that period have left ugly pockmarks on the face of America. They show themselves, for example, in the form of congressional investigating committees still empowered to call citizens to account for eccentricities of thought and association. They show themselves in the form of a Subversive Activities Control Board that, when it does anything at all, presumes to tell Americans which, among their multitudinous voluntary associations, are approved by their government and which are condemned. And, most disfiguringly of all, they show themselves in the survival of those procedures for the screening of government employees which were adopted in the late 1940s and perfected in the early 1950s and which, in all their essential features, remain in full force and effect today.

The survival strength of those procedures is illustrated by two developments recently in the news. One is a bill whooped through the House of Representatives just a fortnight ago, designed to extend the same system of selection to all manner of private contractors and private projects having even the most nebulous relation to national defense. It would give the President almost unlimited power to order investigations of persons or groups, whether or not they were under consideration for access to classified matter; and it would, in effect, make conventionality of opinion the standard for determining suitability for employment.

Representative Louis Stokes, who wrote a dissenting opinion about the bill when it came out of the House Internal Security Committee, said that under its language "the President would be justified in barring a worker employed in a defense industry because he took part in peaceful picketing of a chemical company in protest of its manufacture of napalm."

The other recent manifestation of the persistence of pollution in the political environment is to be seen in an announcement last month by the Secretary of Health, Education and Welfare that his department would drop its system of pre-appointment security checks for science advisers, a system that has produced a lengthy blacklist of eminent American scientists, including at least one Nobel Prize winner.

Calling present practices "archaic," Secretary Robert H. Finch said, "Today's decision is the first step in a long overdue updating of our appointment procedure." Indeed the procedure is "archaic" and indeed an updating of it is "long overdue." But it may be seriously doubted that a perversion so deeply embedded in departmental practice is going to be dislodged by a mere command from the head of the department.

And what is to take its place? Why, scientists called upon for consultation and counsel will be required to sign an affidavit swearing that they do not advocate the violent overthrow of the government or belong to any organization that advocates it; and security checks are to be conducted only to make sure that an appointee has not committed perjury in subscribing to this incantation. One wonders whether anybody over the age of ten places the slightest reliance on such a ritual.

The most conspicuous case in which a scientist was declared ineligible on security grounds to serve as a consultant to his government was the case of Dr. J. Robert Oppenheimer. . . .

Dr. Oppenheimer was probably the most brilliant scientific genius to be born and bred in the United States. A man who, according to one of the greatest of his peers, "did more than any other man to make American theoretical physics great" and a man who, by the common judgment of physicists, did more than any other man to develop the atomic bomb was denied clearance as a consultant by the Atomic Energy Commission out of "concern for the defense and security of the United States."

It would be hard to say which constitutes the greater absurdity: that a man should be denied access to the secrets he himself has discovered; or that a government should deny itself access to a man's unique skill and knowledge—and do it in the name of national security.

In his concluding plea to the board that "tried" Dr. Oppenheimer, the physicist's counsel, Lloyd Garrison, said, "America must not devour her own children, Mr. Chairman and members of this board. If we are to be strong, powerful, electric and vital, we must not devour the best and most gifted of our citizens in some mechanical application of security procedures and mechanisms."

The program by which the government of the United States selects the men and women to be entrusted with the general safety and welfare is a program which suffers from two corrupting vices. The first of these is that it equates trustworthiness with conformity, eliminating from government service by a process of natural selection the most daring, innovative and eccentric personalities and giving preference to orthodoxy and mediocrity.

The second is that it relies for judgment as to an individual's security—or "suitability," the standard now in vogue—upon allegations made by unidentified informants.

The consequences are disastrous alike for the country and for many of the individuals subjected to judgment by this system.

Stashed away in the supposedly sacrosanct files of the Federal Bureau of Investigation are dossiers on millions of Americans. And additional dossiers are steadily being compiled as new applicants and employees come under consideration. These dossiers are filled with allegations which the "subject" has no means of correcting or refuting because he does not know who made them, does not even know that they are there.

Worse than this, the officials who are to judge his suitability for employment have no way of finding out who supplied the information concerning him, for the FBI does not disclose its sources of information. Often the allegations will be cabalistically identified as coming from informant V-8 or T-9. And those who are to decide on the "subject's" suitability must guess whether it was obtained from some sage or from the village idiot, from a malicious personal enemy of the "subject" or from a detached observer, from a foreign agent or from a patriot.

Judgment in such circumstances is an impossibility. No private employer would dream of choosing his personnel in such a manner. Anonymous sources are less reliable than no sources at all. One might more safely hire by horoscope—or by lottery.

The FBI, moreover, is not the only federal agency compiling dossiers on the political foibles and inclinations of citizens. An article in the January issue of *Washington Monthly* by Christopher Pyle, a former captain in Army Intelligence, tells of a vast computer-bank operation conducted by the Army, containing dossiers on the politics of law-abiding citizens for use in case of riot or insurrection. Referring to this, Senator Sam Ervin said on the floor of the Senate the other day:

> The Army political surveillance program is only one of the many data systems in the hands of an ever curious executive branch. In the total recall of vast computer systems rests a potential for control and intimidation which is alien to our form of government and foreign to a society of free men. Regardless of the purpose, regardless of the confidentiality, regardless of the harm to any one individual, the very existence of government files on how people exercise first amendment rights, how they think, speak, assemble, and act in lawful pursuits, is a form of official psychological coercion to keep silent, and to refrain from acting. Because it is more insidious, it is a coercion far more effective and intimidating than any tyranny experienced by the Founding Fathers.

The most pernicious part of all this is that no one knows—no one can have the means of knowing—whether he himself is a subject of a dossier carefully preserved in the vaults of the FBI or filed in the remorseless data bank of Army Intelligence. It makes no difference that he may never have sought a government job; someone may have suggested his name, proposed him for a place he never dreamed of taking. And so he can never guess what doors of opportunity may have been closed to him simply because some faceless accuser slipped a little slander into the data collection process. Nor can he tell how widely the slander has been whispered among government officials.

This is not a system of security becoming to a free people. It is a system which at once betrays security and betrays freedom.

The question that needs to be asked about the security system is what it is that security is supposed to secure. It is not an abstraction; it is not a value or an end in itself. The only valid function of security is to secure liberty.

CONTROLLING THE FBI*

In thinking about the future of the FBI it may be useful to look at its origins and at the pattern of its growth. The FBI was created in 1924 by Harlan Fiske Stone when he was Attorney General of the United States, before his elevation to the Supreme Court. One of his first acts when he took charge of the Department of Justice was to abolish the Division of Investigation, which had become mired in politics and had played an ugly part in the arrest and deportation of aliens under the Attorney Generalship of A. Mitchell Palmer. In its place, Stone established a Bureau of Investigation, choosing a young man named J. Edgar Hoover as its director. In doing so, the Attorney General issued the following statement defining the bureau's role:

> There is always the possibility that a secret police may become a menace to free government and free institutions because it carries with it the possibility of abuses of power which are not always quickly apprehended or understood. . . .
>
> It is important that its activities be strictly limited to the performance of those functions for which it was created and that its agents themselves be not above the law or beyond its reach. . . . The Bureau of Investigation is not concerned with

*Article, the Washington *Post*, July 7, 1975.

political or other opinions of individuals. It is concerned only with their conduct and then only with such conduct as is forbidden by the laws of the United States. When a police system passes beyond these limits, it is dangerous to the proper administration of justice and to human liberty, which it should be our first concern to cherish.

These are words worth remembering, worth rolling reflectively on the tongue. For they are not only prescient and prophetic, they are alive with political realism—the kind of realism that led the Founders of the Republic to limit the powers of government by a written constitution.

As everyone knows, the new bureau flourished, achieving a great reputation for honesty about money matters and for efficiency in capturing automobile thieves, bank robbers and kidnappers. Mr. Hoover had a flair for publicity as well as genius for effective organization. Soon the FBI, with its laboratories and advanced crime-detection techniques and daring G-men, became not only the scourge of criminals but the most admired of all federal agencies.

It should be said in defense of Mr. Hoover that he did not initially reach out for power; power was thrust upon him. In 1939, with American involvement in the Second World War at hand, President Roosevelt instructed the FBI to take charge of all investigation "relating to espionage, counterespionage, sabotage, subversive activities, and violation of the neutrality laws." There were three things wrong with this:

First, it was without any statutory basis. Congress had authorized a Division of Investigation in the Department of Justice which afforded an adequate foundation for a Bureau of Investigation to do what Attorney General Stone empowered the bureau to do in the area of law enforcement. But Congress had not then, and has never since, authorized any agency of the Department of Justice to take charge of counter-intelligence although it has, to be sure, repeatedly approved appropriations to carry on such activities. Mr. Roosevelt went still further. He authorized the FBI, with the approval of the Attorney General, to tap telephones in national-security cases, although this entailed a direct violation of an Act of Congress, the Federal Communications Act of 1934.

Second, this assignment took the FBI into a field where it had no real competence or experience. Counter-intelligence is not the normal work of a law-enforcement agency and is far too important to be left to policemen. Mr. Hoover seriously believed that actors and actresses who gave ambulances to Loyalist Spain or entertained at Soviet-American rallies when the two countries were allied in war were perils to American security. He seriously believed that a minister of religion who militantly sought equal rights for black Americans was bound to be a Communist agent. Mr. Hoover sincerely equated political heterodoxy with disloyalty and pursued it relentlessly as "subversive."

Third, the President's directive not only tremendously expanded the FBI's power but also radically changed its focus. Indeed, it brought the FBI right back into the political area from which former Attorney General Stone had removed it, the constitutionally protected area of political opinion and association. Subversive activities are essentially political activities displeasing to those in power but not necessarily criminal in character.

A few years later, in 1947, President Truman—also without any legislative authorization—gave the FBI full responsibility under the Federal Employee-Loyalty Program for investigating the suitability and trustworthiness of government employees and of applicants for government jobs. Relying on accusations by unidentified informers, many of them former Communists, the FBI became, in effect, the definer of patriotism, the arbiter of political acceptability.

No wonder Mr. Hoover became a kind of Lord High Executioner, a law unto himself. No President governed him, no Attorney General ruled him, no Congress fixed boundaries for his roving authority. And so, step by step, we got unlimited surveillance, indiscriminate bugging and tapping and reading of our mail, Cointelpro and black-bag jobs and official blackmail and all the other attributes of a police state that have become the commonplace in newspaper reports in recent weeks. The FBI became,

in truth, precisely what Attorney General Stone warned against—
"a menace to free government and free institutions."

Stone's words are still not heeded, moreover. The incumbent
director of the FBI found himself capable of saying in 1975—
without a perceptible tremor of embarrassment—that "we must
be willing to surrender a small measure of our liberties to preserve
the great bulk of them." Is liberty really now no more than a
luxury, and a liability, in a nation that has grown to greatness
under it? Echoes of the tragic past! Must we destroy the Constitution in order to save it?

The FBI is not going to be brought under control by any congressional oversight committee—which will be told no more than
the FBI wants it to know. It can be brought under control only by
first being cut down to size—by having its role firmly defined by
Congress, so that it becomes what it was meant to be in the first
place, a law-enforcement agency concerned, as Harlan Stone put
it, "only with such conduct as is forbidden by the laws of the
United States."

The elephantine growth of the FBI is superbly symbolized—
perhaps it would be better to say embodied—in the mammoth,
and monstrous, edifice that now stands athwart Pennsylvania Avenue like a brooding Bastille and is identified by golden letters
across its portals as the J. Edgar Hoover FBI Building. If it cannot
be razed, could the House of Representatives not take it as a
fourth, fifth, or sixth office building, instead of taking the new
Congressional Library annex? Then the FBI could be appropri-
ately returned to the Department of Justice as a subordinate agency
of that instrument of government.

At the very least, can it not be renamed—say, the Harlan Fiske
Stone Building—as a memorial not to our past folly but to the
true character of our country, where liberty is valued alike as a
means and as an end, and where a government of laws still prevails?

FOUR

The Heritage of Civil Liberties

The arguments over the loyalty-security programs, the congressional investigations and the FBI's activities brought into question two fundamental aspects of the American constitutional system. The first was the Bill of Rights—what values, what rights, did the men who established the American government really intend to protect when they wrote the first eight Constitutional Amendments? The second was the role of the Supreme Court in enforcing those rights—was it interpreting the Bill of Rights correctly? Was it acting within the scope of its authority when it did so? The questions arose because some politicians and legal scholars argued that the court was turning the Bill of Rights into a "suicide pact" when it enforced the grants of freedom of speech and of the press, the right of privacy included in the Fourth Amendment, and the guarantee of due process of law, in ways that limited the power of government to prosecute suspected Communists and criminals successfully. The men who founded the nation, it was argued, could not be assumed to have written a document intended to curb so sharply the ability of government to defend itself against threats to national security and its citizens against criminals.

Alan Barth regarded this "suicide pact" argument as hogwash. The men who founded the nation, he believed, knew that there were risks in elevating freedom above order and liberty above efficiency. But those men chose to take those risks, first in 1776 when a rebellion was mounted and again in 1787 and 1789 when a Constitution and Bill of Rights were drafted; they wanted no part of a government which provided order and efficiency, even in the pursuit of national security and justice, if it did not first provide freedom and liberty.

In his search for the source of the early Americans' profound taste for what we now call civil liberties—with a push in that direction by Justice Hugo L. Black—Barth came upon the English Levellers of the seventeenth century. The Levellers are given little space in most history books; they were quite unsuccessful in their day. Yet the ideas they espoused—freedom of religion, a government of laws, freedom of speech—came to have great influence in subsequent Anglo-American history.

Barth turned to the story of the Levellers again and again over the years to explain the importance of the Bill of Rights to free men, the correctness of the Supreme Court's interpretations of those Amendments and the essential nature of the court's role in interpreting them. The following essay, which synthesizes two of his lectures, is the fullest explanation of the debt he believed Americans owe to this obscure group of rebellious Britishers.

THE ROOTS OF LIMITED GOVERNMENT*

Americans are much given to saying with pride—with more pride, perhaps, than understanding—that they live under a government of laws and not a government of men.

*This essay is a combination of two lectures—the Lawrence Memorial Lecture delivered on October 18, 1962, at Connecticut College, New London, Connecticut, and the Gertrude C. Bussey Memorial Lecture delivered on October 13, 1964, at Goucher College, Towsen, Maryland.

But laws, of course, are man-made. The Constitution of the United States itself, the supreme law of the land, was framed by mortal men. Ordinary mortals legislate in Congress, administer the laws in the executive branch of the government and interpret the laws in the judicial branch. These laws were not delivered to us on tablets from Mount Sinai; they are not self-executing; and there are inevitable conflicts about the application and construction of them.

What we really mean by a government of laws is that the men who wield power in the name of the public do so not arbitrarily or capriciously but in conformity with certain settled rules and certain fundamental standards of fairness. And we mean also that those who wield power are always subject to check and correction by other elements in the government.

Finally, and most important of all, we mean that there are limits to what the government may do. This is the very essence of what we call civil liberty, which has, as I understand the term, a single, simple meaning. Civil liberty consists of restraints on the power of government.

The government of the United States, for all its majesty, is a government of limited powers. It operates under the terms of a fundamental charter—a written Constitution—which specifies what it may do, and also what it may not do, and which fixes certain procedures for its dealings with its citizens.

If a Constitution is to have force and meaning, the restraints which it imposes on the government—which is to say on the will of the majority—must be implemented by men as detached as may be from political pressures and popular passions. In the American governmental structure, this responsibility is assigned to a Supreme Court.

In recent years the Supreme Court has turned its attention in an unprecedented degree to the protection of private rights against public power. It has needed to do this because in modern times government has been used increasingly to promote the public welfare in ways previously left to private enterprise; and thus the scope and impact of governmental power has been immeasurably extended.

I do not mean at this time to argue whether this is good or bad or merely inevitable; and I do not mean to canvass the whole roster of recent court decisions affecting individual liberty. Roughly, it may be said that they fall into four main categories.

First, the court has said that the Constitution forbids racial discrimination in public facilities or publicly supported places. Since this upsets long-established patterns in a large section of the country, it has aroused a loud outcry against the court.

Second, the court has insisted that the Constitution requires the states to conform to higher standards of fairness in dealing with persons accused of crime. Since this conflicts with a widespread desire to wage a ruthless war on crime which has increased frighteningly in proportion to the urbanization of American life, this too has produced a loud outcry against the court.

Third, the court has insisted that the Constitution calls for substantially equal apportionment of seats in the House of Representatives and in both houses of state legislatures, applying the general and basically democratic principle of one man, one vote. Since this would upset entrenched political organizations and destroy rural supremacy in American politics, it has engendered the loudest hullabaloo of all. . . .

Fourth, the court has acted to protect the separation of church and state decreed by the First Amendment. It declared that the Constitution requires of government absolute neutrality in regard to religion. This necessitated saying that school authorities could not require the recitation of a prayer in public-school classrooms. Since this ran counter to the religious impulses and desires of innumerable Americans—motivated by the loftiest aims to promote virtue and morality—it stirred up a veritable whirlwind of outrage. . . .

The decision in this case, whether you happen to agree with it or not, is a kind of decision which it is peculiarly the function of the Supreme Court to make in the American political system—a decision in which the court operates, if you please, as an antidemocratic influence, as a check on the popular will.

I want to talk about this veto power of the Supreme Court— about this role of the court as a restraint upon majority rule—

because it is, I think, an important aspect of civil liberty and an aspect indispensable to the idea of a government of laws. . . .

The Bill of Rights appended to the Constitution limits the power of the United States government in two ways. First, it restricts the reach and range of governmental authority; it says that there are certain areas—the areas of conscience, expression and association—into which the government may not penetrate at all. It says that the law-making body of the government may make no law whatever respecting religious worship or respecting freedom of speech or publication or restricting the right of the people to join hands freely in voluntary associations for the accomplishment of common political purposes.

Second, the Bill of Rights fixes certain forms which the government must follow in dealing with the people. The Fourth, Fifth, Sixth and Seventh Articles of the Bill of Rights specify procedures designed to keep the government from acting arbitrarily or capriciously or unfairly. These articles declare, among other things, that people living in this country are not to be arrested or imprisoned without judicial authorization, that their homes are not to be subjected to unreasonable searches, that they are not to be tried twice for the same offense, nor required to be witnesses against themselves, nor be deprived of life, liberty or property without due process of law.

The reasons why the authors of the Constitution saw fit to limit the powers of government are set forth candidly and clearly in that extraordinary document, the Declaration of Independence, in which they explained why they were severing their political connections with the English crown. The Declaration sets forth three basic assumptions, or premises, so commonly accepted among the educated people of the eighteenth century that they were referred to as "self-evident."

What are these self-evident premises? First, that all men are created equal; second, that they are endowed by their Creator with certain unalienable rights; and, third, that it is precisely in order to secure these rights that governments are instituted among men, deriving their just powers from the consent of the governed.

Now, it is plain that these ideas have religious roots. They grow out of a belief that the individual human personality is possessed of an innate worth and dignity by reason of its divine origin—by reason of the supposition that man was created in the image of God. Because man is God's creature, he is born free. He possesses inviolable immunities. There is in him a shrine of conscience which no temporal power may invade. John Milton expressed this belief eloquently:

> Our liberty is not Caesar's. It is a blessing we have received from God himself. It is what we are born to. To lay this down at Caesar's feet, which we derive not from him, which we are not beholden to him for, were an unworthy action, and a degrading of our very nature.

These ideas have ancient and diverse origins, of course. The sense of man's worth as an individual child of God finds expression in the Old Testament and is the central premise of Jewish thought and theology. It finds expression equally in the New Testament as the keystone of Christianity. And its sources are no less discernible in classical Greece and Rome.

But for the political implementation of these ideas, one must look to English history in particular. There was a foreshadowing of them in Magna Carta—although one could hardly call Magna Carta a democratic document. Nevertheless it did provide that "No free man shall be taken or imprisoned or dispossessed or outlawed or banished, or in any way destroyed . . . except by the legal judgment of his peers or by the law of the land."

It was in the first half of the seventeenth century, however, that the idea of individual liberty and the concept of limited government as the indispensable condition of liberty came into full focus. This was perhaps the most tumultuous and teeming half-century in English history—a span of years that embraced the death of Elizabeth, the accession of the Stuart kings, the production of the King James version of the Bible, the poetry of John Milton, the rise of Parliament, the Civil War, the Regicide—and the brief glory of the Leveller Movement.

The bitter and terrible English Civil Wars of the 1640s revolved around two main issues. One was a matter of religion. It was a time in which religion was the paramount fact of social and political life. Religion was inextricably involved in government, for in England church and state were indistinguishable; the King governed both, and prelates like Archbishop Laud exercised great secular authority. The first Civil War became in large degree a struggle between the Episcopalian nobility and gentry on the one side and the Presbyterian gentry and merchants on the other. It would be hard to say on which side lay the greater degree of dogmatism and intolerance.

The other principal matter at issue in the Civil War was a struggle for supremacy between King and Parliament. All through the reign of King James, as he more and more asserted the claims of royal prerogative, Parliament more and more asserted that it, and it alone, was the essential source of law and authority.

Sir Edward Coke, Attorney General alike under Elizabeth and under James—and later Chief Justice of the Common Pleas—became the champion of Parliament against the King. Acts of Parliament, he held, bound the sovereign as well as his subjects. And royal edicts in violation of those acts had no validity.

Coke went still farther: not only was the monarch subject to acts of Parliament, he asserted, but Parliament itself was subject to the common law—that ripened harvest of judicial decisions rooted in long experience and representing the wisdom and conscience of the community.

But King James, and after him his son, King Charles, accepted no such limitations on their authority. They believed themselves divinely anointed. King Charles, a fellow not without some very attractive qualities, regarded the people as wards to be guided and governed by him conscientiously, but in his absolute discretion. As he saw it, the people had no rights save those he chose to confer upon them. And these rights, in any case, were rights they might assert against their fellow subjects but not against their sovereign. G. M. Trevelyan quotes him as expressing . . . [such] views with his dying breath upon the scaffold. . . .

Just before it condemned poor King Charles to death, Parliament adopted a resolution expressing its own ideas respecting the locus of supreme power. The resolution declared:

> That the people are, under God, the original of all just power; that the Commons of England, in Parliament assembled, being chosen by and representing the people, have the supreme power in this nation; that whatsoever be enacted or declared for law by the Commons in Parliament assembled, hath the force of law, and the people of this nation are concluded thereby. . . .

One serious trouble with this resolution lay in the simple fact that the Parliament which passed it could not be said by any stretch of anyone's imagination to have been chosen by or to be representative of the people. This was the Rump, or remnant, of the Long Parliament, which had, in any case, not been subject to any popular election for a decade. Most of its members, after the Presbyterians of the Long Parliament had been evicted by Oliver Cromwell, were country gentry and the rest were lawyers or merchants, for the most part the younger sons of the land-owning families. They represented, in short, only a particular class and interest of the English people.

Most Englishmen could not realistically count themselves as being a part of the "original of all just power." They had no voice whatever in the selection of their government. And to some of them it seemed no better to be ruled by the absolute fiat of a House of Commons than to be ruled by the absolute fiat of a King.

There developed among the men who had fought for freedom under Fairfax and Cromwell and Ireton in the New Model Army a strong feeling that they would have fought entirely in vain if they merely exchanged the tyranny of King Charles for the tyranny of a Parliament which would dictate to them without limitation in all matters of conscience—and a Parliament in which, besides, they were largely without representation. . . .

[T]here has never been an army like . . . [this New Model Army] before or since anywhere on earth—or in Heaven either, for that matter. . . . This was truly a people's army in which any ambitious private might hope after a few years' service to command a regiment and in which there was hardly any class barrier between officers and men. The code of discipline was strict; but off duty all ranks met as equals. They met and they argued. They argued incessantly about politics and religion—which in that time were much the same thing. This was, in [H. N.] Brailsford's fine phrase, a "God-drenched" army which prayed as it rode and credited God with all its victories. It regarded religious liberty as the central aim of politics.

It was among the enlisted men and the junior officers of this remarkable army that the Leveller Movement found its principal support in the brief period, 1646 to 1649, that it exercised influence—largely the interval between the two English Civil Wars. The Leveller Movement was in reality a political party—probably the first political party, in the modern sense of the term, ever formed. The name "Leveller" was applied to it, in derision, by its critics, who charged it with wanting to level all property in a kind of premature seventeenth-century communism. But in point of fact the interest of the Levellers was simply in religious and political democracy.

The leaders of the Leveller Party were an extraordinary group, most of them officers in the New Model Army. Foremost among them was John Lilburne, whom Lord Acton once characterized as "the boldest thinker among English democrats." Bold he was; and brash as well. Among the people of London who loved him for his indomitable independence, he was known affectionately as "Freeborn John."

When he was still a very young man, apprenticed to a merchant in the cloth trade in the City of London, John Lilburne made a trip to Holland and, on his return, was arrested and haled before the Court of Star Chamber on suspicion of having smuggled "factious and scandalous books" into England. The suspicion was probably very well grounded. But Lilburne, who had learned a little law, insisted that no freeborn Englishman could be compelled to answer questions except in response to specific charges and, in any case, could not be required to serve as a witness against himself.

For this contumacy, Lilburne was fined £500, a staggering sum for a young apprentice, was tied to a cart and, his body bared, was whipped through the streets of London all the way from the Fleet Prison to the Palace Yard at Westminster. And all the way, as the cart moved along and the lash fell upon him, John Lilburne, blessing God for having called him to this service, declaimed to the crowd about his wrongs and about their rights.

At Westminster he was placed in a pillory, bowed down with his neck in the hole and his lacerated back bared to the sun; and there he stood for two hours cheerfully exhorting all who would listen to resist the tyranny of the bishops. When he was told to be quiet, he refused; and so he was gagged, so cruelly that his mouth bled. And then, in a gesture as magnificent as it was theatrical, he plucked from the folds of his robe three copies of the pamphlet that had caused all the controversy and flung them to the crowd.

After this, Lilburne was thrown into the Fleet Prison—for ten days in solitary confinement with irons on his hands and legs and with nothing to eat. For two and a half years he remained in prison—until, at last, the Long Parliament set him free. Soon after, in 1641, it abolished the Court of Star Chamber forever.

Lilburne was, no doubt, a most difficult and intractable fellow. There was an epigram written about him on his death which tells a good deal about his personality:

> *Is John departed and is Lilburne gone?*
> *Farewell to Lilburne and farewell to John.*
> *But lay John here; lay Lilburne there about,*
> *For if they ever meet, they will fall out.*

How much the world owes to obdurate—perhaps cantankerous—individuals like John Lilburne is quite beyond calculation. He defied power for the sake of principle; but the principle, in those days when power was only beginning to be curbed by law, was not generally accepted nor embodied in any Bill of Rights. It was on his own courage and conscience that John Lilburne had to stand—on his own sense of what constituted fair procedure.

To John Lilburne's indomitable independence we owe in no small measure the general recognition today that men are not to be arrested on suspicion and interrogated at random and compelled to convict themselves out of their own mouths. Except in certain congressional investigating committees, the modern analogue of the Star Chamber, random questioning in the hope of eliciting some damaging admission from a suspect is no longer countenanced among free men.

Now, let me try to tell you, briefly, about some of the novel and daring ideas the Levellers espoused—novel and daring in their time, however self-evident they may seem to us three hundred years later.

Not long after a time when men were hanged, drawn and quartered, and burned at the stake for religious deviation, the Levellers advocated complete religious toleration. They sought freedom of worship not alone for Episcopalians and Presbyterians and the innumerable Puritan sects that flourished then, but even for Catholics and Jews. "If God have revealed more light of the Gospel to one than another," Richard Overton wrote, "shall the more knowing trample the ignorant under his feet?"

They were opposed to any establishment of religion. An established Presbyterian Church, supported and made official by the government, seemed to them no more desirable than the established Episcopal Church which had been official under King Charles. They were also opposed to any centralized ecclesiastical authority.

They believed, rather, in gathered churches in which each congregation would be free to choose its own forms of worship and its own minister. They stood, in short, for a wall of separation between church and state, believing that each would be stronger by reason of complete independence.

The spirit of toleration colored their view of political as well as religious differences. They favored free speech for utilitarian reasons—because they believed that only through unfettered discussion—"liberty of discourse" was Walwyn's phrase for it—could they arrive at truth or ensure enjoyment of civil liberty.

At the heart of the Leveller philosophy was a belief in democracy. The Levellers sought a dramatic enlargement of the franchise to include not only landowners but free men of every condition throughout England. The cornerstone of their creed was a conviction that the just powers of government had to be derived from the consent of the governed. Thomas Rainsborough put it this way:

> For really, I think that the poorest he that is in England hath a life to live, as the greatest he; and therefore, truly, sir, I think it's clear that every man that is to live under a government ought first by his own consent to put himself under that government; and I do think that the poorest man in England is not at all bound in a strict sense to that government that he hath not had a voice to put himself under.

Now, I must turn to the most important fact of all about the Levellers, the most important contribution made by them to political science. Believing as they did in the idea that men possess inalienable rights, believing also that governments can exercise only such powers as are conferred on them by the people, the Levellers proposed to create a new government in England by compact. They proposed a fundamental charter—a written constitution, if you please—which would define and limit what the government could do. They called this charter "An Agreement of the People." And they proposed to go about the country and ask the people to sign the agreement, thereby through their own consent putting themselves under the government they were to establish.

As you know, the Agreement of the People did not succeed, and England has never adopted a written constitution. In theory, parliamentary power knows no bounds; in practice, it pays deference to the common law and to settled principles of individual rights.

It was in the new world, however, that the Leveller vision

became a political reality. Puritans who came to these shores because they could not find in seventeenth-century England the religious toleration they desired brought with them the Leveller idea of limited government. And when Americans established a government of their own, they fixed boundaries for its powers.

The Agreement of the People found its full flowering in the Constitution of the United States. That Constitution erected a fortification for freedom. It furnished safeguards against ourselves, against our passions and extravagances. It set forth in a Bill of Rights those "unalienable rights" which no Congress, no government, no majority of the people could invade or violate.

It is far easier to lose liberty than to win it. The loss comes about, like so many losses, from forgetfulness, from carelessness.

I am fearful not only that the Levellers have been forgotten but that their legacy has been forgotten, too. Again and again in recent years—in the name of national security, in the name of public safety, in the name of convenience masquerading as necessity—we have tolerated constitutional short-cuts which involved serious trespasses on individual rights.

Think, for example, of the degree to which we have institutionalized in our federal government a system of personnel investigation in which men may be dismissed and disgraced on the basis of whispered accusations by faceless informers—without any opportunity to confront and cross-examine their accusers.

Think of the extent to which we have allowed congressional investigating committees to probe into the affairs of universities and newspapers and even churches—into areas where Congress is forbidden to legislate. Think how often we have permitted these committees to question men about matters of association and belief—and to punish them by publicity for offenses which are not punishable by law.

Think of how often we let law-enforcement agencies cut the corners of procedural restraints—let them arrest men on mere suspicion and hold them for interrogation in the lonely, intimidating atmosphere of a police station, or let them tap telephones at random, or invade the privacy of homes with unwarranted searches. Think, if you will, of how carelessly we have tended to dismiss the procedural protections of the Constitution—those protections which limit the power of the police—with that mischievous catchphrase "mere legal technicalities," when, in simple truth, they constitute the essential bulwarks of a free society.

Think, to take just one more instance, of the hullabaloo that was raised recently when the Supreme Court ruled that the Regents of the State of New York could not require the recitation of a prayer in public-school classrooms. How could Americans have so completely forgotten the reasons which led the authors of the Constitution to forbid any "establishment of religion" in the United States! In his eloquent and compelling opinion for the court, Mr. Justice Black reminded us of those reasons:

It is a matter of history that this very practice of establishing governmentally composed prayers for religious services was one of the reasons which caused many of our early colonists to leave England and seek religious freedom in America. . . . By the time of the adoption of the Constitution, our history shows that there was a widespread awareness among many Americans of the dangers of a union of Church and State. These people knew, some of them from bitter personal experience, that one of the greatest dangers to the freedom of the individual to worship in his own way lay in the Government's placing its official stamp of approval upon one particular kind of prayer or one particular form of religious service. . . . The first Amendment was added to the Constitution to stand as a guarantee that neither the power nor the prestige of the Federal Government would be used to control, support or influence the kinds of prayer the American people can say—that the people's religions must not be subjected to the pressures of government for change each time a new political administration is elected to office.

All this is a legacy of the Levellers. It is the essence of what they learned in a bitter civil war and in the jails where they were flung because they would not bow the head or bend the knee in worship at the command of any government.

The most vital part of the Leveller legacy lies in the idea that civil liberty depends upon restraints on the power of government. And in a democracy this means, of course, restraints upon ourselves.

The Constitution is a limitation not alone upon the government. It is a limitation on the people, on *us*. Sometimes it keeps us from doing what we would like to do. That is the purpose of a Constitution. That is the essential meaning of limited government. That is the indispensable condition of a government of laws.

The Supreme Court of the United States has served valiantly, at least in recent years, as a bulwark of individual liberty against the potentially oppressive power of the state—against the impatience of majorities. But free men can never rely upon courts alone for the preservation of their freedom. Courts can give warning of danger. But they are really powerless to protect us from ourselves. They can remind us of our heritage. But they cannot preserve that heritage for us.

A free society is a society in which there is wide tolerance of diversity—tolerance of religious convictions which may seem to the majority to be leading to perdition, tolerance of political opinions which the majority may deem dangerous and even disloyal, tolerance of the largest possible range of individual eccentricities and idiosyncrasies. It is a society in which there is respect for privacy, respect for individuality.

What we have to remember above all else as a self-governing society is that it is we, the people, who must be controlled. And it was precisely in order to control *us*—to fix boundaries for our power—that the United States Constitution was ordained and established.

FIVE

Respecting Freedom

Alan Barth's love for the First Amendment went beyond its application to political speech, political action and political association. While he regarded those rights as essential to the ability of citizens to control their government and their destiny, he also believed that the other rights guaranteed by the First Amendment were an essential part of the liberty the Constitution was written to ensure. He believed an uncensored press and the freedom to demonstrate peaceably against the government were handmaidens of free speech in the quest for political liberty. He believed that the right to read or look at whatever material caught a citizen's fancy was an essential element of intellectual freedom. And he believed that freedom of religion and separation of church and state were vital to human liberty.

Barth's interpretation of the First Amendment was much like that of Justice Hugo L. Black—doctrinaire, with no tolerance for the idea that the rights it guarantees could or should be subordinated to other interests of either citizens or governments through any "weighing" or "balancing" process. He believed that the First Amendment barred all American governments—federal, state and local—from placing any limits on the exercise of the rights it guaranteed. He did distinguish sharply, however, between speech and conduct, between peaceful and rowdy demonstrations, and between the rights of adults and of children. And his personal views of what citizens *should* do in matters of politics, religion and morality were clearly divorced from his views of what citizens *could* do in those areas without governmental interference.

This view of the First Amendment led Barth to defend the Supreme Court's decision barring organized prayer exercises in the public schools and to attack proposals aimed at public reimbursement to parents for the costs of religious education; he feared that once the wall of separation between church and state was breached, either government would eventually come to control religion or a particular religion would come to control government. This view also led him to defend with equal passion the right of Nazis to have their say in public places and of the anti-war demonstrators of the late 1960s to express their displeasure with the government vigorously enough to disrupt the normal flow of life in Washington; it also led him to denounce demonstrators whose conduct, as contrasted with their speeches, breached reasonable regulations established to maintain public order and safety. It is worth noting that the anti-war demonstrators were opposing a policy supported by the same editorial page on which Barth's frequent defenses of their right to demonstrate appeared.

Similarly, Barth argued for the elimination of any censorship over books, newspapers, magazines and movies; he did not believe that the public's consumption of political propaganda or of salacious material could endanger the national security or the morality of the American people; he did, however, contend that government had power to limit the distribution of pornographic material to children.

Like Justice Holmes, Barth believed that when ideas—political, social, religious or moral—are tested in the marketplace, the best will survive. He knew there was a risk in this; there is always a possibility the worst may survive. But for him, this was the risk willingly accepted by those who wrote the Constitution and the First Amendment because they believed, as he did, that without accepting the risk there can be no democracy, freedom or liberty.

IN BEHALF OF RELIGION

JUNE 26, 1962

The Supreme Court's decision respecting prayer in the public schools is an act of liberation. It frees schoolchildren from what was in effect a forced participation by rote in an act of worship which ought to be individual, wholly voluntary and devout. It frees the public schools from an observance much more likely to be divisive than unifying. And most important of all, perhaps, it frees religion from an essentially mischievous and incalculably perilous sort of secular support.

The main thrust of Mr. Justice Black's learned, illuminating and richly eloquent opinion for the court is to show that one of the principal purposes of the First Amendment was to preserve religion in the United States from the inevitably corrupting influence of secular authority. The Establishment Clause, he wrote, "stands as an expression of principle on the part of the Founders of our Constitution that religion is too personal, too sacred, too holy, to permit its 'unhallowed perversion' by a civil magistrate." It would be wholly absurd to treat this concern for religious liberty as reflecting any indifference, let alone hostility, to religious worship. Speaking of that faith in the power of prayer which animated so many of the authors of the Constitution, Mr. Justice Black went on:

These men knew that the First Amendment, which tried to put an end to government control of religion and of prayer, was not written to destroy either. They knew rather that it was written to quiet well-justified fears which nearly all of them felt arising out of an awareness that governments of the past had shackled men's tongues to make them speak only the religious thoughts that government wanted them to speak and to pray only to the God that government wanted them to pray to. It is neither sacrilegious nor antireligious to say that

127

each separate government in this country should stay out of the business of writing or sanctioning official prayers and leave that purely religious function to the people themselves and to those the people choose to look to for religious guidance.

There is no doubt that this decision will be disappointing and painful to many deeply conscientious ministers of religion and to laymen who believe that public education ought to be infused with some measure of religious faith. But religious faith is best inculcated in the home or in places consecrated to religion. And the freedom to inculcate it in accordance with private conviction is best fortified by a jealous exclusion of civil authority from all forms of religious activity.

A prescribed prayer, however non-denominational it may be, is a form of enforced orthodoxy and is therefore an inescapable enemy to religious liberty. Let children speak to the teachers appointed to instruct them in forms and language prescribed for their education. But let them speak to God in the forms and language prescribed by their individual consciences.

ALL-PURPOSE PRAYER

APRIL 30, 1964

When Representative Becker appeared before the House Judiciary Committee Tuesday to defend his school prayer and Bible-reading proposal, he was asked, "Who would prepare the prayer?" This is the key question, the vital question, for a people whose political system is rooted in the idea of an absolute separation of church and state. But for a man who wants to amend the Bill of Rights, Mr. Becker was irresponsibly vague. He proposes to leave it to "various school districts and localities to determine the prayers" to be recited. What a formula this offers for conflict all over the country.

Representative Cahill asked him, "Who is to determine what version of the Bible is to be read?" And again he answered: "Local people." Earlier, Mr. Becker had said that when he attended school, "No one suffered a dilemma when passages were read from the King James Version of the Bible, although I am a Roman Catholic." He is entitled, of course, to speak for himself. But many Catholics, including officials of the hierarchy, have objected strongly, on grounds of principle, and with complete justification in our judgment, to school use of the King James translation as a form of proselytizing for Protestantism.

To many conscientious persons, forms of worship are of great significance. Mr. Becker speaks cavalierly of a "non-denominational" prayer satisfactory to everyone; but no such prayer has yet been devised in any land under the sun. And every attempt by public authorities to offer any prayer or other form of religious observance as suitable for all men has produced bitter division and dissension.

Mr. Becker may make light of doctrinal differences; but they have been a prolific source of man's most hideous inhumanity to man. When Michael Servetus went to the stake for heresy in sixteenth-century Geneva, he was heard to pray from the flames, "O Jesus, thou Son of the eternal God, have pity on me!" It is said that if he had been willing to confess Jesus, the eternal Son of God, he might have been saved. But because he took an unorthodox view of the Trinity, he put the adjective in the wrong place.

In thousands of school districts all over the United States, school boards, or school principals or school teachers—public officials all—will be empowered, under Mr. Becker's proposal, to say what is orthodox in worship for their pupils. It would be hard to find a more certain prescription for discord. It would be hard to contrive a more futile coercion of conscience. The First Amendment was devised precisely to save this country from such attempts to fix an official orthodoxy.

PERMISSION TO PRAY

APRIL 21, 1968

The [District of Columbia] Board of Education went on record Wednesday night—with only two dissenting voices—as "having no objection to the voluntary participation" of school personnel in prayer sessions before school starts in the morning. This action was in response to a request signed by three teachers for "permission" to undertake this act of religious worship. It seems to us that the request was mischievous and the granting of permission by the board altogether misguided.

The three teachers were, of course, not really asking permission to pray. No board, no public authority of any sort, has power in the United States to grant or withhold such permission. Individually, teachers, like other Americans, are wholly free to communicate with God at any time, in any place and in any way they please. The Board of Education should have told them that it has nothing whatever to do with such a request.

What the teachers were really requesting, however, was permission to use a school building—constructed and maintained by public funds for a secular purpose—in order to conduct a religious exercise. They can, of course, hold prayer meetings in their homes or in their churches. But for the Board of Education to authorize their use of a schoolroom for an act of worship is to lend its support and encouragement to such worship. And this is precisely what the First Amendment as construed by the Supreme Court forbids any public authority to do in the United States.

It is not a derogation of religion but a protection of religious freedom to exclude public authority from any encouragement of worship. "The place of religion in our society is an exalted one, achieved through a long tradition of reliance on the home, the church and the inviolable citadel of the individual heart and mind," Mr. Justice Clark wrote for the Supreme Court five years ago. "We have come to recognize through bitter experience that it is not within the power of government to invade that citadel, whether its purpose or effect be to aid or oppose, to advance or retard. In the relationship between man and religion, the state is firmly committed to a position of neutrality.''

Members of a Board of Education really ought to understand a fact so fundamental to the American system.

THE FIRST AMENDMENT
AND THE SCHOOL-AID ISSUE

MARCH 3, 1971

The fashionable ruse just now for funneling public funds into support of religious schools is to set up a voucher system under which tuition grants are paid to the parents of children attending such schools. It is argued that, by avoiding direct payment to church institutions, this will somehow serve to circumvent the constitutional prohibition against any establishment of religion in the United States. Possibly so, if five Supreme Court Justices can be persuaded to squinch their eyes tight shut to the realities of the situation. At the same time, however, it will almost certainly open the floodgates to a tide of trouble—the very sorts of trouble which the authors of the Constitution sought to avert when they adopted the First Amendment.

In Maryland, Governor Marvin Mandel, following the recommendation of the Kraushaar Commission, has just recommended a $12.1 million scholarship program for the state's 120,000 private elementary and secondary school pupils, eighty-three per cent of whom are enrolled in Catholic parochial schools.

From the Governor's point of view, this endorsement would probably shift the burden of decision to the electorate as a referendum item in the November 1972 general election. But, as one legislative leader put it succinctly, "I wish that the damn thing would just go away. It'll tear this state apart.''

No doubt it will tear the state apart, and not just in 1972 either but year after year as Catholics and non-Catholics vie with each other for division of the public purse in a rivalry bound to have ugly religious implications. That rivalry has created bitter and intolerant antagonisms in every country where it has been allowed to fester.

In New York State just a fortnight ago, Governor Rockefeller announced that he definitely favored some form of aid for parochial schools, an assertion comforting to his Catholic constituents. What he has in mind is hard to guess; but he definitely drew the line at any form of tuition-aid legislation, asserting that such a bill would create "a very effective lobby for doubling the amount the following year." And he added, realistically, that "the amount would go up every year until it reached the point where the state would be funding" non-public schools almost totally.

The First Amendment has two main purposes. One was to keep religion out of the country's political life. The authors of the Constitution had seen in Europe how Protestants in power persecuted Catholics and how Catholics in power persecuted Protestants; and how both of them persecuted Jews. And they were determined to spare the new country they were creating that sort of religious enmity and strife.

The other purpose was to keep the authority of the state out of religion in order to assure absolute freedom of conscience. Government support of religion, the founders knew, would lead to government control of religion. . . .

There is not and there never has been any hostility to religion in this neutrality, this abstention from governmental intrusion into the area of religious worship. There has been only a protective restraint, born of the knowledge that individual freedom to worship—or to refrain from worship—would be lost if government could put its official stamp of approval on any particular form of religious observance—or even upon religion in general.

Americans have every right, of course, to seek for their children a religiously oriented education and to send their children to private schools which provide the sort of religious orientation they want. But they have no more right to ask the general public to pay for such schools—and for the religious instruction they provide—than to ask the general public to pay for the churches in which, happily, they are free to gather for prayer and for worship as they please.

It is very loosely said that if the country's parochial schools do not soon receive public support, they will be obliged to close their doors. If this is so, it can mean only that these schools are not sufficiently important to the parents who prefer them or sufficiently important to the church that sustains them to warrant the sacrifices that continuance of them would entail.

It is true, to be sure, that if the parochial schools ceased operation, the children now attending them would have to be accommodated in public schools; and this would undoubtedly entail an enlarged public expense. But it is an absurdity to argue from this that parents who do not now use the public schools are entitled to a rebate amounting to the value of the public facilities not used by them.

Parents who want the benefits of private schooling and yet do not want to pay for them need to reckon the real costs of seeking public support. Public support, in the end, must mean public control. And in the field of religion, this is wholly stultifying.

The Supreme Court has already said that prayers or Bible readings may not be prescribed in any school supported by public funds. What an empty victory it would be for these who seek public support for religious schools to gain that support and then find that in consequence the schools could not be used for any religious observance.

In two states recently, referendums were held on the subject of state aid to church schools and other non-public schools. In Michigan, voters approved a constitutional amendment banning all state aid, direct or indirect, to private schools. And in Nebraska, voters turned down a proposal for state aid to private schools, now prohibited. But perhaps in other states the decision will go the other way. In any event, the struggle will be deeply divisive. And to whatever degree the private schools gain from it, the public schools will lose—lose in terms of money and in public support.

The religious schools are organs of a church. The public schools are organs of a secular authority, the state. Would it not be wiser, as the founders of the Republic concluded, to keep church and state altogether separate?

TAKE IT EASY

DECEMBER 28, 1965

Tolerance is always the first casualty of war. Criticism of the government—especially any opposition to its war aims and purpose—is likely to be regarded as sympathy and solicitude for the enemy and therefore as an expression of disloyalty. In truth, of course, criticism of prevailing public policy may be the most courageous and the most useful form of patriotism. But when passions run high and the nation's security seems threatened from outside, a critic is even less likely than a prophet to find honor in his own country.

The thought may be worth remembering in time of tension. Young men who burn their draft cards in public places or who sit-in at the offices of local Selective Service Boards no doubt seem very unattractive to a majority of their fellow citizens and perhaps altogether odious to other young men who have been sent to risk their lives in Vietnam. But their protests or their bravado or their folly—call it what you will—do not really constitute any immediate or serious danger of wrecking the government or even of impeding the war effort. They may well be a nuisance but they can hardly be considered a menace.

If these demonstrators break any law, they ought to be prosecuted and punished. But it cannot be looked upon as anything other than an expression of national hysteria to put a boy in prison for five years because he is guilty of a foolish and futile gesture, such as setting fire to his draft card—a gesture that cannot affect in the slightest degree his liability for military service. This gesture, like a draft-board sit-in, is not an ordinary criminal act; in intent it is a form of protest—which is to say an expression of opinion—and entitled, therefore, to considerate protection under the First Amendment. Stifling such protest is far more dangerous to the country than tolerating it.

In a different but not wholly unrelated area, a jury last week convicted a young Harlem Negro, William Epton, in Criminal

Court in New York of conspiring to riot, of advocating the over-throw of the New York State government and of conspiring to overthrow it. The statute under which Epton was prosecuted was the same repressive criminal-anarchy statute under which Benja-min Gitlow was prosecuted forty years ago—and against which Mr. Justice Holmes protested so eloquently.

Epton, outraged by what he deemed injustice and police brutal-ity in Harlem, was one of those who talked with the most impru-dent intemperance a few hours before the Harlem riot of July 1964. But to pretend that he was solely, or even principally, re-sponsible for the violence that followed is simply to seek a scape-goat instead of a solution for a social problem of the most complex causation. Maybe he deserves punishment, but surely not the twelve years in prison to which he could be sentenced under New York's repressive statute.

President Johnson has spoken out in support of the right to dissent. It might be useful for him to do so again—and more specifically in regard to draft protests. For he has a Selective Service director who seems bent upon using the draft as a device to punish political non-conformity. And he has a newly appointed assistant director of the FBI who makes public speeches denounc-ing "non-conformists." Such speeches fan the fires of intoler-ance. This would be a good time to recall the values Americans are fighting to defend and the principles that distinguish them from their enemies.

PEACE DEMONSTRATIONS

AUGUST 12, 1967

What is the purpose of the demonstrators who have been protest-ing American action in Vietnam in recent days on Capitol Hill and at the White House? What do these Americans, most of them manifestly moved by conscience, hope to accomplish by coming here? We presume that they seek to show Congress and the country and the world outside of America that there are Americans opposed to the country's policy in Southeast Asia; and they seek to express moral indignation against the cruelty and killing which are inescapable consequences of that policy.

To say that they are misguided and unrealistic, that they fail to face the terrible consequences of a failure to fight in Vietnam, is not to say that they ought to be silenced and forbidden to protest. To condemn them for a lack of patriotism would be as unjust, uncharitable and unintelligent as they were themselves, some of them at least, in condemning President Johnson for indifference to the suffering of children in Vietnam. To dismiss their concern as of no consequence would be as simple-minded as they seem themselves when they suggest that peace can be achieved in Vietnam by a simple unilateral declaration of peace.

Moreover, street demonstrations are too vital and honored an element of the democratic process to be carelessly curtailed. The line between allowable demonstrations and mob action or riotous violence is not a line always easy to discern. It is fair to say categorically, however, that until they trespassed on the Capitol grounds these demonstrators did not cross it; their protest did not get out of hand or threaten the safety of life and property, and its purpose was to persuade, not to coerce. They were, therefore, entitled to considerate treatment by the police and to protection against such louts as George Lincoln Rockwell's Nazi henchmen who threw red paint on them.

Demonstrations such as the one at the foot of Capitol Hill on Monday present great difficulties for the police. We think that Inspector James M. Powell, new Chief of the Capitol Police, and Howard V. Covell, Deputy Chief of Metropolitan Police, showed sound judgment and great forbearance in letting the crowd approach the Capitol grounds and in warning its leaders not to invade those grounds. Those who disobeyed them were evidently courting arrest; and after a remarkable display of patience by the police, some 260 of them were arrested and hauled off to jail. There were complaints from some of the demonstrators that the police handled them roughly and insensitively. But in the main, we think, the Capitol Police, Park Police and Metropolitan Police acted with restraint. No one was seriously hurt; the law was firmly and effectively upheld; and the demonstrators said what they came to say.

The general good order of this group and the non-violent principles to which it is committed raise some retrospective questions about the wisdom and necessity of the number of arrests that were made. A few symbolic arrests might have achieved the same vindication of the law. But the police deserve some sympathy for what was done in the heat of the occasion. They might well examine their tactics to make sure that in future situations they do not give to such episodes a distorted importance. The sheer number of arrests must mistakenly convey to citizens elsewhere the false notion that this was a large and significant expression of dissent.

While the mistakes of the police, if there were any, have some justification because of the necessity for instant action, the same cannot be said for any undue severity in the courts. They have the time to coolly examine the seriousness of the threat to public order, and in retrospect it does not seem to have been a threat so serious as to justify severe penalties. We hope that when the cases have been ultimately disposed of, the sentences will have been meted out in proportion to the good intentions of the demonstrators and not in proportion to their bad judgment.

AN APPEAL TO REASON

OCTOBER 20, 1967

The Americans who plan to march tomorrow from the Lincoln Memorial to the Pentagon in protest against the war in Vietnam have an indubitable right to do so. This form of expressing dissent from a policy of their own government is honored by tradition and protected by the Constitution. It bears witness to a freedom which is at once a source of strength to America and an essential element of American life. When all this has been said, however, it is vital for the marchers to remember that the constitutional right which they exercise is a right to assemble *peaceably* and that it must be exercised in good order and in conformity with valid laws.

Leaders of the March have conferred with government representatives, and reasonable rules have been formulated as to routes, permits and appropriate places for demonstration. The government has manifested, as it should, a genuine tolerance for, if not hospitality to, a demonstration against itself; and the General Counsel of the General Services Administration, Mr. Harry R. Van Cleve, Jr., has accorded full recognition to the civil-liberties issues involved.

Not all of the March leaders have responded in kind. These leaders are diverse in background, interest and aim. Their organization appears unstructured. And while some have been genuinely concerned to keep the protest peaceable, others have talked quite irresponsibly about civil disobedience and even violence. There may be a few, indeed, who seek disorder for its own sake— or for the sake of concealed interests not primarily concerned with peace and justice.

There are confused appeals to the marchers, some of them couched in the language of incitement. One publication of the National Mobilization Committee to End the War in Vietnam declares, for example: "Direct action is planned for THOSE WHO ARE PREPARED TO CLOSE DOWN THE PENTAGON WAR MACHINE. . . . The general plan is for persons to enter the Pentagon and to block the staircases, hallways, and doorways by the traditional non-violent sit-in techniques; in doing this we will disrupt the war machine's normal functioning."

The duty of the local, state and federal law-enforcement authorities in this situation is quite clear. They have a responsibility to let the March and the subsequent planned demonstration run their course—so long as they remain orderly and confine themselves to the routes and locations assigned to them; and they have a corollary responsibility to protect the marchers from any violent interference or disruption by citizens who disagree with them. But it is equally clear, of course, that the law-enforcement authorities have a responsibility to protect the public safety and to prevent any disruption of governmental activity.

It is a puerile form of anarchy to talk about closing down the Pentagon. These marchers had better acquaint themselves with the facts of life: they are not going to be allowed to close down the Pentagon "war machine" or any other kind of United States government machine.

The police ought to use as much force as may be necessary— as much and no more—to maintain order and prevent law-breaking. Persons who interfere with the normal functioning of government or otherwise break the law should be arrested and taken as promptly as possible to a court; there will be a number of judges on hand to deal with them according to law. No resort to clubs and disabling gases can be justified save by absolute necessity to stop mob action. The essential task of the police in this difficult situation will be to contain violence, not to punish it or to become engulfed in it.

The world will observe what happens in Washington tomorrow and will judge America accordingly. Feelings run very high about the war in Vietnam. But emotional tension cannot justify lawlessness or violence. The right of peaceable assembly is a right to appeal to the reason and conscience of the country. It is not a right to induce anarchy.

PREPARATION FOR THE MORATORIUM

NOVEMBER 11, 1967

Citizens may disagree with official policy, even in time of war, and still be patriots. But they must be free to express their disagreement. Dissent that is suppressed tends inevitably to become rebellious, just as any force too narrowly confined tends to become explosive. That is why protest against prevailing policy— even when a President feels that it may hamper the execution of that policy—needs to be accorded the fullest freedom consonant with public safety.

Nothing is clearer from the Constitution and the traditions of the American people than that citizens have a right to come to the capital of the United States and demonstrate dramatically to their representatives in Congress and to their President that they oppose a national policy. It is true that such a demonstration may cause a lot of inconvenience; it may snarl traffic, interfere with people engaged in their normal activities, put the government to great expense in maintaining order. But to forbid or frustrate such a demonstration would be at once dangerous and un-American in the truest sense of that abused term.

We set forth these general observations with the thought that they ought to guide the government in dealing with the anti-war demonstration planned here for November 13, 14 and 15. It would be folly to ignore the potential dangers involved in this demonstration. No one can say with any certainty how many demonstrators will come here. No one seems able to speak with authority for the demonstration as a whole. While there is no doubt that an overwhelming majority of those who will assemble here mean to do so peaceably, there is evidence that others mean to take advantage of the occasion to foment disorder and violence; and there is always a risk that excitement can lead to upheaval even among the well-meaning.

So there is every reason for the District authorities and the Department of Justice to take precautions and to be prepared to deal with trouble. The sooner the rules governing the demonstration can be clearly fixed and made widely known, the better the chances for avoiding disorder. Those rules ought to be generous and reasonable. In a statement Tuesday night, Justice Department officials indicated that they want to scale the November 15 march down to a "symbolic" movement of a few people. There is no warrant for such constraint. Pennsylvania Avenue is a traditional place for parades; and there is no good reason why the demonstrators should not use it if they do so lawfully and in good order.

The aim ought to be to maximize the opportunities for orderly expression, while minimizing the opportunities to foment violence. If there are to be several hundred thousand demonstrators here next week, there is good reason for forbidding them to ring the White House itself because of the dangers that grow out of confining so large a number in so small an area. But they could safely, we should suppose, be allowed to march around the complex comprising the White House, the Treasury Department and the old State, War and Navy Building.

Latitude and hospitality in dealing with demonstrators worked well for this city in the great Civil Rights March of 1963, in the creation of Resurrection City and in the Moratorium Day of last month. They worked a great deal better than the hostility and repression with which the Chicago authorities greeted the demonstrators at the Democratic National Convention of 1968. Local as well as national authorities ought to participate in the planning for this event, for local as well as national interests are involved, and the people who live here need full representation.

Specifically, both Mayor Walter Washington and the City Council ought to be speaking out and exerting their influence in every way possible, publicly as well as privately, to maintain the record that has been established here of respect for liberty as well as order.

Let the rules be respectful of freedom. Let them be promulgated with as much clarity as possible. And let the force be on hand to see that they are resolutely maintained. The Americans who live here need not then be fearful of fellow-Americans who come to the capital to exercise their rights as free men.

PERSONALLY SPEAKING*

NEW YORK CITY—As the motto for his *Historical Review*, Benjamin Franklin chose this sentence: "They that can give up essential liberty to obtain a little temporary safety deserve neither liberty nor safety."

---

*Column, the Beaumont (Texas) *Sunday Journal*, May 23, 1937. Reprinted with permission.

By way of illustrating his point, New York has just served as guinea pig for a magnificent object lesson to the country. The legislature of this state, in the closing hours of its session, railroaded through, without public hearings and without debate, a piece of moralistic legislation called the Dunnigan bill. It provided that the license commissioner of New York City should have power to close any show which he might deem immoral.

The purpose of the bill was noble and idealistic; its sponsors were reputable and high-minded and, as far as I know, quite unselfish. What they desired ostensibly was to wipe out the pornography which the burlesque houses have been purveying under the guise of entertainment. This column on a Sunday morning is no place to recite for you the evils of burlesque. They existed, all right, and they were pretty sordid; the decent citizenry of New York had no use for them.

The only trouble with this Dunnigan bill designed to correct them was that it would have given up essential liberty. It would have imposed a blue-law censorship which might have turned New York into the most ridiculous hick town in the United States. It would have put the theater under the dictatorship of one man's sense of decorum. It would have stifled the expression of ideas, for to some minds the naked truth is as shocking as a naked torso. It would have meant convictions without trial by jury.

No legislature can define that term "immoral." Morals simply aren't static. An editorial in the *Enterprise* some days ago recalled the furor which was raised by the moralists over Paul Chabas' famous painting "September Morn." "The average American," it said, "thinks to himself, or remarks, 'Why, I've seen that picture—copies of it—thousands of times!' Then he may laugh as he recalls the excitement it created among the prudes and moralists of another era, many of them now in their graves and quite shockproof."

Our definitions of decency and morality not only change, but also at any given time are merely relative. As George Kaufman once remarked, "One man's Mede is another man's Persian." There can never be any sound censorship except by the favor or disfavor of the public itself.

Censorship is just too high a price to pay for any kind of "temporary safety." Dirty picture postcards are a nuisance. But you don't have to ban the whole of art in order to get rid of them.

This Dunnigan bill would have become law if Herbert Lehman, the Governor of New York, had not possessed the courage and intelligence to veto it. I speak of his veto as courageous because it placed him in the uncomfortable position of appearing to sanction the evils of burlesque. He was merely upholding an essential principle of liberty. But Americans are prone to look upon anyone who defends the rights of undesirables as defending the undesirables themselves.

Thus, those who sought to protect the civil liberties of Communists have been labeled Communists. Yet what they were protecting actually is a fundamental feature of American tradition. Those who urge freedom of speech for unpopular minorities are urging only a freedom which is indispensable to American democracy.

This confusion of thought was carried to its logical absurdity in a book called *The Red Network*, published some time ago by a well-meaning woman named Elizabeth Dilling. It catalogued as radical anyone who had ever lifted his voice for essential liberty in any form. Such persons as Jane Addams of Hull House, the Rev. John Haynes Holmes, Senator George W. Norris were classed as "Reds," not because they enunciated any radical ideas, but because they defended the rights of others to express such ideas in a free America.

The right to preach any sort of political gospel is just as vital a part of the Constitution as the right to preach any sort of religious gospel. And no service is done to essential liberty in the United States by jailing the candidate of an unpopular political party—as, for example, in Port Arthur, Texas, as well as in Terre Haute, Indiana.

Moralists and patrioteers have this in common—that they are inclined to be reckless about the price they pay for what they want. And what makes it so hard to persuade them to any reasonable economy or restraint is that the things they want are in themselves so eminently desirable. When men are disgusted or outraged by something that seems to them evil, nothing is more difficult than to convince them that arbitrary suppression is in itself a greater evil.

They are in a great hurry for the millennium—in so great a hurry that they are willing to knock over the foundation in order to build the superstructure more rapidly. Sure, we would all like to see the theater freed from obscenity or the nation freed from social unrest. But censorship or suppression are ruinous prices to pay. They are of a piece with lynchings or the "treat 'em rough" school of policing which punish particular infractions of the law but encourage lawlessness in general.

We have a birthright too valuable for recklessness. We just can't afford "a little temporary safety" at the expense of essential liberty.

MOVIE FREEDOM

JUNE 10, 1952

The movies have won a significant second round in their growth to full freedom from censorship. In the case of *The Miracle,* the Supreme Court ruled that they are included within the free-speech and free-press guarantees of the First and Fourteenth Amendments; and it said specifically that New York could not ban the showing of a film on a mere finding that it was "sacrilegious." A week later, in connection with a picture called *Pinky,* the Supreme Court upset without an opinion a decision by the Texas Court of Criminal Appeals which upheld a Marshall, Texas, ordinance authorizing local censors to ban movies "of an immoral character, or of such character as to be prejudicial to the best interests of the people of the city." The standard is a ludicrously vague one; it was used to forbid the showing of a film which offended certain local racial prejudices.

Just where the boundaries of motion-picture freedom are to be drawn must be left to the gradual process of judicial inclusion and exclusion on the basis of successive specific cases. It is clear, however, that the movies have been given a new birth of freedom—so far as legal censorship is concerned. They are no longer to be considered, as the Supreme Court considered them in 1914, "a business pure and simple." But the important question remains whether *they* will consider *themselves* something more than this— and behave accordingly. The question, in short, is whether the movies will live up to the freedom conferred on them by the court.

The movies have been notoriously cautious in censoring themselves voluntarily through their Production Code Administration and they have been notoriously responsive to the prejudices of any group of potential spectators large enough to fill more than a row of theater seats. Moreover, the movie producers have been so servile in their genuflections to governmental inquisitors such as the House Committee on Un-American Activities that one could not help wondering if they had any desire for independence. The court's recognition that they have come of age is cause for congratulation. We hope that they will accept and measure up to the responsibility.

WHAT'S FIT TO READ

DECEMBER 17, 1959

It took five separate Supreme Court opinions to deal with a Los Angeles obscenity statute on Monday. Here is further illustration of the difficulties that develop when men are told that they may determine by law what their fellow-men may read. Having decided in the *Roth* case that obscene speech and writings are not protected by the constitutional guarantees of freedom of speech and the press, the Supreme Court is bound to find itself called upon in case after case to pass upon local definitions of obscenity and to serve as a Supreme Censor of local boards of censorship. It is not an enviable, or even, perhaps, a manageable, responsibility.

Los Angeles adopted a statute prohibiting possession of obscene books in a bookshop. It convicted a bookseller for having in his store a novel, *Sweeter Than Life,* which was judged to be obscene. Mr. Justice Brennan, writing for a majority of the Supreme Court, reversed the conviction because no proof had been presented that the bookseller knew the book to be obscene. "Penalizing booksellers, even though they had not the slightest notice of the character of the books they sold," said the Justice, would tend to restrict the dissemination of books which are not obscene. And he concluded his opinion with the observation that the door barring intrusion into the area protected by the First Amendment "cannot be left ajar; it must be kept tightly closed and opened only the slightest crack necessary to prevent encroachment upon more important interests."

The logic of this assertion seems to us as confused as the metaphor. Mr. Justice Black made a compelling response to it: "I do not believe that any Federal agencies, including Congress and this Court, have power or authority to subordinate speech and press to what they think are 'more important interests.' " It is tempting to try to cure obscenity by censorship, just as it is tempting to try to cure a headache by morphine; but the cure is deadlier than the disease. "Censorship," as Mr. Justice Black said, "is the deadly enemy of freedom and progress."

The most reassuring aspect of the court's decision in this case is that the Justices were unanimous, for one reason or another, in striking down the conviction. They are in full agreement that censorship is dangerous and must be very narrowly confined, if tolerated at all. The Postmaster General and other censors would do well to read, and weigh, their words.

THE CHILDREN'S DOWER

NOVEMBER 7, 1960

All who love literature and all who cherish the right to decide for themselves what books they wish to read must rejoice that *Lady Chatterley's Lover* has been found not guilty of obscenity in an

English court. The celebrated novel by D. H. Lawrence about love in the machine age was put on trial in England and in Canada just as it was not long ago in the United States.

In London's Old Bailey a jury of nine men and three women decided on Wednesday that under the standards fixed by a new statute the book as a whole—lately brought out in England for the first time in an unexpurgated edition by Penguin Books—does not tend to deprave and corrupt those who "having regard to all relevant circumstances" are likely to read it. In Montreal last summer—in the same month that *Lady Chatterley's Lover* was finally cleared by the United States courts and certified as safe for distribution through the mails—a judge ruled it to be obscene under a new Canadian obscenity ordinance; the New American Library, publisher of the novel's unexpurgated version in Canada, has promised to appeal.

At the trial in London, the Bishop of Woolwich told the jury that Christians ought to read the novel—an old-fashioned way of finding out for themselves whether they like it or not. But the prosecutor said the members of the jury should ask themselves: "Would you approve of your young sons and young daughters reading it? Is it a book you would have lying around in your own house? Is it a book you would even wish your wife to read, or your servant?"

These are interesting questions. We should suppose they would be answered variously by various heads of families. But in any case they afford a very poor basis, we think, for determining whether the government should suppress a book and forbid anyone to read it. What one man may consider meet for his children or his wife or his servant may to another man seem altogether poisonous.

English and Canadian censors, like those in the United States, are forever trying to limit the literary diet of adults to the intellectual pablum they think suitable for children. They are despoilers of the past. But worse than that, they impoverish the future. There is no way to measure the losses they inflict. "What matters," said Leo Tolstoy long ago, "is not what the censor does to what I have written but to what I might have written."

FOOD FOR THOUGHT

DECEMBER 21, 1961

"If that's literature, I'll eat it," said Leonard T. Kardy, the well-known literary epicure and, in his spare time, State's Attorney for Montgomery County. Mr. Kardy's prospective repast was that controversial novel of Henry Miller's, *Tropic of Cancer*. He was summing up his case against a Bethesda book dealer who sold the novel, was convicted on Tuesday of violating Maryland's obscenity law and was sentenced by Judge James H. Pugh to six months in the State House of Correction. Mr. Kardy went on to demonstrate his firm independence of taste by adding, "I don't care what the authors say." He persuaded Judge Pugh to forbid testimony as to whether the book is pornography or has literary merit by several authors brought into court as expert witnesses.

Mr. Kardy is confused, we think. If books were to be eaten, it would be feasible of course to have something in the nature of the pure-food-and-drug laws to determine their digestibility and to protect the public from unwholesome ingredients. Excessive use of condiments to titillate the palate or the injection of aphrodisiacs in any form could be sternly forbidden. But even then it might be extremely helpful to have the advice of culinary experts as to whether the limits of the law had been infringed.

In literature, which most people like to digest mentally rather than intestinally, deleterious substances are harder to detect. Literary experts can be especially helpful to a jury in the effort to distinguish the genuine from the spurious. Ordinary jurors are not well equipped for this task. Some of them prefer the work of Edgar Guest to the work of John Keats. Some of them would consider parts of Shakespeare salacious. Authors and critics who have read a great deal and who know something about writing as an art can render invaluable assistance to a jury in understanding a writer's purpose.

In denying the Montgomery County jury this assistance, we

think Judge Pugh and Mr. Kardy erred. The Supreme Court has said that obscenity involves expression "utterly without redeeming social importance." Judge Pugh let the jurors decide that the book repelled them individually. The real question to be determined is whether the book has values which redeem its admitted offensiveness to many readers.

LITERARY FOG

MARCH 23, 1966

The fourteen opinions that came from the Supreme Court on Monday in three obscenity cases bear witness to the court's uncertainty in this murky area. Mr. Justice Brennan, the chief architect of the court's present position, has tried earnestly and resourcefully to fashion a rule—or a set of rules—that will permit wide latitude in the expression of aesthetic ideas while protecting the country from gross forms of pandering to prurient interests. Yet it must be profoundly disquieting to him, as to every lover of liberty, that a man is to go to prison for five years under these rules for the mere publication of words and pictures which, however offensive to some, seem to have redeeming value to others of comparable decency and taste.

The country is left without any clear standards as to what is permissible and what is impermissible in artistic or literary expression. The inevitable result is to put a damper on publication. The production of a book (or of a magazine, a play or a movie) entails a costly investment. If to the uncertainty of popular approval is added a serious hazard of judicial disapproval, the cost is likely to seem prohibitive. And this may mean the discouragement not only of pornography but also of a *Decameron* or *The Rape of Lucrece* or *Ulysses*. The cost, then, would be prohibitive for the country. *Ulysses* did more than shock people by its employment of four-letter words. It liberated literature and revolutionized style.

People have been arguing for two centuries about whether *Fanny Hill* is art or obscenity. It could be both. At any rate, no critic, no judge, no collection of judges is capable of settling the controversy with any permanency. It should constitute a warning of a sort that this widely circulated, much-discussed book, now cleared by the court, was the first literary work ever to be banned in the United States. It has been read, nevertheless, by generations of schoolboys; and it would be hard to show that it has ever hurt any of them. There is, we think, much shrewd common sense behind, an observation made by Mr. Justice Douglas in the *Fanny Hill* case:

> Perhaps the most frequently assigned justification for censorship is the belief that erotica produces antisocial conduct. But that relationship has yet to be proven. Indeed, if one were to make judgments on the basis of speculation, one might guess that literature of the most pornographic sort would, in many cases, provide a substitute—not a stimulus—for antisocial conduct.

We think that Mr. Justice Douglas' dissenting opinion in the *Ginsburg* and *Mishkin* cases was the most illuminating of all the fourteen judicial statements handed down on Monday. He spoke, as an interpreter of the Constitution should speak, for the rights of minorities. And he pointed out that books which seem vulgar, worthless and odious to some may have utility and significance for others. To outlaw books on the ground that they offend public taste is, as he says, "to let majorities rule where minorities were thought to be supreme." Mr. Justice Stewart voiced the same thought: "If the First Amendment means anything, it means that a man cannot be sent to prison merely for distributing publications which offend a judge's aesthetic sensibilities, mine or any other's." And Mr. Justice Black, of course, repeated this view as he has done so eloquently in the past.

There are risks in allowing complete freedom of aesthetic expression just as there are risks in allowing complete freedom of political expression. But these risks are trivial when compared with the risks inherent in suppression. This was the magnificent idea behind the First Amendment. It sought—and found—safety through freedom.

PROTECTING THE YOUNG

OCTOBER 14, 1968

Richard Nixon's proposal to outlaw the mailing of obscene matter to children under sixteen constitutes a thoughtful step in a direction suggested by the Supreme Court. As Mr. Nixon observed, "We can constitutionally restrict from children matter that would not be objectionable to adults." The court was quite clear about this in the most recent of its decisions in this difficult area. It gave approval to a carefully drawn New York statute forbidding the sale of certain magazines to juveniles, although sale of the same magazines to adults admittedly could not have been prohibited without infringing First Amendment rights.

On pragmatic as well as constitutional grounds, this way of dealing with the pornography problem seems to us to make much sense. It is by no means certain that material regarded by most of the public as pornographic or otherwise distasteful does any actual harm to those adults who choose, of their own volition, to look at it; and it is equally uncertain that any social harm flows from the exposure of adults to such material. But children are more likely to be hurt by it and more likely to be exposed to it unwittingly and unwillingly by exploiters of their innocence; and in any case, their parents can reasonably look to the law to protect them from that sort of exploitation. Protection of children can be accomplished, moreover, without limiting the freedom of adults to see whatever they want to see and without the danger of stultifying art or stifling the expression of ideas.

Mr. Nixon took favorable note of the recent proposal of the motion-picture industry to set a classification system that would prevent children from seeing "unsuitable movies." What he now suggests about material sent through the mail would be sensibly complementary. He was not at all specific about the terms of the law he has in mind and, of course, as the court has made plain, they would have to be drafted with great care. But the purpose would be well worth the effort.

THE RIGHT TO RECEIVE IDEAS

APRIL 12, 1969

A unanimous Supreme Court ruled last Monday that "the mere possession of obscene matter cannot constitutionally be made a crime." This seems to us fundamental at once to privacy and to freedom. The ruling grew out of a case in which Georgia law-enforcement authorities, after obtaining a warrant to search the home of a suspected bookmaker for material related to this calling, found instead three reels of an eight-millimeter film which they promptly viewed with the man's projector and characterized as obscene. The man was convicted under a Georgia law making it a crime to "knowingly have possession of obscene matter."

Three Justices would have reversed the conviction on the simple ground that "because the films were seized in violation of the Fourth and Fourteenth Amendments, they were inadmissible in evidence at the appellant's trial." But a majority of the court chose to deal with the invasion of privacy involved in the case. "Whatever may be the justification for other statutes regulating obscenity," they said, "we do not think they reach into the privacy of one's own home. If the First Amendment means anything, it means that a state has no business telling a man sitting alone in his own house, what books he may read or what films he may watch. Our whole constitutional heritage rebels at the thought of giving government the power to control men's minds."

Perhaps the court will soon take the next logical and inescapable step beyond this conclusion. If the state "has no business telling a man sitting alone in his own house, what books he may read or what films he may watch,'' it has no business telling him what books he may purchase or what theaters he may enter to watch whatever films he may wish to see. Georgia's law is an exceptionally rigorous one in that it forbids mere possession of obscene material. But many other states forbid sale or exhibition of such material.

Why should a state exercise such control over an adult's voluntary selection of material for his own edification or enjoyment? There is good reason to shield children from ideas or images deemed unfit for their immature minds. And there is ample justification for laws which forbid the intrusion of offensive material on adults who do not wish to view it. Such intrusion is a form of disorderly conduct and punishable as such. But free adults ought to be able to decide for themselves what they wish to see and hear. Mr. Justice Marshall, writing for the court, put it in terms that really admit of no exception: "It is now well established that the Constitution protects the right to receive information and ideas. . . . This right to receive information and ideas, regardless of their social worth, is fundamental to our free society.''

THE SUPREME COURT AS CENSOR

NOVEMBER 14, 1970

Justice Hugo Black went to the root of the problem in his reaction the other day to the argument in the Supreme Court over the Swedish film *I Am Curious (Yellow)*. For his own part, he has no inclination to look at such a film—and has said plainly in the past that he doesn't intend to do so. He did not accept appointment to the Supreme Court to serve as a censor. He believes, moreover, that experience does not qualify him and the Constitution does not authorize him to fulfill such a role. This seems to us a pretty sound, pragmatic position.

I Am Curious (Yellow) is a film which depicts human sexual intercourse openly on the screen. Some eminent and experienced film critics have called it artistic; others, equally eminent and experienced, have called it pornographic. A lot of people in Washington looked at it and formed their own opinion of it during the year it was on exhibition here; and there is no evidence whatever that they, or the community as a whole, were injured by it.

The one point about the controversy over this film that ought to be controlling, we think, is that nobody is obliged to see it. Attendance is absolutely voluntary. Indeed, the exhibitors who have chosen to exploit the widespread interest in it charge a goodly sum of admission. Children are barred. Adults who pay to go in are at liberty to leave at the first sign of anything that may strike them as indelicate or indecent. Why, then, should adults in a free country not be free—if they wish to do so—to decide about it for themselves?

The premise behind the effort to suppress this film is that sexual intercourse is essentially obscene. That seems to us a dubious and dangerous premise. So much of life and of art revolves around sex and the infinite variety of its expressions that it is impossible to fix meaningful limitations upon the representation of it. Is the explicit verbal depiction of sexual intercourse in D. H. Lawrence's novel *Lady Chatterley's Lover* obscene? Are the jokes and cartoons and the innuendoes in a score of magazines in any drugstore more acceptable?

Maryland's Attorney General Burch told the Supreme Court that if exhibition of the film is permitted in Maryland, the next thing will be "couples copulating in the aisles." This argument seems to us to reduce the case to absurdity. Besides, as Justice Black was quick to point out, the court has always observed a distinction between expression and conduct. That distinction would be wiped out if the court were to adopt the line suggested by the Chief Justice that the depiction of conduct is equivalent to conduct.

The proposal to censor is essentially a proposal to permit an official determination of what constitutes good taste. It is better—and on the whole safer—to leave that determination to public opinion and the public interest.

SIX

The Civil Rights
Struggle

The racial revolution that swept America during Alan Barth's lifetime profoundly altered almost everything about relationships between blacks and whites. When he began writing for the *Post,* Washington was a very southern city. Its schools and playgrounds were segregated; its theaters, major hotels and restaurants were closed to blacks; its non-elected government was controlled by whites, with only a token sprinkling of blacks in positions of authority. By the time Barth retired, official segregation had vanished and almost all the major politicians and public office-holders in Washington were black. Changes similar to these had come about elsewhere in the nation, and yet they had come so quickly and some of them were absorbed so easily that many events in the revolution leading to them now seem a part of ancient history. Perhaps no gap in understanding between today's young adults and their parents or grandparents is greater than the gap in their perceptions of how far the nation has moved in racial matters.

This chapter consists exclusively of editorials, in chronological order. They present racial issues as they arose between 1948 and 1971. In one sense, they are vignettes of history, pictures that bring back memories of a troubled and troubling era. In another sense, each one is a window on a man who believed passionately that all men are created equal as he responded to the scene unfolding around him. From restrictive covenants on real estate in 1948 to the location of public housing projects in 1971, Barth followed a consistent path, although his hope that desegregation would be accepted readily in all parts of the nation gradually faded away. Some of the events on which he commented like the desegregation of restaurants and theaters seem almost unreal in the 1980s. But they were major changes when they occurred. Some of his comments may also seem lukewarm by today's standards of commitment to racial equality; but they were made by an advocate of total and immediate desegregation who was trying to find a non-violent path to that goal in a society full of hatred and resistance and petty meanness.

EQUAL PROTECTION

MAY 6, 1948

The Supreme Court decision forbidding judicial enforcement of restrictive realty covenants based on race is perhaps the most effective step in the emancipation of American Negroes since Abraham Lincoln struck off their chains in 1863. Ghetto life is not liberty. And the progressive confinement of Negroes to ever contracting, ever more squalid slum sections of American cities, in the North no less than in the South, has been a root cause of all the other disadvantagements suffered by their race. From it has flowed the high incidence of disease among Negroes, the tendency to juvenile delinquency and crime, the principal ground for segregation in schools, playgrounds and places of public entertainment, the extortionate rentals which sapped Negro earnings, the cramped conditions which stultified the development of Negro children. The stamp of the ghetto, in other words, has given the Negro just those attributes which have made him seem an undesirable neighbor to so many whites.

No one need either hope or fear that the Supreme Court's action will change this situation quickly. The ghetto wall is merely breached, not demolished. As the court made clear, restrictive covenants remain valid where the contracting parties wish to observe them; and they will continue, no doubt, to exclude Negroes from many areas. That is a social consideration. Economic considerations will, for a long time at least, prove an even more formidable barrier so far as the more expensive and "fashionable" white residential sectors are concerned. Thus the depreciation of real-estate values feared by the defenders of restrictive covenants is unlikely. All that the Supreme Court has done is to strike down a legal barrier to the gradual integration of Negro citizens in the American society—an integration which is the necessary eventual solution of a dilemma burdensome to white and colored Americans alike. . . .

"SEPARATE BUT EQUAL"

OCTOBER 11, 1949

The Supreme Court has consented to review a case that may have great historic significance—the case of Elmer W. Henderson against the United States of America, Interstate Commerce Commission and Southern Railway Co. The case will test the validity of a Southern Railway regulation, approved by the ICC and upheld by a divided three-judge Federal District Court, requiring passengers to be segregated according to their color in the railway's dining cars. . . .

The case originated when Henderson, a Negro, traveling as a field representative for the wartime Fair Employment Practices Committee, was denied service in a Southern Railway diner, in accordance with company regulations, because the two end tables, curtained from the rest of the car and supposedly reserved for Negroes, were being used by white passengers. The Interstate Commerce Act provides that "it shall be unlawful for any common carrier . . . to subject any particular person . . . to any undue or unreasonable prejudice or disadvantage in any respect whatsoever." The company reconciled its regulations with the law on the ground that the furnishing of separate but proportionately equal facilities entailed no discrimination. The ICC upheld this justification.

The doctrine that segregation is not discrimination rests upon an 1896 decision of the Supreme Court in *Plessy v. Ferguson*—perhaps, with the single exception of the Dred Scott case, the worst decision in the Supreme Court's entire history. The court at that time dismissed the contention that "the enforced separation of the two races stamps the colored race with a badge of inferiority," and blandly observed that "if this be so, it is not by reason of anything found in the act, but solely because the colored race chooses to put that construction upon it."

The sophistry and callousness of this judgment were roundly scored by Justice Harlan in one of the court's great dissents. "Our Constitution is color blind," he said, "and neither knows nor tolerates classes among citizens. . . . We boast of the freedom enjoyed by our people above all other peoples. But it is difficult to reconcile that boast with a state of the law which, practically, puts the brand of servitude and degradation upon a large class of our fellow citizens, our equals before the law. The thin disguise of 'equal' accommodations . . . will not mislead anyone, nor atone for the wrong this day done."

The "thin disguise" has been used ever since to justify segregation in public schools, state universities, public transportation and other public facilities. The whole structure of discrimination by law has been based upon it. All experience has shown not only that separate facilities are never, in fact, equal but that enforced separation is imposed deliberately to humiliate Negroes and to emphasize their inferiority. It serves that purpose well. It creates inequality by imposing a caste status upon the group at which it is aimed. . . .

EQUAL EDUCATION

MARCH 2, 1950

The federal government, through Solicitor General Perlman, has again asked the Supreme Court to strike down the legal fiction that segregated facilities for Negroes can be considered equal facilities. Recently the Solicitor General filed a brief as a "friend of the court," supporting the suit brought by Heman Marion Sweatt, who was excluded because of his color from the all-white Texas University Law School, and the suit of G. W. McLaurin, admitted to the graduate school of the University of Oklahoma but required to sit at a special desk set aside for him in the doorway. . . .

[These] cases illustrate the essential absurdity of the "separate but equal" doctrine. The State of Texas has offered Mr. Sweatt a new law school set up especially for him and the few other Negroes in the state qualified to enter it. But it is, of course, a law school in name only, no matter what its physical facilities. It cannot give Mr. Sweatt the contact with fellow-students and the collision of ideas which are essential parts of a legal education. Mr. McLaurin has actually the same physical facilities as his white fellow-students but is denied membership in their community in a manner patently intended to humiliate him. To pretend that this is equality of educational opportunity is to ignore the very purpose for which the segregation is imposed.

The "separate but equal" fallacy was enunciated in *Plessy v. Ferguson* in 1896. . . . It is high time for the Supreme Court to overrule it.

INTERRACIAL PLAYGROUND

MAY 26, 1952

A photograph reproduced in *The Washington Post* Sunday shows a score or so of children seated at a long table, their hands clasped in a symbolic gesture of devotion to their common Creator. They are saying grace. They are about to have juice and snacks—a customary morning interlude at pre-school play centers such as the one they are attending. The only aspect of this scene that is not customary is that it includes white and Negro children.

The two races are together here at the playground adjacent to the Raymond School (white) because the playground was designated an open unit by the Recreation Department last July and because the mothers using it decided to make it inter-racial. It has been so since the first of the year. You can see other pictures of the children at play—gay and friendly, as children should be. Next year, when they are old enough to enter kindergarten, they will be separated in accordance with the color of their skin. But this year, free from prejudice, they are practicing democracy—learning a lesson in human brotherhood which, perhaps, no segregated school system will ever be able wholly to erase.

EQUAL EDUCATION FOR ALL

MAY 19, 1954

The Supreme Court's historic decision in the school-segregation cases brings the United States back into the mainstream of its own best traditions. Segregation is a hangover from slavery, and its ugliest manifestation has been in the schools. Rooted in a denial of human equality, it has always been, like the evil institution that spawned it, a blight upon American life. Its effect was divisive.

It separated Americans into superior and inferior races, and by subordinating one to the other gave the fiction a semblance of reality. Now, at last, the equality of opportunity which is a fundamental premise of the American society is to become a fact in regard to education—which is, after all, the key to opportunity. The effect will be to establish a new and invigorating unity.

The Chief Justice's twin opinions in the segregation cases are informed by a compelling logic. They eradicate, and unequivocally, the "separate but equal" doctrine contrived by the Supreme Court nearly sixty years ago in *Plessy v. Ferguson.* . . . Monday's decision is a resounding vindication of the wisdom expressed by Mr. Justice Harlan in his eloquent dissent in the *Plessy* case: "In view of the Constitution, in the eye of the law, there is in this country no superior, dominant, ruling class of citizens. There is no caste here. Our Constitution is color blind, and neither knows nor tolerates classes among citizens."

Education, as Chief Justice Warren declared in his opinion,

is the very foundation of good citizenship. Today it is a principal instrument in awakening the child to cultural values, in preparing him for later professional training, and in helping him to adjust normally to his environment. In these days, it is doubtful that any child may reasonably be expected to succeed in life if he is denied the opportunity of an education. Such an opportunity, where the state has undertaken to provide it, is a right which must be made available to all on equal terms.

But of course it cannot be made available to all on equal terms if it is provided for some on terms that are profoundly humiliating and that remove them from free association with their fellows. Segregated schooling imposes insuperable psychological handicaps. The court came, therefore, to an inescapable conclusion: "Separate educational facilities are inherently unequal."

The manner in which this decision was rendered reflects judicial statesmanship of the highest order. The court was long in coming to a conclusion that would inevitably disturb a settled pattern of race relations and entail difficult adjustments in some parts of the country. We think the delay was wise and salutary. It allowed the event to grow naturally out of the womb of time—a development long foreshadowed and recognized as inevitable even by those who opposed it. We think, too, that there was wisdom in the respite automatically provided by the court's decision to rehear arguments in the fall respecting application of its doctrine. The decision brings an era to its end; those who sought zealously and worked patiently to accomplish this result can afford now to display a measure of patience in letting those who resisted the result accommodate themselves to it. Moderation is likely to beget moderation.

Some of the reactions from the South—Senator Russell's and Senator Eastland's extravagances, for instance—reveal the real magnitude of the problem. But such views are countered by more enlightened attitudes which perhaps more genuinely reflect the temper of the South today. The time lag permitted by the court will facilitate an orderly working out of the difficult problems involved in integration. The nation can be confident that the South will bring to the handling of these problems intelligence and adaptability and good will. We have no doubt that the South will embrace its new era and find in it a general enrichment and emancipation.

It is immensely heartening to observe reaction to the court's edict in the District of Columbia, even among those who felt resistance toward it. The Commissioners, the Board of Education and the Superintendent of Schools have moved swiftly and with exemplary spirit to bring this community into accord with the new interpretation. Machinery is already in motion to inaugurate a single school system next fall. There is every reason to hope that Washington will carry out President Eisenhower's expressed wish that it serve as a model to the nation.

It is not too much to speak of the court's decision as a new birth of freedom. It comes at a juncture in the affairs of mankind when this reaffirmation of basic human values is likely to have a wonderfully tonic effect. America is rid of an incubus which impeded and embarrassed it in all its relations with the world. Abroad as well as at home, this decision will engender a renewal of faith in democratic institutions and ideals.

THE MANNER OF INTEGRATION

JUNE 1, 1955

Having enunciated a year ago the fundamental principle that "racial discrimination in public education is unconstitutional," the Supreme Court has now dealt with the practical problem of "the manner in which relief is to be accorded." Its decision seems to us a common-sense one. It will anger those who refuse to recognize racial equality either as a fact of life or as an imperative of democracy; and it will disappoint those who wish that integration could be accomplished overnight by edict. But it will enable state governments and boards of education and school superintendents to meet the complex problems involved in merging dual school systems and to move with orderly progress toward eliminating all racial discrimination from public education.

The Supreme Court chose a flexible rather than a doctrinaire approach to the problem. It chose in large part, indeed, the approach recommended to it by the Solicitor General—remanding the several cases to the Federal District Courts for decrees which will take into account local conditions, revision of local laws and regulations, problems arising out of available physical facilities and other such circumstances which may vary greatly from place to place. It seems to us that this flexibility was wise and that it is better calculated to hasten integration than any peremptorily fixed schedule of compliance. The trouble with a fixed schedule is that it must be in the nature of a lowest common denominator—fixed, that is, in accordance with the conditions of the locality where integration will be slowest; and it operates, therefore, to retard integration in localities where it can move much more rapidly. The approach chosen by the Supreme Court allows, and invites, every locality to bring itself into conformity with constitutional requirements as speedily as possible.

Although no deadline was set by the Supreme Court, its decision requires "a prompt and reasonable start toward full compliance." It authorizes the District Courts to permit delay only after such a start has been made; and it places on those asking for delay the full burden of establishing that it is genuinely necessary in the public interest. Chief Justice Warren's opinion made it quite clear, moreover, that the existence of prejudice is not to be counted among the local conditions warranting delay. . . .

Every reasonable consideration has been given to the difficulties which some communities will experience in bringing about a radical change in the pattern of race relations. The Supreme Court has already—and deliberately, one supposes—allowed a full year to elapse since it announced the constitutional principle involved. That year should have served to adjust men's minds to a change which must be accepted. We may all hope that it will be accepted with the grace and good will, the spirit of accommodation and the respect for republican institutions which have long characterized Americans and held them together as a people.

POLITICS AND CIVIL RIGHTS

FEBRUARY 16, 1956

. . . We are at a climactic stage in the development of race relations in the United States. A historic pattern is being swept away. Ancient wrongs which find their only justification in a tradition based on bigotry are at long last being righted. It is only natural that Negroes who have suffered these wrongs should be impatient to inherit their full rights as citizens of the United States. Justice is so clearly on their side that it is almost an affront to ask them for moderation and continued patience. Nevertheless, moderation and continued patience are likely to bring them to their goals much more speedily than intransigence and intemperance.

If the school-segregation issue falls into the hands of the extremists and the political exploiters, an evolutionary process which came to maturity as a result of American economic and social growth—and which the Supreme Court merely recognized and ratified—will be frustrated and delayed. For it is plain that a harmonious integration of different races is one of the many matters that cannot be accomplished by the points of bayonets. This is by no means to say that justice and law and order ought not to be resolutely enforced by governmental authority. It is to say simply that kindliness, tolerance, mutual trust and good will are indispensable ingredients of every social adjustment.

"It is my conviction," Hamilton Basso wrote the other day in a distinguished letter to the New York *Times,* "that once the South is rid of its fear that it will be required to reorganize the whole of its society within a few months or years it will begin noticeably to obey those impulses of decency, kindness and honorable behavior which, because of the statements of its extremists, would now seem to be blocked off." The South's extremists respond to extremists from the North—and *vice versa.* No doubt it was this consideration that led the Supreme Court to order integration in flexible terms attuned to varying conditions; it ordered a "prompt beginning," not an immediate completion. And it ordered compliance to be judged in the judicial atmosphere of federal courts, not in an executive agency subject to political pressures. The firmness with which such action can be taken was demonstrated yesterday by a federal court in New Orleans which declared Louisiana's 1954 segregation laws unconstitutional.

This is preeminently a time when the test of statesmanship is restraint. The change in customs and institutions demanded of the South involves the birth of a new era. Birth is never without birth pangs. It calls for compassion and understanding.

DISINTEGRATION

APRIL 16, 1956

Dangerous steps toward disintegration of the Federal Union are being taken these days with a recklessness that ought to arouse deep concern in the heart of every American devoted to the preservation of the United States as a nation. The direction and the accelerating pace of these steps ought to sound, in the ears of the President of the United States above all, a call to action. For these steps, once taken, will be extremely difficult to reverse.

The latest of these steps has been taken in North Carolina—commonly counted among the more advanced and enlightened of the southern states. The North Carolina Advisory Committee on Education, following the lead of the Gray Commission in Virginia, has filed a report recommending that state constitutional changes be made authorizing financial grants "to be paid toward the education of any child assigned against the wishes of his parents to a school in which the races are mixed." Here is another transparent effort to evade a decision of the United States Supreme Court.

"I do not think the United States would come to an end," Justice Oliver Wendell Holmes once said, "if we [the Supreme Court] lost our power to declare an Act of Congress void. I do think the Union would be imperiled if we could not make that declaration as to the laws of the several states." The truth of this seems almost self-evident. If every state legislature could construe the Constitution in accordance with its own lights and without deference to any final constitutional authority, disintegration would be the inescapable consequence. Fallible as it may be, the Supreme Court is the final authority established by the Constitution to determine the constitutionality of legislative acts.

It cannot be doubted that there are men in the South as well as in the North who, for the sake of maintaining a nation to which they are devoted, are prepared to submit to duly constituted federal authority even when they disagree with it. A nation can endure only so long as it is guided by such men. But they are submerged in the South today by those who shout defiance of federal authority while pretending that they are patriots. The South is not monolithic. It does not speak with one voice, however much its zealots may assert that it does. And the task of national leadership is to give the more sober voices a chance to be heard. . . .

The beginning of statesmanship in this situation is to give status to those who recognize federal authority and seek a solution within its terms, and to isolate those who would destroy the Union rather than submit to it. The President's own immense prestige and the respect in which he is held in every part of the country can be a wonderfully healing and unifying influence. But to be influential, he must assert leadership.

LAW AND ORDER

SEPTEMBER 4, 1957

The terms "law" and "order," so commonly bracketed, are not invariable companions; and sometimes, as in Little Rock, Arkansas, the one is sacrificed for the sake of the other. It was in the name of order, not of law, that Governor Orval Faubus of Arkansas threw a cordon of armed National Guardsmen around Little Rock's Central High School yesterday and ordered them to bar the entrance of Negro students. The law says plainly that the Negroes ought to be admitted; a United States District Judge has instructed the Little Rock school board to begin desegregation of the high schools and has issued a broad injunction forbidding any persons to interfere with this desegregation.

But Governor Faubus suddenly came to the conclusion, just as desegregation was about to begin, that order could not be maintained in Little Rock if "forcible integration" proceeded. It was not quite clear what the Governor means by "forcible" integration; integration as planned in Little Rock by the local school board was not designed to be any more "forcible" than anything else required by law. Those who oppose desegregation in Arkansas and who threaten violence to prevent it are guilty of lawlessness. Unhappily, it was on the side of those who threatened to defy the law that Governor Faubus intervened; and it is their conception of order, rather than the law's conception, that he has used National Guardsmen to maintain.

Responsible sources in Little Rock say that there was and is very little tension in the Arkansas capital. What threat there was to orderly desegregation of the schools arose in very large measure, in the opinion of these sources, from the Governor's own rather panicky warnings. The performance becomes the more curious in light of the fact that Mr. Faubus is not known as a diehard segregationist. The Governor had been under some pressure from the white citizens' councils, but not long ago he defeated by a two-to-one margin a candidate espousing the views of the citizens' councils.

Moreover, desegregation is not wholly a novelty in Arkansas. The state university has admitted Negroes for some years. The towns of Hoxie and Fayetteville and Charleston have desegregated their public schools. The desegregation plan adopted by the elected school board of Little Rock was an exceedingly careful and conservative one, extending the process over a period of years; it must have had considerable community support. Indeed, observers familiar with the situation in Little Rock say that its people were ready to accept desegregation.

It would be tragic indeed if Governor Faubus had responded to a manufactured scare, to a threat of violence fabricated by lawless elements in no sense representative of the community. One wonders at any rate whether the Governor did all that he could have done to promote and encourage observance of the law—whether, in this situation, order might not have been coupled with law for the maintenance of both. Certainly the Governor has placed himself—and the federal courts and the Department of Justice—in an extremely complicated legal box. One must hope that Mr. Faubus himself will find a way out of the predicament he entered so precipitately and apparently so needlessly.

PAYING GUESTS

AUGUST 30, 1959

A man's home being his castle, it goes without saying that he need invite nobody to enter it except at his own pleasure. This applies to his dining room, his swimming pool, his private beach if he possesses one. And if it pleases him to choose his guests on the basis of race or religion, why, no one can contest his right to do so—although one may reasonably, we think, doubt his wisdom. When he invites the general public, however, offering admittance to his dining room or his swimming pool or his private beach for a fee, his practices become at once a matter of public concern. The public becomes entitled, then, to insist on his observance of standards of safety and sanitation. It becomes entitled also to insist on his observance of principles of public policy.

To permit discrimination on account of race or religion in places of public entertainment is contrary to sound public policy for a variety of reasons. One, it subverts the root premise of a democratic society, that men are created equal and must be accorded equality of opportunity. Two, it offends and injures law-abiding, well-behaved citizens by subjecting them to a humiliating exclusion from the company of their fellow-citizens, and thus it promotes friction instead of harmony in the community. Three, it diminishes the prestige of the United States in a world groping toward the ideal of human freedom and equality.

For these reasons, and others, the states of the American Union, in an exercise of their police powers, ought to forbid racial discrimination in places of public entertainment. Twenty-one states now do so. Maine is the latest to join the cavalcade with a statute which goes into effect next month. It provides punishment by fines ranging from $100 to $500 and jail sentences up to thirty days for any action of "discrimination by reason of race, color, religious creed, ancestry or national origin at places of public accommodation." If Maryland were to follow suit, there would be a prompt end to the ugly and embarrassing incidents of racial exclusion which have been reported of late at those so-called "private" beaches catering to the public on Chesapeake Bay. Virginia, equally, needs to put a stop to racial discrimination in its restaurants. When a host takes paying guests, he relinquishes some of the prerogatives of privacy.

PASSIVE PROTEST

FEBRUARY 24, 1960

All over the South, Negroes and some sympathetic white citizens have adopted a form of passive and orderly protest against racial discrimination which it will be very hard for segregationists to overcome. In recent days the protest has been leveled mainly at stores which welcome Negro customers so long as they remain standing but forbid them to sit down with white customers at counters where food is served. Negroes and white sympathizers have been occupying seats at such counters—and in some instances have been arrested for their pains.

Passive resistance, if wisely led and kept carefully within legal bounds, is a nearly irresistible weapon. It sufficed, in time, to win independence for India. It may well serve to win equality for Negroes in the United States.

Behind these protests lies a long record of Negro patience and of stubborn refusal from some white persons to make any adjustment to social change. To the Supreme Court's mild and flexible formula for desegregation of the public schools, parts of the deep South replied only with massive resistance. To the moderation of Congress, which a few years ago withheld drastic civil-rights legislation and pared down the measure it adopted out of consideration for southern sentiments, parts of the deep South replied only with intensified discrimination against Negroes at the polls. To Negro hopes and to the country's assumption of a good-faith effort at accommodation with the Constitution, parts of the deep South replied only with blindness and bitterness.

The protests will grow in volume and in strength. They are protests against a denial of the dignity that is due every human being and against a denial of rights guaranteed to every American citizen by the Constitution of the United States. These protests have behind them the full force of humanity and justice.

MORAL SUASION

AUGUST 12, 1960

The news that a group of major chain-store executives have agreed to desegregate lunch counters in their outlets in sixty-nine southern communities heralds a major social change—a change as heartening as it is inescapable. Credit for hastening the change belongs in part to the chain-store executives, who have exhibited real mercantile statesmanship; in part to Attorney General Rogers, who gave them a timely prod; and, most of all, to those patient and peaceful demonstrators in various southern cities whose valiant "sit-ins" pointed the way to a moral imperative. . . .

Mr. Rogers has shown the chain-store executives what should have been obvious from the outset—that they have a bread-and-butter economic interest in desegregation. Negroes cannot be expected to patronize other departments of stores which deny them service at lunch counters; and they cannot be expected to patronize other outlets of chains which insult and discriminate against members of their race in the South.

We have no doubt that their local competitors who continue to discriminate will feel impelled before long to follow their lead. Attempts by some southern states to require lunch-counter segregation by law are clearly at cross-purposes with the Constitution; and it is immensely encouraging that Mr. Rogers has indicated that the Department of Justice can be counted upon to give legal aid, at least at the appellate level, to any stores prosecuted for violation of such unconstitutional laws.

The sit-ins which sparked the change in the South began as spontaneous protests by local groups of Negro students aided by some sympathetic white students. They have been conducted, almost without exception, in a marvelously dignified and disciplined manner by young men and women avoiding any resort to force and subjecting themselves to the hazards of violence at the hands of rowdy mobs and unruly local police. Their technique of peaceful protest will spread; it is already beginning to be used to penetrate those most sanctimonious sanctuaries of segregation, the churches. And it will prevail, as other instances of moral suasion have prevailed in the past, because its cause is just.

TOWARD EQUALITY

AUGUST 21, 1960

There are symptoms of acceleration in the slowly evolving pattern of race relations. Nothing very dramatic has occurred; nothing sensational is impending. But the pace seems to be quickening.

If one looks at the map prepared by the Southern Regional Council showing the counties in southern states where school desegregation was in effect in the spring of this year, one must acknowledge that segregation is still overwhelmingly prevalent. In Louisiana, Mississippi, Alabama, Georgia and South Carolina, there has been no change at all. In Florida, Arkansas, Tennessee, North Carolina and Virginia, only an occasional school district has allowed white and colored children to sit in the same classrooms. Texas, Oklahoma, Missouri, Kentucky, West Virginia, Maryland, Delaware and the District of Columbia range, however, from extensive to complete desegregation of schools.

If this is far from perfection, it is at least progress. The latest instances of it can be seen in the assignment by Virginia's Pupil Placement Board of two Negro students in Richmond and nine in

Roanoke to formerly all-white school systems. There is implicit in this an acceptance of change, however reluctant—a recognition that those ingeniously evasive private-school schemes won't work, that massive resistance is, in the long run, a mirage.

There is a nascent awareness, moreover, that desegregated schools do not automatically usher in miscegenation or even mixed cocktail parties and that they are not incompatible with good education. The South can still have its own rich culture and its best traditions even if it accords Negroes their constitutional rights.

Apart from schools, there are other indications that ancient barriers are crumbling. In public transportation, at lunch counters, in recreational facilities, in places of entertainment, discrimination is gradually diminishing. And the experience of association between whites and Negroes cannot fail to break down ancient prejudices and misconceptions. The quiet courage of the Negro students who have engaged in peaceful sit-in demonstrations has had an incalculable impact. The beginning of effective influence by the federal government, as in the desegregation of chain-store lunch counters and in the enforcement of civil-rights legislation, has given backing to the proponents of moderation and accommodation in the South.

Even the tension and anxiety and friction that exist today in the South are more indicative of progress than the old complacency. If to the inescapable pressure of economic conditions there can now be added the moral influence of the South's churches and the leadership of the Presidency, a tremendous transition can be achieved. The time is ripe for it. The nation desperately needs to make it.

CHAIN-GANG JUSTICE

OCTOBER 27, 1960

The pictures published yesterday of the Rev. Martin Luther King, Jr., handcuffed and on his way to prison, will haunt the state of Georgia for a long time to come. There is a pretext for the prison sentence imposed on Dr. King: Last month he was fined $25 and given a twelve-month suspended sentence on a charge of driving without a Georgia driver's license—although he possesses a valid Alabama driver's license. On Tuesday he was ordered to serve four months in prison on the ground that his participation in an Atlanta sit-in demonstration had violated the suspended sentence in his traffic case.

The pretext will deceive no one. The whole world will understand that Georgia has railroaded this minister of religion to jail because he dared, as a Negro, to ask for decent and equal treatment for Negroes in Atlanta. The store in which the sit-in demonstration took place has pressed no charges against Dr. King; the Mayor of Atlanta has made it plain that the "City of Atlanta has no charges against any of the sit-in demonstrators" and that "the trial and incarceration of Dr. King are the responsibility of De-Kalb County and the State of Georgia."

This is the kind of chain-gang justice for which Georgia used to be notorious. This is the kind of racism which Americans hoped was confined by now to the Union of South Africa. Surely there are Georgians in high office with enough pride in their state and enough sense of fairness to put an end to this shabby perversion of justice. Let them speak out to save their state from shame.

"ORGANIZED ROWDYISM"

JANUARY 13, 1961

It is time for a showdown at the University of Georgia. Two Negro students admitted to the university in conformity with a federal court order have now been suspended—by order, as it were, of a mob. If the state of Georgia cannot or will not provide protection for their rights as citizens, then it must be provided by the United States. The mob cannot be permitted to prevail.

The admission of the two Negroes to the university took place initially without disorder or difficulty. They were treated with courtesy and respect by university officials. More than fifty girls living in the dormitory to which Charlayne Hunter was assigned called on her in her room, introduced themselves and welcomed her. If the student body as a whole did not welcome her and Hamilton Holmes, the other colored student, it at any rate overwhelmingly accepted their presence. Only a small and noisy minority, stirred up by outsiders, made trouble.

The trouble, such as it was, was kept well under control until Wednesday night. There developed then what the Athens, Georgia, chief of police termed "organized rowdyism, led by strangers from out of the city." The Mayor of Athens asked at 10 p.m. for State Police assistance in maintaining order. No help came until 12:20 a.m.

To suspend the two Negro students because their safety was threatened by "organized rowdyism" is to penalize the victims of law-breaking instead of penalizing the law-breakers. And it is also, of course, to stultify the law—to allow it to be warped by intimidation. If Governor Vandiver won't protect the rights of Miss Hunter and Mr. Holmes, we trust that Federal Judge Bootle will—with the help of the United States marshals if necessary. . . .

DARKEST ALABAMA

MAY 16, 1961

Alabama calls itself, presumably with pride, the "Heart of Dixie"— which must mean that it cherishes the traditions of the Old South, chivalry, hospitality, kindness. But some of its citizens showed precious little understanding of those traditions on Sunday when they burned and stoned two buses, one in Birmingham and the other just outside of Anniston.

The buses carried mixed loads of white and Negro passengers, calling themselves "Freedom Riders" and striving to demonstrate, under the auspices of the Congress of Racial Equality, that the guarantees of the United States Constitution are valid throughout the length of this long land. This was their sole offense. The "Freedom Riders" engaged in no disorderly conduct and did nothing to provoke violence—save to exercise a constitutional right. The police dispersed the crowds after one of the buses had been destroyed by fire and after several of the passengers had been injured. But no arrests were made.

Why does this happen in Alabama? The buses had come into the state from Georgia, where nothing untoward had occurred. But Alabama has a Governor who encourages contempt for the Constitution of the United States and who preaches incendiary racist nonsense. The plain fact is that Americans cannot be assured in Alabama of the equal protection of the law guaranteed by the Fourteenth Amendment. . . .

TIME TO MOVE AHEAD

SEPTEMBER 27, 1961

Seven years have gone by since the Supreme Court of the United States ordered the country's public-school authorities to end segregation "with all deliberate speed." Yet in more than two thousand school districts not the slightest start has been made toward compliance. And in many parts of the country, northern as well as southern, desegregation has been partial, grudging and has been vitiated by gerrymandering of school districts.

The Civil Rights Commission—its six members representing all sections of the country—has reached a unanimous judgment that the pace of desegregation must now be advanced. In all conscience, the commission is quite right. There has been ample opportunity for a gradual change in the pattern of race relations. An abundance of time has been accorded to the sensibilities of white Southerners reluctant to see any change in a way of life which has been quite comfortable for them, however uncomfortable it may have been for Negro children. There has been quite enough deliberation; the need now is for speed.

Accordingly, the commission has offered recommendations that Congress supplement the Supreme Court's order with some enforcing legislation. The commission thinks that Congress ought to require every segregated school district to submit plans to the federal government within six months for concrete first steps toward desegregation and for full desegregation as speedily as feasible. In addition, the commission wants Congress to give financial and technical assistance to local school systems undertaking desegregation, provide federal protection for children, parents, citizens and school officials carrying out desegregation plans, and pass a law speeding up federal court action in school cases.

There is nothing novel about the legislative measures recommended by the commission. Most of them were recommended— nay, pledged—in the Democratic Party's 1960 platform. They would serve to throw the force of federal authority effectively behind the Supreme Court's [decision] for the first time. How likely they are to win congressional approval is, however, uncertain.

Gradualism has undoubted virtues in bringing about a difficult social adjustment. But gradualism ought not to be made a mask for immobility. To let desegregation lag indefinitely is to let resistance harden into outright rebellion. It is to entrench discrimination rather than alleviate it. And for a generation of Negro schoolchildren it has meant a frustration of the hope and promise held out by a court which is this nation's supreme arbiter of its Constitution. For the children who have waited for a chance to go to desegregated schools these past seven years, the clock can never be turned back; for them the years of childhood are gone forever. The promise and the hope must be redeemed for the children who will be going to school in the years immediately ahead.

SHOWDOWN

SEPTEMBER 29, 1962

Patience and forbearance are appropriate attributes to power. The United States, dealing with a recalcitrant state, is in something like the situation of a firm father dealing with an unruly child. It is prudent and possible to tolerate temper tantrums up to a certain point. But when that point has been reached, it becomes necessary to assert authority unmistakably and conclusively.

Attorney General Kennedy has been well advised, we think, to put up with Ross Barnett's antics until now. His patience has avoided needless violence. It has afforded the Governor of Mississippi every reasonable opportunity to come to his senses. It has allowed full scope to the operation of such conciliatory and persuasive influences as could be brought to bear on the inflamed situation. It has made the legal issues completely clear.

But now that Governor Barnett has willfully defied the order of the Fifth Circuit Court to appear before it in New Orleans and show cause why he should not be judged guilty of contempt, a finding that he is in contempt seems inescapable. The Governor's direct legal responsibility has not been established until now. If he does not purge himself of contempt by Monday, we think the United States must move against him with whatever power may be needed to make its authority fully effective. If this requires using the armed forces of the United States, let them be used. If it requires jailing the Governor of Mississippi, let him be jailed as the law-breaker he has made himself. The authority of the United States, justly determined through its courts of law, is not to be ignored.

"Mr. Meredith will be registered," Attorney General Kennedy has said unequivocally. The United States, being committed to this result, can do no less. It is clear, however, that it will have to do a great deal more. It will have to assure the safety of that very brave young man in a situation made desperately dangerous by the recklessness of Mississippi's officials. Governor and Lieutenant Governor alike have been whipping up a mob hysteria calculated to produce violence. Lieutenant Governor Paul B. Johnson was quoted as saying, for example, "If the state troopers hadn't been at Ole Miss . . . that Negro wouldn't have lasted as long as it takes to aim a shotgun." This is nothing less than an incitement to assassination.

Oxford, Mississippi, is now crowded with state troopers mobilized by a Governor apparently determined upon some sort of Hitlerian immolation. Given the incorrigibility of folly, they may have to be thrust aside by force. Let us hope, and indeed pray, that enough sanity will prevail in Mississippi to forfend so terrible an event. But the United States cannot now settle for less than full vindication of the law.

LIVING PETITION

AUGUST 29, 1963

Freedom—the sound and spirit of the word alike—reverberated yesterday across the grounds of the Washington Monument. At the end of the Mall, inside the great memorial erected to his memory, the gaunt, grave, silent figure of the Great Emancipator sat and listened, remembering, perhaps, the words of other marchers for freedom long, long ago: "We are coming, Father Abraham, three hundred thousand strong." Surely Abraham Lincoln yesterday heard the voices singing "Glory, Glory, Hallelujah," demanding fulfillment at last of the promise for which he lived and died, and shouting with simple faith in themselves and in their fellow Americans: "We shall overcome . . . we shall overcome."

They came from every portion of America. California had a throng there under a proudly held banner of the state. There was a delegation from West Memphis, Arkansas. The NAACP of Evansville, Indiana, turned out in strength. So did the NAACP of Shreveport, Louisiana, and of Erie, Pennsylvania, and of Pittsfield, Massachusetts, and of an endless catalogue of the towns and cities of the land.

Every kind and class of American was there. The Vermont Stone Cutters Association formed a goodly group. The Amalgamated Meat Cutters and Butcher Workers of North America, the United Automobile Workers, the civil-libertarians of every hue, the Protestants, Catholics and Jews, white men and black men, black women and white women, children and their parents and their grandparents, the humble and the great—all were present. America sent to that great meeting in her capital the representatives of every one of her manifold aspects and estates.

It was part picnic, part prayer meeting, part political rally, combining the best and most moving features of each. It was a happy crowd, much more gay than grim, full of warmth and good feeling and friendliness, instinct with faith and high hope, united in a sense of brotherhood and common humanity. It was a most orderly march, not with the precision of a military parade but with the order that grows out of a clear sense of common purpose, a fixed and certain destination.

No one could view that vast sea of faces turned upward toward the Lincoln statue without an awareness of commitment and dedication. No one could hear the scourging words spoken yesterday by A. Philip Randolph and Martin Luther King and others without a sense of guilt and grief and shame. No one could hear the tones of Marian Anderson's deep and beautiful voice singing, "He's Got the Whole World in His Hands" without profound emotion and involvement.

If the words spoken yesterday were heard by Abraham Lincoln at one end of the Mall, let us hope that they were heard by the Congress of the United States at the other end. For this was something much more than a mere outlet for emotion. Dr. King was altogether right in saying that "Those who hope that the Negro needed to blow off steam and will now be content will have a rude awakening if the Nation returns to business as usual. There will be neither rest nor tranquillity in America until the Negro is granted his citizenship rights. The whirlwinds of revolt will continue to shake the foundations of our Nation until the bright day of justice emerges."

There is a magnificent opportunity at hand to cut out once and for all a cancer in America demeaning and degrading to all Americans. Not Negroes alone, not white libertarians alone but Americans in general marched yesterday—and must march in unity and in brotherhood tomorrow and tomorrow.

TROUBLE IN ALABAMA

FEBRUARY 6, 1965

Before condemning the Rev. Martin Luther King and his followers for breaking a law in Selma, Alabama, one needs to consider the law that was broken and the reasons for breaking it. Dr. King and 263 adults were arrested on charges of parading without a permit. Whether the Selma ordinance requiring a permit for a parade is constitutionally valid—and whether the marchers were, in fact, parading or merely, as Dr. King put it, "walking down to the courthouse"—are matters which courts will have to decide. There is no doubt, however, that Dr. King deliberately defied duly constituted authority in Selma—a serious responsibility for any citizen.

Dr. King is not a lawless or irresponsible man, and his defiance of authority in Selma was certainly not selfishly motivated or recklessly undertaken. He wants to enable Negroes to register and vote in Selma. It is an indisputable fact that Alabama's voter-registration requirements are rigged to discriminate against Negroes; and in Selma particularly, difficult literacy tests and slow procedures have been employed by registrars to keep Negroes from exercising their rights as citizens.

It was against this pattern of discrimination that Dr. King was protesting. If the demonstration he led violated a local ordinance, it was, nevertheless, orderly, peaceful and dignified. No one can charge him with violence or rioting or endangering property rights or public safety in any way.

Is his conduct, then, morally justifiable? Is it right for a minister of religion to lead followers in such a defiance of duly constituted authority? We think so. We have no doubt that the Rev. Martin Luther King, released on bond yesterday from the Selma jail, is as much at peace with his conscience as Martin Luther himself was when he nailed his ninety-five theses on the door of the castle church at Wittenberg 450 years ago in defiance of clerical and secular authority.

It is a social evil that Dr. King is attacking. And he is attacking it by the one method which has proved genuinely effective in recent years. His defiance of authority and his imprisonment focused the attention of Selma, Alabama, and of the whole nation, on the evil that persists in that southern city. It evoked the "indignation" which President Johnson expressed at his news conference on Thursday and which he said all Americans should feel "when one American is denied the right to vote."

If Dr. King has broken the law in Alabama, he has done it to make known the ancient pattern of law-breaking which has taken place there. "If Negroes could vote," he declared, ". . . there would be no oppressive poverty directed against Negroes, our children would not be crippled by segregated schools, and the whole community might live together in harmony." If Negroes could vote, in short, they could break the chains that bind them to misery; if they were given political responsibility, they could be held responsible for their own condition. If they could vote, they would have no need to demonstrate in demand of so basic a right. Denial of that right to vote has denied them their lawful remedy.

Alabama cannot silence Dr. King and his followers by putting them in prison. It can only make the echoes of their protest reverberate more resoundingly. Dr. King and his followers can be silenced only by giving them their rights as Americans.

GRENADA

SEPTEMBER 14, 1966

Human beings everywhere must be revolted by what happened on Monday in Grenada, Mississippi. To some Mississippians, it appears to have been an occasion for laughter to see children clubbed and maimed by adults armed with ax handles, pipes and chains. But to the civilized world, this is a spectacle too abhorrent to be longer countenanced.

The Mississippi mob vented its wrath on children lawfully attending two public schools in Grenada on the opening day of the new school year. One was an elementary school, the other a high school. As the children left their classrooms, screaming grown-ups fell on them. According to the Associated Press, "One Negro youth ran a gauntlet of cursing whites for a full block, his face bleeding, his clothes torn. Another youth was thrown to the ground and stomped. . . . Men did all the beating but many women were present, cursing and yelling."

Every community has its scum, of course. And if this were no more than the brutality of a few hoodlums momentarily out of hand, it could perhaps be regretted and dismissed as an aberration. But the ugliest aspect of what happened was that the law-enforcement authorities of Grenada watched it all, not raising a hand to protect the helpless children. What manner of men can these be? There seems to have been such a default of moral and political leadership in Mississippi—by successive Governors, by the state's U.S. Senators in Washington, by local authorities—that the population as a whole has been corrupted and degraded to insensibility.

This is not an isolated incident in Mississippi. It is part of a pattern, fostered by official callousness, fomented by official contempt for the law. It is of a piece with the shooting of James Meredith when he walked on a Mississippi highway last June and akin to the mobbing of the civil-rights marchers who came after him. It is in keeping with the killing of Medgar Evers in Mississippi in 1963 and with the murder of three civil-rights workers in the state's Neshoba County in 1964. From January 1961 through May 1964 there were more than 150 serious incidents of racial violence reported in Mississippi. Most of these went altogether unpunished. "Every assault or murder which goes unpunished," the Civil Rights Commission warned in its report of last fall on Law Enforcement in the South, "reinforces the legacy of violence—the knowledge that it is dangerous for a Negro to depart from traditional ways."

The United States is directly concerned in this Mississippi primitivism. It is federal law and the edict of federal courts that Mississippians over and over again have flouted. And it is the image of America in the eyes of civilized mankind that Mississippians have grimed and disgraced.

Let us now put an end to it. If the state can't control its thugs, the United States can. Governor Johnson's initial reaction to the Grenada situation was to say that state troopers will be "as active as the situation requires where the local authorities call on them for help." But it is evident that the local authorities don't want help. Later, and more realistically, the Governor sent 175 highway patrolmen in full riot dress into Grenada to protect the Negro children. Let us give them one more trial. But if they fail again, let us quit paltering and send federal troops into the state to maintain order. A touch of martial law might just be a civilizing influence to these barbarians.

REACTION

SEPTEMBER 30, 1966

An ominous and dangerous reaction has gripped the country. Its immediate pretext, of course, is the riotous disorder that has afflicted so many American cities in recent weeks. But it is, nevertheless, a reaction not alone against rioting but against race as well. It is, in truth, a reaction against extending to Negroes the civil rights that belong to all American citizens. And the apt and inescapable term that must be applied to all who participate in such a reaction is "reactionary."

The signs of it are everywhere. They were evident in the defeat of the Civil Rights Bill. They are readily discernible in the apathy about home rule for the District of Columbia. The primary triumphs of George P. Mahoney in Maryland and of Lester Maddox in Georgia are glaring examples of the reaction. But the most dismaying indication of all is the turnabout in the Senate over the administration's desegregation "guidelines"—and particularly Senate Majority Leader Mike Mansfield's defense of that turnabout.

The Senate on Tuesday approved overwhelmingly a rider on an appropriation bill which would authorize white Medicare patients to occupy hospital quarters separate from Negroes, if doctors say it will contribute to their health. No one can seriously doubt that this means the continuance of segregated hospitals at least in the deep South. And it endorsed an Appropriations Committee report denouncing the HEW guidelines for school desegregation. Senator Mansfield on Wednesday endorsed this action at least as to hospitals. "I think they have gone too fast," he said.

Too fast? In the decade that passed between the Supreme Court decision that school segregation violated the Constitution and the congressional enactment of the 1964 Civil Rights Act, fewer than two per cent of the Negro children in the eleven states of the deep South were admitted to schools attended by white children. A year after adoption of the Civil Rights Act, six per cent of the Negro children in those states were in classes with white children. There are 1800 school districts in the South with over a million schoolchildren which still, today, maintain dual school systems. It is monstrous for the government of the United States to continue financing this outright defiance of the Constitution.

Congress and the President and the country came to a recognition in 1964 that the deep South was going to obey the Constitution only if the federal government required it to do so. That is why Congress passed the 1964 Civil Rights Act, implementing it with Title VI, which forbade the distribution of federal funds to segregated hospitals and schools. The Department of Health, Education and Welfare has not been too fast in applying the plain terms of Title VI. Congress meant them to be effective. If anything, HEW has been too cautious and too slow. Segregation is still the rule rather than the exception in the South. . . .

The Civil Rights Acts were not passed by Congress as largesse to Negroes. They were passed as indispensable to the health and welfare and sense of justice of the whole American people. To retract them now for the purpose of punishing a few Negro leaders who mouth slogans about "black power" is to injure the whole Negro race insensately and, indeed, to injure the whole American people. . . .

WHITE POWER

OCTOBER 27, 1966

"Violence, even in self-defense," Dr. Martin Luther King, Jr., writes in *Ebony* magazine, "creates more problems than it solves." The experience of the past few months has pretty amply demonstrated the melancholy truth of this observation, as the momentum of the civil-rights movement has come to a grinding halt in the wake of rioting in a dozen major cities across the nation.

"These violent eruptions," says Dr. King, "are unplanned, uncontrolled temper tantrums brought on by long-neglected poverty, humiliation, oppression and exploitation. Violence as a strategy for social change in America is nonexistent. All the sound and fury seems but the posturing of cowards whose bold talk produces no action and signifies nothing."

This seems to us precisely right. It puts in perspective the ranting about "black power" and about Negro separatism—as though Negro aims and Negro rights were to be achieved by seeking a head-on collision between nascent black power and an overwhelmingly developed white power. Yet no more than a day or two ago the hotheaded young director of the Congress of Racial Equality, Floyd McKissick, delivered himself of the dictum that "the civil rights movement is dead as a doornail and what we have now is a black revolution, for black people to take what they can for themselves."

It really would be difficult to cram a greater quantity of egregious, mischievous nonsense into any single, simple sentence. If the civil-rights movement were, in fact, dead, Mr. McKissick would surely have to stand trial as one of its principal assassins. But it is not dead; it is merely momentarily derailed. The reaction to violence and to the talk about "black power" has taken its toll. . . .

But the civil-rights movement—and the men and measures promoting it—remain very much alive. They remain alive because they express the considered moral convictions and the real interests of the whole American people, black and white alike. There is not the slightest doubt that Negro demonstrations, led in large part by Dr. King, played an indispensable role in awakening the white conscience. And it is equally plain that litigation and championship of constitutional principles by such Negro organizations as the NAACP were vital in bringing about white recognition of the need for reform and the correction of injustice. CORE and SNCC and other militant groups did valiant work for a while in organizing Negroes in the peaceful assertion of their rights.

But Negro equality is going to be achieved in the United States not because Negroes wrest it by force from a white majority but because the white majority is brought to realize that the whole country will be better off economically and ethically when all men really become equal in opportunity and before the law. Discrimination against Negroes has been a blight and a blot on America. The extirpation of it will mean liberation for both races. The inevitability of history is behind this movement.

EQUALITY AND THE LAW

DECEMBER 26, 1966

The Duke University Law School did some valuable teaching in North Carolina the other day. It publicly severed relations with the state Bar Association because that body—every member of which has taken an oath to support the Constitution of the United States—refused to admit as a member a Duke University law graduate who is a Negro. The graduate passed the regular state bar examination and was duly admitted to practice before the North Carolina bar. The dean of the Law School, pointing out that exclusion from the Bar Association would be an obstacle to professional advancement, said that the school felt it has the same responsibility to Negro students as to all others.

This is no empty gesture. It should shock and shame the lawyers of North Carolina—and perhaps impel them to right a wrong. But it has another even more significant value. It reminds the world that there are powerful voices of conscience speaking in the South. No one can doubt that they will eventually prevail. To give them expression is surely the highest function that an institution of learning can fulfill.

SCHOOLS AND BUSES

NOVEMBER 13, 1967

The schoolbus, it seems, is not a very formidable additive to the schoolroom. In the wake of the Supreme Court's decision of 1954 holding that segregated schools amounted to a denial of the equal protection of the laws to Negro children, there was a widespread notion that integrated schools could, of themselves, overcome Negro disadvantagement. With some support from the Office of

Education, busing of pupils from one neighborhood to another was undertaken in a number of cities. But a couple of recently published small-scale studies—one conducted in New York City, the other in San Francisco—suggest that busing is not the panacea that it was once hopefully, if naïvely, supposed to be.

In the words of the New York report, the bused children "gain in terms of classroom functioning, particularly in terms of participation and verbal fluency" but "there is no evidence of steady long-term improvement in reading level." The busing did no harm, the report concluded, to the quality of education in the receiving school but appeared to skim off the ablest and most ambitious children from the slum schools. The more simple, though "very tentative" conclusion of the San Francisco study was that "nothing major has happened."

This should hardly be surprising when one thinks about it. What handicaps children in school achievement is not their skin color but the deprivation so many of them suffer in home environments and cultural backgrounds. When children, disadvantaged in this way, are grouped together in schools, they handicap each other. One interesting finding of the New York study is that achievement scores show that the Negro students bused under New York's Open Enrollment program generally work at higher levels than the average in the slum-neighborhood schools they leave behind. But the explanation of this superiority probably lies simply in the fact that the busing opportunity attracts the more highly motivated and thus the more able Negro students. . . .

THE PHILADELPHIA PLAN:
HALF A LOAF AT LAST

JANUARY 14, 1970

There is a piety about the attacks on the Philadelphia Plan—a program for diminishing the discrimination against black workers in the construction industry—which is almost as sickening as the discrimination itself. In the Philadelphia area, where Negroes constituting about thirty per cent of the population hold about one per cent of the jobs in the key building trades, the Contractors Association of Eastern Pennsylvania has gone to court to obtain an injunction to outlaw a clause in U.S. government contracts which would require that they make a "good faith" effort to meet reasonable goals in raising minority employment. The contractors insist that they are fervently in favor of enlarging job opportunities for Negroes but they are afraid that the Civil Rights Act forbids them to do so.

The Comptroller General of the United States is right with them—if not, indeed, behind them. He, too, is "not against greater opportunities for minority groups"—not at all. He, too, thinks, however, "that the 'Philadelphia Plan' is clearly in conflict with Title VII of the Civil Rights Act of 1964." And he declares that the real question involved is not one of removing racial discrimination from government contracts but simply "the unwillingness of the Department of Labor and the Department of Justice to accept the authority of the Comptroller General" to rule on the legality of a congressional appropriation.

The summit of sanctimony was undoubtedly attained, however, by the president of the AFL-CIO, Mr. George Meany, who told a National Press Club audience on Monday that the real trouble with the Philadelphia Plan is that it sets hiring goals only for federally financed construction jobs while an AFL-CIO program envisages bringing blacks into jobs financed by private as well as by government contracts. This protestation of virtue on the part of unions which have systematically excluded Negroes from jobs or even from apprenticeships for most of the past century has an Alice-in-Wonderland quality that leaves one breathless. Mr. Meany may be right in saying that the Philadelphia Plan was devised to win the Nixon administration a few "Brownie points"; but if it works the way it should, the points will be well deserved.

If there is one matter that ought to be clear in all this, it is that Congress was not trying to perpetuate discrimination when it adopted the Civil Rights Act. Title VII of that act, it is true, forbade the setting of quotas for employment. And there is, it is also true, a superficial semantic similarity between a quota and the kind of goal for minority employment sought through the Philadelphia Plan. But there is also a difference between them far outweighing the similarity.

Quotas are understandably abhorrent to those seeking to do away with discrimination. A quota in this context means a ceiling. Some years ago, when colleges were accused of discriminating against religious minorities in their admission policies, they fixed quotas in percentage terms for these minorities based upon their ratio to the general population and not upon their ability to meet competitive entrance tests; these quotas then became a maximum for the admission of minority-group students. The goals embodied in the Philadelphia Plan constitute a floor, not a ceiling, a minimum rather than a maximum; they constitute an agreement to enlarge job opportunities for minority workers, not restrict them; and so they are in complete conformity with the essential spirit and purpose of the Civil Rights Act.

The difference between the quotas forbidden by the Civil Rights Act and the goals sought by the Philadelphia Plan is like the difference between telling a hungry man he may have no more than half a loaf of bread and telling him that he is assured at least half a loaf. Or, more simply, it is like the difference between help and hindrance.

DAMN THE RESISTERS:
FULL SPEED AHEAD

JANUARY 20, 1970

The essential point to bear in mind in reading the Supreme Court's Wednesday order telling public-school authorities in five southern states to desegregate now—at once, instanter, immediately, forthwith and without delay of any kind—is that it was handed down sixteen years after the court's initial order to desegregate the public schools "with all deliberate speed." The court can hardly be called heedlessly impatient. It has simply had all the delay and all the deliberation it could stomach without sacrifice of its authority. And the government of the United States has looked on at the South's flouting of the Supreme Court with a complacency that invited Negroes to lose all faith in the judicial process—and in the whole idea of orderly social change.

The inaction and indifference of the Eisenhower administration in the 1950s, so far as implementation of the original desegregation ruling was concerned, had much to do with the rise of "massive resistance." The President, in the 1950s, withheld the support of his own leadership and moral authority from the court decree and maintained a neutral aloofness from the great national struggle for equal rights. Non-compliance became a general pattern throughout the old Confederacy in consequence.

The Nixon administration has been lending much the same sort of encouragement to entrenched patterns of segregation in the South. The Department of Justice seems always able to find sympathy for the travail of white citizens who must make a painful adjustment to the ideal of racial equality, yet is rarely able to muster up much feeling for blacks who have had to adjust to inequality for the whole of their lives and seek something better for their children.

There was a positive effrontery in the assertion of the Department of Justice that it would undertake an all-out program of lawsuits to desegregate the entire South this fall if the court would only postpone the deadline for compliance to next September. Will the department now sulk idly in Washington because it has not had its dilatory way?

Further delay in desegregation is a misfortune for everyone in the South—for whites no less than for blacks. It simply perpetuates turmoil and compounds confusion. The change to unified schools has simply got to be made. The sooner it is made, the sooner the South will be able to deal with the manifold problems of improving its educational system for the children of both races. Acceptance of the idea of change, of equality, is the key to progress, alike in education and in the economy of the deep South.

FORCED SEGREGATION

MARCH 26, 1971

In his televised conversation with the President the other evening, Howard K. Smith made a brief statement and asked a clear question which, together, go right to the heart of the problem of racial discrimination in America. "It is clear after a generation of trial," Mr. Smith said, "that the greatest block to integration of any form is segregated suburbs. I have asked you about that before, and your answer has been that you opposed forced integration. But does that not mean, in effect, the perpetuation of discrimination in housing, and isn't that against the law?"

Mr. Smith got no more than a partial answer to his question—and an extremely dusty one at that. Mr. Nixon appeared to concede the premise—that is, "that the greatest block to integration of any form is segregated suburbs." But he asserted that the "situation is caused by economic considerations rather than by racial decisions," that it would be unfair for the federal government to put a low-cost housing project into a neighborhood where people have purchased their homes and "break it up from an economic standpoint, because those homes are too expensive for some people to move into." And then the President said again what he has said before: "I do not believe that that kind of forced integration is constitutional, and it certainly is not required by law."

To say that ability to buy a house is a function of economic considerations alone and not of racial discrimination is to ignore the close causal connection between the two. It is somewhat like saying that anyone, rich or poor, may come to a party, provided he wears a tuxedo, or that children and grown-ups alike will be admitted to a theatrical performance, provided they are more than five feet tall. Blackness and poverty have been closely correlated in America for two hundred years precisely because racial discrimination meant denial of opportunity.

Children reared in a ghetto are likely to live in a ghetto as adults—and to rear their own children there—not because an actual wall or a law confines them but because their environment subjects them to crippling disadvantages—overcrowded housing, malnutrition, sordid surroundings, inferior education, cultural barrenness, discouragement of ambition. To say that they have the same chance as children reared in more favorable surroundings to buy a house in the suburbs is about like saying that children who suffered from rickets or polio in childhood have the same chance as healthy children to win a footrace.

Setting aside any moral qualms about the justice or injustice of ghetto surroundings from the point of view of those subjected to them, there remains an ineradicable fact that ghettos are bad for society as a whole. They are breeding places of disease, crime and depravity; they hike the community's costs for health care, law enforcement and welfare; they stunt the tax base, diminish productivity and impair national security.

It was with the general welfare in mind that Congress enacted laws—housing laws and civil-rights laws—designed to put an end to ghettos and to the racial discrimination that created them in the first place. And so we think President Nixon is simply mistaken when he says that "forced integration"—if the term can be said to have any reasonable application to the selection of a suburban site for a low-cost housing project—"is not required by law."

If all low-cost housing projects are confined to inner cities, they will serve simply to create, perpetuate and enlarge ghettos instead of eradicating them. They will simply make ghetto life more crowded, more disadvantaged and more hopeless. That is precisely why the housing laws and the civil-rights laws were designed to prevent excessive racial concentration in the selection of public-housing sites. Low-cost public housing is the only kind of housing that many black families can afford.

To say that "forced integration" in the suburbs is not required by law is to say, at least in effect, that forced segregation in the inner cities *is* required by law. Mr. Smith was absolutely right in suggesting that the President's policy means "the perpetuation of discrimination in housing"—with all that that implies in terms of a divided and impoverished nation. Rights have meaning only when they are bracketed with opportunities. The right to live where one pleases can be real only if it is accompanied by a chance to realize it.

ONE MAN'S HOPE

MAY 23, 1970

Loyalty is tested in adversity. For many Americans today, there is a crisis of confidence in American institutions and in the viability of the American political system. For black Americans more than any others, that crisis must be a poignant one. So it is with a keen feeling of sympathy that we note the remarks of Dr. Martin D. Jenkins, president of Morgan State College, at a news conference after he emerged from a meeting at which he and fourteen other presidents of predominantly black colleges told President Nixon that his policies had led to "anger, outrage and frustration" among the nation's Negroes.

"I have hope and confidence," Dr. Jenkins said. "There is little in the historical record which would lead to this conclusion, and yet, as a black and an American, I must believe—if I believe in this nation—I must believe that it will move forward, and that it will move forward under the President of the United States. I can take no other position than that."

This constitutes, perhaps, the highest form of loyalty—loyalty not to a particular government or administration but to the ideals and purposes for which that government was established. What Dr. Jenkins was saying was that against admittedly great odds and in the face of the available evidence, he clings nevertheless to a conviction that the American people are still going to make good on the promise of American life.

Consider that Dr. Jenkins made his statement only a few days after six black men, all shot in the back by police firearms, were found dead in Augusta, Georgia. He made the statement in the immediate aftermath of a grand-jury finding that Chicago police, on the pretext of making an arrest, had wantonly fired nearly one hundred rifle shots into a Black Panther hangout, killing a Black Panther national leader. He made the statement on the heels of the tragedy in Jackson, Mississippi, where two college students were killed and nine more were wounded because state highway police poured a fusillade of shots into a dormitory. And he made the statement immediately after talking to a President whose Department of Justice had announced support for tax exemption for private schools set up in the South to circumvent the civil-rights laws and the Supreme Court's school-desegregation decision.

Was Dr. Jenkins foolish? Was he naïvely idealistic? It's hard to say what black men ought to do today. And perhaps white men have no right to say it, anyway. Marching through Georgia doesn't seem to be getting them anywhere. The political process seems to be up against the southern strategy. Revolution is really a suicidal mirage. So there is Dr. Jenkins left believing—as he says he must believe—that "this nation will move forward under the President of the United States." Does any President care to tell him that he's wrong?

SEVEN

———◆———

Restraining the Police

At the center of the Bill of Rights are provisions that deal primarily with the protections afforded persons accused of crime. Found mainly in the Fourth, Fifth and Sixth Amendments, they guarantee, among other things, the rights of individuals to avoid self-incrimination, to have the assistance of counsel, to be free from unreasonable searches and to be arrested only upon "probable cause." The interpretation of these guarantees—the meaning of the constitutional language and the way in which it should be enforced—has brought the courts into conflict with the police, the politicians and the public. This conflict was probably inevitable; each of these constitutional rights makes the solution of crime more difficult, and in an era of increasing concern about crime, any obstacles to law enforcement tend to be seen as "legal technicalities" that protect the guilty.

This conflict did not arise early in American history because of the way constitutional law evolved. Originally, the Bill of Rights limited only the federal government and its officers. The states and state officers, who have the primary role in law enforcement, were free, so far as the federal Constitution was concerned, to ignore the Fourth, Fifth and Sixth Amendments. This situation began to change after ratification of the Fourteenth Amendment in 1868. That Amendment barred the states from depriving per-

sons of life, liberty or property without "due process of law."
Early in the twentieth century the Supreme Court began what
became a long process of applying one provision of the Bill of
Rights after another to the states through the due-process clause.

During the 1950s and 1960s the Supreme Court speeded up
this process and effectively nationalized the procedural side of the
criminal law. All local police forces and prosecutors, for the first
time, were required to recognize and abide by most of the limitations on their practices written into the Bill of Rights. In 1963,
for example, the court said that the federal Constitution requires
states to provide free legal counsel for all indigents charged with
serious crimes; prior to that, all federal courts provided such free
counsel, as did most states, but a few states told poor people to
defend themselves. Indeed, before 1932, when the court ruled
that lawyers must be provided for all indigents charged with capital crimes, some states had executed people convicted at trials in
which they had received no effective legal assistance at all.

This nationalization has often been described as a revolution in
the criminal law. It was, in many states. Those were the states
which did not have state constitutional provisions identical or
similar to the federal Bill of Rights or whose courts had interpreted or enforced such provisions so as to give individual rights
less protection than they received in the federal courts. In these
states the Supreme Court's decisions forced drastic changes in the
procedures police and prosecutors used in making arrests, conducting searches and questioning suspects. Because those changes
made successful police work more difficult and because they coincided with—critics of the court argue they caused—a sharp
increase in crime, a series of bitter confrontations arose between
the court and those who thought such decisions proved the Justices
were "soft on crime."

Alan Barth was one of those who believed that these changes
in law-enforcement practices were not only required by the Constitution but long overdue. He argued for them before they were
made and he fiercely defended the court's decisions. In his view,
the Founding Fathers were well aware that the Bill of Rights made
the detection and solution of crime more difficult; that was one of

the prices they were willing to pay for individual freedom and liberty. This was the message of his third book, *The Price of Liberty*, published in 1961.

Two of the issues on which judicial and public debate was most heated in the 1960s and '70s were the "exclusionary rule," which bars from use in criminal trials illegally seized evidence, and the restrictions placed on the use as evidence of incriminating statements made by those accused of crime. These debates go on year after year, and efforts—both judicial and legislative—continue to ease some of the limitations the court has placed on police conduct.

ORDER AND LIBERTY*

Law enforcement is forever at odds with civil liberty. Law, by definition, imposes limitations on individual conduct. This is not to say, however, that law itself is an enemy of liberty. "For law, in its true notion," as John Locke has told us, "is not so much the limitation as the direction of a free and intelligent agent to his proper interest, and prescribes no farther than is for the general good of those under that law. Could they be happier without it, the law, as a useless thing, would of itself vanish; and that ill deserves the name of confinement which hedges us in only from bogs and precipices. So that however it may be mistaken, the end of law is not to abolish or restrain, but to preserve and enlarge freedom. For in all the states of created beings, capable of laws, where there is no law there is no freedom."

Enforcement of the law against those who violate it—that is, against those who impair the freedom of others—entails power. But power is always dangerous. It must be wielded by men; and

**The Price of Liberty* (Viking Press, 1961; copyright, 1961, by Alan Barth), pp. 19–21, 32–34. Footnotes omitted.

men empowered to administer the law fall easily into the notion that they are empowered also to interpret and to shape it. Thus the power intended to prevent oppression by law-breakers becomes, if not constrained and bounded, a means of oppressing the law-abiding. Power intended to preserve liberty may also imperil it.

Liberty, therefore, requires a dual protection. It requires law enforcement by governmental authority for maintenance of the order which is indispensable to enjoyment of liberty. And it requires at the same time limitation of governmental authority to prevent an extension of authority beyond the need for it. Order and liberty are closely kin. It is important to remember, however, that order is not an end in itself; it is but a means to an end, and the end it seeks is liberty.

Limitation of governmental authority is accomplished by a basic code or charter, written or unwritten, and commonly called a constitution.

• • •

The unique quality of the American Bill of Rights at the time it was adopted lay in the fact that it was designed to protect the people from themselves. When, in 1688, James II renounced the throne of England, and the Prince and Princess of Orange were invited "by the will of the people" to succeed him, Parliament drafted the English Bill of Rights and required the new monarch to subscribe to it. This Bill of Rights, which asserted the sovereignty of Parliament and reasserted the liberties of Englishmen, was designed to serve as a protection against the dangers of oppression or arbitrariness by the King.

But the American Bill of Rights a century later was designed for a republic. The danger of royal tyranny had been dealt with by dispensing with royalty. But the threat of popular tyranny was perhaps even greater. For it entailed dangers of two sorts: the danger that officials vested with authority to maintain order might use it to suppress liberty; and the danger that a majority of the people, impatient to accomplish some purpose, might override all opposition, silence dissent, crush diversity and deal arbitrarily with any who might resist its will. James Madison discussed this second danger in a remarkable letter to Thomas Jefferson on October 17, 1788, arguing for the addition of a Bill of Rights to the Constitution:

> Wherever the real power in a Government lies, there is the danger of oppression. In our Governments the real power lies in the majority of the community, and the invasion of private rights is *chiefly* to be apprehended, not from acts of Government contrary to the sense of its constituents, but from acts in which the Government is the mere instrument of the major number of the constituents. . . . Wherever there is an interest and power to do wrong, wrong will generally be done, and not less readily by a powerful and interested party than by a powerful and interested prince.

Madison was not naïvely sanguine about the restraining power of a Bill of Rights. In the same letter, indeed, he observed that "experience proves the inefficacy of a Bill of Rights on those occasions when its control is most needed. Repeated violations of these parchment barriers have been committed by overbearing majorities in every State." Nevertheless, he favored such a bill because he believed it would at least "counteract the impulses of interest and passion." Jefferson, replying from Paris, said that "though it is not always efficacious under all circumstances, it is of great potency always and rarely inefficacious. A brace the more will often keep up the building which would have fallen, with that brace the less."

In his letter to Jefferson, Madison made one other observation of great significance. "It is a melancholy reflection," he said, "that liberty should be equally exposed to danger whether the Government have too much or too little power, and that the line which divides these extremes should be so inaccurately defined by experience." Here, in point of fact, is the essence of political science, the chief difficulty in the reconciliation of order and liberty.

The men who sat in the Constitutional Convention of 1787 were certainly not indifferent to the protection of property or the main-tenance of order. They sought a government strong enough to enforce the law yet not so strong as to become a law unto itself. They stipulated, therefore, in a Bill of Rights, that the range of that government's authority—the range of popular authority—should be limited and that the application of authority should conform to certain standards of fairness summed up in the concept of due process of law. The procedural guarantees of the Bill of Rights—even more than its substantive guarantees—operate, so long as they are observed, to make possible the happy boast of Americans that they live under a government of laws rather than of men. They operate to keep order the guardian and guarantor of liberty.

PUBLIC SAFETY AND
PRIVATE RIGHTS*

It seems to me that the threat to civil liberty in the United States has shifted somewhat in the past few years from a neurotic anxiety about Communist subversion to an almost equally neurotic anxiety about protection of the community against crime. But if the focus of the threat has somewhat shifted, the origin and the essential nature of the threat remain, I think, the same. These arise out of a tendency which our Fourth of July orators like to designate as peculiarly a failing of the Communists—a tendency to consider worthy ends a justification for unworthy means.

In the frenzied decade following the last world war, when we

*Barth spoke on this topic many times, tailoring his text to fit each audience. This is an amalgam of several of those speeches. It relies primarily upon texts used on May 5, 1961, at the University of Wisconsin in Madison, Wisconsin, and on November 1, 1961, at the First Unitarian Church in Omaha, Nebraska. Other versions were delivered on December 9, 1959, at Vanderbilt University, Nashville, Tennessee, on May 9, 1960, at Brandeis University, Waltham, Massachusetts, and on January 11, 1961, at the University of Michigan, Ann Arbor, Michigan.

were in such a hysteria to protect the country from subversive influences, we countenanced a number of measures which ran violently counter to settled American principles of fair play. In the name of national security, we justified—and continue to justify—a good many short-cuts—reliance on faceless informers, for example—which involved serious trespasses on individual rights.

Just so, it seems to me, we are coming more and more these days, in the name of law enforcement, to justify short-cuts by the police which involve serious trespasses on the individual rights guaranteed to American citizens by the Constitution.

There is a very widespread disposition on the part of the press and the public alike to be indifferent about the procedural rights of persons pursued by the police—especially when those persons are guilty, or presumed to be guilty, of some heinous crime.

There are a couple of obvious reasons to account for this indifference. In the first place, procedure is prosaic. The procedural protections of the Fourth, Fifth and Sixth Amendments seem less glamorous and more difficult to understand than the great substantive guarantees of the First Amendment. People often dismiss them as "mere legal technicalities."

In the second place, it is difficult for respectable and law-abiding citizens to identify themselves with persons accused of crime. Those whose procedural rights are violated by the police are, for the most part, the scum of society—vagrants, purse-snatchers, pickpockets, dope peddlers, robbers, rapists and others who present an indisputable threat to law and order and the safety of the community. It is not easy to make ordinary citizens recognize that their own rights are bound up intimately with the rights of such outcasts. Yet, no political observation is more valid than that the rights of the best of men will be observed only so long as the rights of the worst of men are respected.

There has been an undoubted and very disquieting increase of crime in the post-war years—and especially of violent crime. The causes are too complex to permit analysis here—even if I possessed competence to analyze them. But certainly among the causes are factors which lie far beyond the power of the best of police departments to correct—factors which grow out of the nature of our society—the urbanization of American life, the development of vast slum areas in huge, impersonal cities, a general sense of uprootedness, the impact of mass media of communication devoted to the values of merchandising, the brutalizing influence of two world wars. It may be, in short, that crime is simply a symptom of a general sickness in our society and can be corrected only by curing the sickness that causes it.

Protection of the community against crime is, of course, an immensely important and legitimate public interest. The authors of the Constitution were not indifferent to the maintenance of law and order. They were men with a lively regard for property rights. But they were also men who had an over-riding regard for individual rights—for protection of the individual against the potentially oppressive power of the State.

I think I ought to furnish you with some definition of the way in which I mean to use this word "rights." One often hears it said, in reply to those who urge a respect for the rights of subversives, criminals and other social outcasts, that the community has rights, too—and that these public rights should not be ignored out of a sentimental concern for private rights.

Those who take this view tend to conceive of the community as having an independent existence distinct from the individuals who comprise it. But American traditions and the fundamental idea of the American Constitution are rooted in a conviction that the interests of the individual and of the community are inseparable. "Those who won our independence," said Mr. Justice Brandeis in the greatest of his opinions, "believed that the final end of the State was to make men free to develop their faculties. . . . They did not exalt order at the cost of liberty."

The authors of the Constitution believed that men could best be made free to develop their faculties in a political system which limited the powers of government. They conceived of rights, therefore, as restraints on governmental power. The Bill of Rights which they appended to the Constitution was simply a list of proscriptions forbidding the government in a variety of ways to interfere with individual activity. In the sense in which I employ the word, then, the government, or the public, or the community, as you prefer, has no rights. Rights are privileges or immunities of the individual against public interference.

There is nothing in the least sentimental about this emphasis on respect for private rights. It constitutes one of the essential distinctions between a police state and a free state. A totalitarian society, by definition, is one in which the totality is given primacy over its component individuals. The free society is one in which government is no more than an instrument for the accomplishment of specified collective purposes.

Those who so glibly dismiss as "mere legal technicalities" the procedural guarantees of the Constitution limiting law-enforcement activities forget that nothing is more basic to civil liberty than freedom from arbitrary arrest and imprisonment by policemen who are masters, not servants, of the law. The most characteristic symbol of the police state is the ominous rap on the door at night. Freedom from the fear of that rap is the basic condition for the exercise of every other form of freedom. "The history of liberty," Mr. Justice Frankfurter once observed, "is the history of the observances of procedural safeguards."

For as long as men have sought to be free, arbitrary arrest has been a mark and measure of despotism. In every land and time, men have protested and fought against it. It has been a principal cause of every major uprising against established government. It was one of the grievances of the English barons against King John in 1215 and prompted their insistence in Magna Carta that "no free man shall be taken or imprisoned . . . except by the legal judgment of his peers or by the law of the land." Bitter resentment against capricious arrest and incarceration was one of the prime causes of the French Revolution. And so the Declaration of the Rights of Man and of the Citizen stipulated that "No man should be accused, arrested, or held in confinement, except in cases determined by the law, and according to the forms which it has prescribed."

Arbitrary arrest and arbitrary searches conducted under the infamous writs of assistance and general warrants were among the bitterest grievances against George III recited in the American Declaration of Independence. When they established their independence, Americans were determined that no government of their own creation should ever engage in these forms of despotism. Accordingly, they imposed heavy restraints upon police activity in the Fourth Amendment to the Constitution.

The Fourth Amendment says in sweeping terms that "the right of the people to be secure in their persons, houses, papers, and effects, against unreasonable searches and seizures, shall not be violated, and no warrants shall issue, but upon probable cause, supported by oath or affirmation, and particularly describing the place to be searched, and the papers or things to be seized." It is this Amendment that protects American citizens against arbitrary arrest and that makes of every American home a fortress safe from arbitrary intrusion by the police.

The Amendment means, among other things, that Americans may be arrested only when probable cause exists to justify the arrest. And the existence of this probable cause is to be determined not by policemen in their unchecked discretion, but by a judicial officer. Probable cause means something more than mere suspicion. It means evidence substantial enough to justify a reasonable man in forming an opinion that a particular suspect has committed a particular crime.

Ideally, an arrest is to be made only after an arrest warrant has been issued by a judge, instructing the police to bring the arrested person before him forthwith. But the exigencies of law enforcement have made it necessary to authorize the police to make arrests without a warrant when they have probable cause to believe that someone has committed a felony. When the police arrest without a warrant, the law provides in the federal jurisdiction—and something very like it is true, I believe, in every state of the Union—that the arrested person must be taken "without unnecessary delay" before a magistrate.

It is then the business of the magistrate to determine whether the police really had probable cause to justify the arrest. If probable cause exists, the magistrate advises the arrested person of his rights—the right to a preliminary hearing, the right to remain silent, the right to counsel. He warns the arrested person that anything he says may be used in evidence; and he then admits him to bail or commits him to prison pending trial. In short, the law lets policemen arrest, but delegates to magistrates the judgment whether to detain.

At this point it would be useful, I think, to look at the facts of a particular case in point. Let me tell you briefly about the case of Andrew Mallory, a semi-moronic Negro who was convicted of rape in the District of Columbia and whose conviction was subsequently upset on "technical" grounds by the Supreme Court of the United States.

The rape occurred in 1954 in the basement of a Washington apartment house, where the victim, a young married white woman, had gone to do some laundry. The man who attacked her wore a mask, and she was unable to identify him beyond saying that he was a young Negro. The police arrested Andrew Mallory and two other colored youths who lived in the building, took them to a station house and questioned them there intensively for six or seven hours. All three were given lie-detector tests. In the course of the lie-detector test, Andrew Mallory broke down and confessed that he had committed the crime. It was by then late at night, and he was not taken before a magistrate for arraignment until the following morning. On the basis of his confession, he was convicted and sentenced to death.

The Supreme Court unanimously reversed this conviction, although there was no serious doubt about Mallory's guilt. In an opinion by Mr. Justice Frankfurter, the court reminded the police that the rule regarding prompt arraignment was adopted in order to check "resort to those reprehensible practices known as the third degree." And then it went on to read the police an elementary lesson in law-enforcement practice.

"The police," it said, "may not arrest upon mere suspicion but only on 'probable cause.' The next step in the proceeding is to arraign the arrested person before a judicial officer as quickly as possible so that the issue of probable cause may be promptly determined. The arrested person may, of course, be 'booked' by the police. But he is not to be taken to police headquarters in order to carry out a process of inquiry that lends itself, even if not so designed, to eliciting damaging statements to support the arrest and ultimately his guilt. . . . It is not the function of the police to arrest, as it were, at large and to use an interrogating process at police headquarters in order to determine whom they should charge before a committing magistrate on 'probable cause.' "

Nevertheless, this is standard operating procedure for the police almost everywhere in the United States. And almost everywhere it is winked at by the courts, by the press and by the public. Nearly every state in the Union admits as evidence confessions obtained after arrests made on mere suspicion and as a result of police interrogation during a period of unlawful detention.

Arrests without a warrant have become so much a commonplace in this country that, to tell the truth, an arrest warrant is now a rarity—a relic of some distant law-abiding and law-respecting past. It has been estimated that about ninety per cent of the felony arrests made in the United States are made without a warrant.

Unfortunately, a great many arrests are made not only without a warrant but also without any semblance of the probable cause which would be required to obtain a warrant—and which the law requires for an arrest without a warrant. You don't need to go beyond official statistics to test the truth of this assertion. If you will look at the Uniform Crime Reports for the United States compiled by the Federal Bureau of Investigation for 1959—the most recent year for which these figures are available—you will find arrests in cities of more than 2500 population listed by categories: it shows, for example, a total for the United States of 2610 arrests for murder and non-negligent homicide; a total of 15,379 arrests for robbery; 4002 for forcible rape; 323,353 for disorderly conduct. And then, running your eye down the list, you will come to a curious category of crime—a category called "suspicion." And you will find that there were 99,663 arrests in 1959 for "suspicion."

But suspicion is not a crime anywhere in the United States. There is not a state in the Union that makes it criminal to suspect—or even to be suspected. What this means, of course, is that 99,663 persons were arrested and brought into police stations by policemen who wanted to question them—but without enough evidence against them even to file a specific charge.

In the District of Columbia the fashion in police circles is to arrest "for investigation." Go down to police headquarters in Washington and look at the police blotter—the arrest book—and you can see written over and over again, unblushingly, in the space where the arrest charge is supposed to be specified, the simple word "investigation." There were 7367 persons arrested for investigation in the District of Columbia in 1958; and every one of them was subsequently released without any other charge.

There is no penal offense known as "investigation."

Now, these figures do not take into account the undeterminable number of additional persons unlawfully arrested on mere suspicion—that is, because the cops wanted to question them—concerning whom evidence to support a charge was subsequently uncovered—very likely through a confession obtained during a period of unlawful detention.

Neither do these figures reflect the vast number of persons who are arrested all over the country on vague, blanket charges such as "vagrancy" and "disorderly conduct" used loosely by the police to cover a multitude of sins which are not crimes. Most of these, too, are released without prosecution.

The police in most cities are fond of showing their zeal and energy whenever a particularly heinous crime is committed by rounding up and arresting every suspicious person they can lay hands on. For example, the victim of a 1958 robbery in a Washington restaurant reported that it was perpetrated by three stocky young Negroes, one of whom slugged her. The police immediately rounded up no fewer than ninety suspects in a precinct-wide dragnet operation. Few of them were either young or stocky; a number, in fact, were over fifty years of age. Sixty-seven of them were held overnight at police headquarters. None of the ninety was ever charged with the crime. A charge was brought subsequently against another man, not one of those arrested.

Later on, there was an inquiry into the circumstances of this roundup. The Superintendent of Police, testifying, said that "large-scale interrogations" of this sort were not unusual. He cited a recent investigation involving four murders in the course of which 6170 persons were detained by the police. The roundup in the 1958 restaurant robbery, he acknowledged, had gone "a bit too far" but he said that he had issued no written orders to prevent similar roundups "because every crime must be investigated on its merits."

This is the kind of investigation pursued by most police departments. Arresting suspects in order to ask them questions is the easiest way to investigate. It saves a lot of energy that would otherwise have to be expended collecting evidence. Presumably it helps keep a detective from becoming a flatfoot. Nevertheless, there is one serious defect about it. It is plainly against the law. Policemen may, of course, ask questions of anyone they please. But they may not arrest and detain anyone for the purpose of asking questions.

Policemen not only like to arrest on suspicion in order to ask questions. They like to do their questioning in the lonely, often intimidating atmosphere of a police station. Even if there is no resort to third-degree investigating tactics, the threat of violence is always in the air. It loosens men's tongues—and especially if they are poor or friendless or ignorant and do not know much about their constitutional rights.

During the course of a trial in Federal District Court in Washington, the prosecutor candidly if unintentionally blurted out the reason why police prefer to question suspects in a police station prior to arraignment. In his argument to the jury, the prosecutor declared: "They say why didn't we put him downstairs"—in jail, that is, after a magistrate had advised him of his rights—"and call him back the next morning. Why? We would find the place crawling with attorneys telling him 'You don't have to talk to the police.' "

Professor Caleb Foote of the Pennsylvania University Law School, who has made an extensive study of police investigating methods, made a grim observation: "It is probable that most American police prisoners are held incommunicado prior to preliminary examination, with no right to use the telephone or contact friends, relatives, or lawyers."

This, too, is altogether unlawful. It breaches not only the law but important constitutional rights as well—the right to counsel, the right to bail, the privilege against self-incrimination, even the basic right of *habeas corpus*.

The American Civil Liberties Union of Illinois in 1959 published a report titled "Secret Detention by the Chicago Police." A study of more than two thousand arrest cases showed that fifty per cent of the police prisoners produced in Felony Court had been held without charge for seventeen hours or longer; another thirty per cent could not be accounted for in terms of pre-booking detention because of police failure to complete the arrest slip. One out of every ten Felony Court defendants in the sample had been held for forty-eight hours or longer. One out of every twenty had been held for sixty hours or longer; one out of every forty had been held for *at least three days* before he was charged with an offense.

Now, let me offer one more illustration of the police tendency I have been talking about. Some of you may remember a case much in the headlines about a year and a half ago—the case of Willem Van Rie, a young Dutch radio operator on the steamer *Utrecht* who was arrested for the murder of a young woman, a passenger on the ship, whose body was found in Boston Harbor. Let me read you the headline in the New York *Herald Tribune* which told about the breaking of that case:

SHIP'S RADIO MAN IS HELD,
HE WAS SLAIN GIRL'S LOVER
Quizzed 20 Hours, Admits
Romance Though Married

This man, unfamiliar with American law, not wholly at home with the English language, was questioned relentlessly for twenty hours, without having a charge lodged against him, without arraignment, without being allowed to get in touch with a lawyer, or even with the Dutch consulate, until at last he made damaging admissions which provided the probable cause for committing him to jail and indicting him. The police had little more ground for arresting him than for arresting the three others from the freighter whom they brought in, interrogated and released. The Constitution of the United States, the Constitution of New York, the laws of New York were all violated by the police procedure in this case.

Yet, to the best of my knowledge, no New York newspaper made the slightest protest against it. And judging from the *Herald Tribune*'s headline trumpeting the fact that the suspect was quizzed for twenty hours, that newspaper wasn't even aware of any police misconduct.

Newspaper naïveté of this sort is not at all unusual. One frequently sees news stories which report that someone was arrested on suspicion of murder or on suspicion of robbery—written evidently by reporters who have no idea that suspicion never affords a valid basis for arrest. The sad part of this is, however, that the reporters are generally quite accurate in what they have written.

Now, let me turn . . . to the invasions of privacy which occur so commonly and so callously as a part of contemporary police activity.

Among the injuries and irritations which led the American colonists to rebel against the rule of King George III, none roused more resentment than the "writs of assistance," which amounted to general warrants authorizing the indiscriminate ransacking of homes and places of business.

The makers of the American Constitution resolved that such general warrants for police searches should never take place in the country they were creating. In the Fourth Amendment they conferred, as against the government, Justice Brandeis wrote, "the right to be let alone—the most comprehensive of rights and the right most valued by civilized men."

The Fourth Amendment forbids only unreasonable searches. But it has long been a settled matter of law that the searching of a home is not reasonable unless there is "probable cause" to justify it, unless the information establishing the probable cause is sworn to by somebody, and unless the search is authorized in advance by some judicial authority. Moreover, to be reasonable, a search must be specific. It cannot be undertaken at random with respect either to the scene of the search or the object of the search.

Nevertheless, as court records make perfectly plain, searches are made all the time in outright defiance of these limits placed by the Constitution on police power. And until very recently many states allowed evidence obtained by unlawful searches to be used in criminal prosecutions. The federal courts have long excluded such evidence. But it was not until last June that the Supreme Court of the United States got around to saying flatly in the *Dollree Mapp* case that "all evidence obtained by searches and seizures in violation of the Constitution is, by that same authority, inadmissible in a state court."

The decision produced much weeping and wailing and wringing of hands on the part of police chiefs and prosecutors who moaned and groaned that they would not now be able to enforce the law and protect the public. But the truth is that they had forgotten what it is they are supposed to protect. Their most important business is to protect "the right of the people to be secure in their persons, houses, papers and effects." If this personal security of the people sometimes affords a shelter for criminals, the authors of the Constitution believed this was not too high a price to pay for that degree of privacy which is indispensable to individual dignity and self-respect.

Now, the alarming aspect of the police practices I have been discussing, as I see it, is not so much that the police sometimes break the law in their zeal to enforce the law. There is nothing novel about this kind of police conduct. And, as everyone knows, there have been periods when police conduct was a great deal worse than it is today—when it was generally corrupt and brutal as well as technically unlawful.

No, the really alarming aspect of the current situation is that to a very large extent the American people have closed their eyes to this cutting of legal corners by the police or have actively prompted and promoted it. Panicked by the incidence of crime in big cities, they have become impatient with the restraints of the Fourth

Amendment—impatient, too, with judicial insistence that the commands of the Amendment be obeyed by the police. You could see abundant evidence of this panic in the careless haste with which the House of Representatives last year passed the Willis-Keating bill designed to overturn the Supreme Court's ruling in the *Mallory* case.

This popular indifference was mirrored in American newspapers. Arrests on suspicion, indiscriminate roundups, prolonged detention, interrogation designed to force confessions—all these were reported in the press with only occasional editorial protest. . . .

The maintenance of civil liberty depends upon a general understanding of what it means, and what it costs—upon a general acceptance of the risks that it entails.

The men who wrote the Constitution did not mean to make the policeman's lot a particularly happy one. They were well aware that the Fourth Amendment would, in some degree, reduce police efficiency and make law enforcement more difficult. But it was no part of their purpose to establish a police state. They were prepared to accept some measure of risk to public safety for the sake of protecting private rights. They did not, as Mr. Justice Brandeis put it, exalt order at the cost of liberty.

If we in the United States become careless of civil liberty, if we think of it as a liability rather than an asset, if we put public safety above private rights, and the protection of the community above the protection of the individual, we shall end by making ourselves over into a mirror image of what we most abhor. And if we do that, we shall have betrayed and lost our richest inheritance.

THE EXCLUSION OF EVIDENCE*

. . . A difficult question of public policy arises . . . when a court discovers defects in the methods employed to bring about the

The Price of Liberty, pp. 94–100.

conviction of an indubitably guilty defendant. Should courts ignore police practices in obtaining evidence so long as they do not entail physical coercion and so long as the evidence presented in court is competent and relevant? The traditional and prevailing rule in English and many American courts is that they should. Or should courts exclude evidence obtained in violation of a defendant's legal and constitutional rights? The latter course has been adopted by the federal courts in the United States—and by about half the states.*

In a landmark case, *Weeks v. United States,* decided in 1914, the Supreme Court dealt with this question and settled it by a unanimous decision so far as the federal judiciary is concerned. The case involved the seizure of some papers in plain violation of the Fourth Amendment. The defendant, charged with using the mails for an unlawful lottery scheme, filed a pre-trial motion to have the papers returned to him. The motion was denied by the trial court; the papers were introduced in evidence and used to convict him. The Supreme Court held, however, that denial of the motion for return of the illegally seized papers amounted to a prejudicial error and, in an opinion by Justice William R. Day, deplored "the tendency of those who execute the criminal laws of the country to obtain conviction by means of unlawful seizures and enforced confessions." The opinion went on to declare:

> If letters and private documents can thus be seized and held and used in evidence against a citizen accused of an offense, the protection of the 4th Amendment, declaring his right to be secure against such searches and seizures, is of no value, and, so far as those thus placed are concerned, might as well be stricken from the Constitution. The efforts of the courts and their officials to bring the guilty to punishment, praiseworthy as they are, are not to be aided by the sacrifice of those great principles established by years of endeavor and

*In 1961, a few months after this was written, the Supreme Court decided that the exclusionary rule established in the *Weeks* case would apply to state as well as federal prosecutions. Thus, all courts in the United States now exclude evidence seized illegally or unconstitutionally.

suffering which have resulted in their embodiment in the fundamental law of the land.

A few years later the Supreme Court went a step farther and forbade even the indirect use of evidence obtained as the result of an unreasonable search. In this case the arresting officers made copies of the illegally seized documents, returned them when ordered to do so, but then issued a subpoena to the defendants to produce the originals. Justice Oliver Wendell Holmes wrote, "The essence of a provision forbidding the acquisition of evidence in a certain way is that not merely evidence so acquired shall not be used before the court, but that it shall not be used at all."

The exclusionary rule is believed by many eminent and thoughtful lawyers to be sentimental and even silly. A criminal trial, they argue, is not a game in which sportsmanship requires the prosecution to handicap itself to the point of futility. They consider it illogical to exclude valid evidence of a crime simply because another crime was committed to obtain it. If policemen breach the law in trying to enforce it, they say, let the policemen be prosecuted like other law-breakers. This view was ably expressed by Professor Edward Barrett of the University of California Law School:

Law enforcement is not a game in which liberty triumphs whenever the policeman is defeated. Liberty demands that both official and unofficial lawlessness be curbed. And in any specific instance it is hard to say that, put to the choice between permitting the consummation of the defendant's illegal scheme and the policeman's illegal scheme, the court must of necessity favor the defendant. . . . It should be noted that the exclusion of the evidence usually results in the defendant's completely escaping punishment for his act, while the admission of the evidence does not constitute a judicial approval of the officer's conduct, and that the officer is still, at least in theory, subject to some form of civil or criminal liability.

. . . The artificiality of this [latter] argument is accentuated by the emptiness of the remedies it suggests. . . . So far as civil redress is concerned, the victim of the wrong is unlikely to have the resources to right it. In most instances he is without much standing or reputation in the community, so that he may find it very hard to prove damages. Very often, moreover, he wants to keep as far away from courts as possible and has no appetite for a protracted lawsuit. There is an added consideration that civil suits involve large legal expenses, and it is rarely profitable to sue a policeman; the chances are against a policeman's being able to pay appreciable damages in the unlikely event that a judgment should be rendered against him.

The suggestion that an offending policeman may be prosecuted as a private individual for his misconduct seems still less related to reality. More often than not his misconduct stems from misplaced zeal or from an error of judgment respecting the limits of the law, understandable in the stress and excitement of making an arrest or seeking to solve a crime; to punish him for trying to do his duty would be a harsh injustice. . . .

Furthermore, police officers and prosecuting attorneys commonly work in cooperation. If the prosecutor does not direct the policeman, he must at least recognize when lawlessness was involved in obtaining evidence; and if he presents that evidence in prosecution, he becomes, of course, a party to the offense. It is unlikely in such circumstances that he will prosecute the policeman who has helped him to win a conviction; at any rate, very few prosecutions of this sort have taken place.

"If police officers know that evidence obtained by their unlawful acts cannot be used in the courts," said Justice Douglas, "they will clean their own houses and put an end to this kind of action." This is, perhaps, an overly optimistic view. The deterrent effect of the exclusionary rule is uncertain, and its corrective influence is extremely limited. Obviously it helps only those persons whose cases are taken into court—and more often than not these are guilty persons. It does nothing for the relief of innocent victims of unlawful police conduct whose cases are dropped without prosecution. . . .

Perhaps both these contentions miss the most important consideration in favor of the exclusionary rule. When courts admit evidence obtained by unlawful police conduct, they lend color and countenance in some measure to lawlessness. The consequence is to undermine respect not only for the courts but for the law of which the courts are custodians. Respect for law is the *sine qua non* of effective law enforcement. A widespread lack of it among Americans is, conversely, the most serious impediment to the work of the police; it leads American juries sometimes to reject or discount prosecution evidence precisely because of a suspicion that it was obtained by questionable means. Thus, dubious police methods defeat the very purpose for which they are pursued. . . .

THE EXCLUSIONARY RULE

JUNE 29, 1971

The Supreme Court found occasion on Monday to remind Attorney General Mitchell, a slow learner, that "when the right to privacy must reasonably yield to the right of search is, as a rule, to be decided by a judicial officer, not by a policeman or government enforcement agent." The case before the court involved a search and seizure by New Hampshire police officers conducted on the basis of a warrant issued by the Attorney General of New Hampshire (who had assumed charge of a murder investigation and was later the chief prosecutor at the trial) acting as a justice of the peace. The Supreme Court reversed a conviction of the accused on the ground that the warrant for the search and seizure did not satisfy the requirements of the Fourth Amendment because it was not issued by a "neutral and detached magistrate." . . .

The judgment of the Supreme Court seems to us natural enough and in clear conformity with the historic meaning of the Fourth Amendment. But one aspect of this case that seems to us surprising is a single-page opinion by Mr. Chief Justice Burger, dissenting in part and concurring in part, which declares: "This case illustrates graphically the monstrous price we pay for the Exclusionary Rule in which we seem to have imprisoned ourselves." . . .

Dissenting in a related case, the Chief Justice observed that "the rule has rested on a theory that suppression of evidence in these circumstances was imperative to deter law enforcement authorities from using improper methods to obtain evidence." And, indeed, there is a great deal of experience, we think, to show that this theory is entirely valid. That it does not always deter police misconduct is no proof that it is without deterrent value. The Chief Justice himself says, "I do not propose, however, that we abandon the Suppression Doctrine (the Exclusionary Rule) until some meaningful alternative can be developed. . . . Obviously the public interest would be poorly served if law enforcement officials were suddenly to gain the impression, however erroneous, that all constitutional restraints on police had somehow been removed— that an open season on 'criminals' had been declared."

The Chief Justice acknowledges that private damage actions against individual police officers afford no "meaningful alternative." As he says with considerable understatement, "Jurors may well refuse to penalize a police officer at the behest of a person they believe to be a 'criminal' and probably will not punish an officer for honest errors of judgment." . . .

The remedy suggested by the Chief Justice is that the government itself should afford "compensation and restitution for persons whose Fourth Amendment rights have been violated." This seems to us reasonable and just, so far as it goes; and we should be glad to see Congress establish the mechanism for such a remedy. But we do not see any reason to suppose that it will effectively curb police carelessness regarding constitutional rights; on the contrary, it may well provide a pretext for ignoring those rights.

More significant than all this, however, is the fact that when courts admit evidence obtained by unlawful police conduct, they lend color and countenance to lawlessness. They become, in a real sense, accomplices in crime. The essential defense of the Exclusionary Rule lies in its indispensability for maintaining the purity of the judicial process. . . .

In our view, the price we pay for the Exclusionary Rule is not nearly so "monstrous"—to use the Chief Justice's own word for it—as the price we would pay, in terms of the corruption of our courts, if we were to abandon that rule.

CONFESSIONS*

What is wrong with a coerced confession? During a long span of history, the truth of what an accused person said was customarily tested by torture. The investigation of crime was often pursued by questioning suspects with the aid of the thumbscrew and the rack. It cannot be said that they were ineffectual devices. Undoubtedly they uncovered a great deal of guilt. But they came to be condemned in civilized societies on two counts. In the first place, it was recognized that confessions obtained by torture were untrustworthy. This is, perhaps, not an insuperable objection, since the validity of confessions, once they have been made, can usually be tested by checking them with known facts about a crime. In the second place, however, the use of torture has been condemned because in civilized communities it came to be regarded as revolting to the civilized sense of justice and inconsonant with the dignity of man.

From the beginning of the American Republic, forced confessions have been inadmissible in federal courts. They offend both the Fifth Amendment's privilege against self-incrimination and its concept of due process of law. In 1936 the United States Supreme Court ruled that such confessions are equally inadmissible in state courts because they violate the due-process clause of the Fourteenth Amendment.

*The Price of Liberty, pp. 52–56, 60.

The case which came to the court involved a conviction for murder based upon confessions obtained through such sadistic brutality that one of the judges of the Supreme Court of Mississippi said of the trial's transcript that it "reads more like pages torn from some medieval account, than a record made within the confines of a modern civilization which aspires to an enlightened constitutional government." The case is worth recounting if only to show to what unspeakable lengths law-enforcement officers may go when not governed by rules of procedure.

Investigating the murder of a white man in Mississippi, a deputy sheriff named Dial, accompanied by others, went to the home of a Negro named Ellington. They accused him of murder. When he denied it, they hanged him by a rope to the limb of a tree, let him down, then hanged him again and let him down again. Even after they had tied him to a tree and whipped him unmercifully, he continued to protest his innocence until, at last, they released him. A day or two later, however, Dial and another man arrested Ellington again, took him across the border into Alabama and there whipped him, saying they would continue the whipping until he confessed. When he agreed to sign any statement Dial would dictate, he was taken to jail. One of the Mississippi Supreme Court Justices, in a dissenting opinion, told of what happened to the other two defendants:

> The other two defendants, Ed Brown and Henry Shields, were also arrested and taken to the same jail. On Sunday night, April 1, 1934, the same deputy, accompanied by a number of white men, one of whom was also an officer, and by the jailer, came to the jail, and the two last named defendants were made to strip and they were laid over chairs and their backs were cut to pieces with a leather strap with buckles on it, and they were likewise made by the said deputy definitely to understand that the whipping would be continued unless and until they confessed, and not only confessed, but confessed in every matter of detail as demanded by those present; and in this manner the defendants confessed the crime, and as the whippings progressed and were repeated,

they changed or adjusted their confession in all particulars of detail so as to conform to the demands of their torturers. When the confessions had been obtained in the exact form and contents as desired by the mob, they left with the parting admonition and warning that, if the defendants changed their story at any time in any respect from that last stated, the perpetrators of the outrage would administer the same or equally effective treatment.

The subsequent trial of the three Negroes was a meaningless procedure. Although counsel for the defendants appointed by the court objected to admission of the confessions and brought before the court the manner by which they had been extorted, and although the deputy, Dial, and others admitted the whippings, the three Negroes were found guilty and sentenced to death.

While the concept of due process allows the states great latitude in trial procedures, it does not countenance compulsion by torture. "Because a State may dispense with a jury trial," Chief Justice Charles Evans Hughes wrote for a unanimous court, "it does not follow that it may substitute trial by ordeal. The rack and torture chamber may not be substituted for the witness stand. . . . It would be difficult to conceive of methods more revolting to the sense of justice than those taken to procure the confessions of these petitioners, and the use of the confessions thus obtained as the basis for conviction and sentence was a clear denial of due process."

. . . In 1944, in the *Ashcraft* case, the court, this time with three dissenting Justices, squarely held a confession to be involuntary, although it had not been coerced by violence, because the convicted man had been questioned almost continuously for thirty-six hours under the glare of powerful lights. The court took the view that this constituted psychological pressure of a sort which robbed him of his mental freedom. . . .

[A] year later a confession was held inadmissible because it had been obtained from a suspect who had been kept in a hotel room incommunicado from eight a.m. to six p.m., completely unclothed for part of that period, in order to "let him think that he is going to get a shellacking."

The rule, then, in state and federal courts alike, is that a confession may be used to convict a defendant only when it has been made of his own volition. It is inadmissible as evidence against him if it was wrested from him by any sort of coercion, physical or psychological. It is also inadmissible if it was obtained as a result of some threat or promise of reward, such as a mitigation of punishment. But coercion, especially when it has been applied by psychological rather than physical means, may be extremely difficult to detect. A beating may leave discernible marks upon a prisoner; prolonged interrogation in the intimidating atmosphere of a police station, threats veiled or open, suffering induced by denying the prisoner food, water or sleep—these are not readily discernible. And a determination of the degree to which such pressures may have induced the confession presents a most delicate matter of judgment.

Interrogation, by itself, in the absence of any coercion, is not forbidden by the Constitution. But the purpose of interrogation— at least if it is at all insistent—is almost inescapably to induce someone to disclose what he would like to conceal. There are, of course, confessions which are completely and indisputably voluntary, as when, for example, a woman calls the police and says, "Come, arrest me. I have just shot my husband." Remorse or an oppressive sense of guilt or a conviction that their crimes were justified or a desire for notoriety may lead men entirely on their own initiative to acknowledge violations of law. About the voluntariness and admissibility as evidence of such confessions there is no uncertainty.

"A confession by which life becomes forfeit," wrote Justice Frankfurter, ". . . must be the expression of free choice. A statement to be voluntary of course need not be volunteered. But if it is the product of sustained pressure by the police it does not issue from a free choice. When a suspect speaks because he is overborne, it is immaterial whether he has been subjected to a physical or mental ordeal. Eventual yielding to questioning under such circumstances is plainly the product of the suction process of interrogation and therefore the reverse of voluntary."

. . . Perhaps the only sure way to avoid what Mr. Justice Frankfurter called "the suction process of interrogation" is to forbid interrogation altogether once a suspect has been placed under arrest—at least until he has been brought before a judicial officer, charged and advised of his rights. For the very fact of interrogation in the loneliness and helplessness which may be induced by the atmosphere of a police station constitutes coercion. And the inescapable intent of interrogation under such circumstances is to coerce—to lead a man to say what he would not say under circumstances which made him feel more free.

QUESTIONING SUSPECTS

DECEMBER 5, 1962

"Questioning," Mr. Justice Jackson once wrote, "is an indispensable instrumentality of justice." Obviously, police officers investigating a crime need to seek information about it from many sources. They have ample authority to ask anyone about anything.

But there are restraints upon police conduct imposed by the Constitution, by local laws and by rulings of the Supreme Court. The Fourth Amendment forbids arrest of anyone without probable cause to believe that he committed a particular crime—which is to say that it forbids arrests on mere suspicion for the purpose of eliciting from a suspect by interrogation the information necessary to establish probable cause for arresting him.

The Fifth Amendment provides that no person "shall be compelled in any criminal case to be a witness against himself"—which is to say that, although the police may ask questions, no one is obliged to answer them if the answers would tend to bring about his conviction for a crime.

In conformity with these commands of the Constitution, the

District of Columbia Code has provided for the past hundred years that a police officer making an arrest without a warrant "shall immediately, and without delay, upon such arrest, convey in person such offender before the proper court, that he may be dealt with according to law"—which is to say that judicial officers, not police officers, are to decide whether probable cause exists to charge a person with a crime and detain him.

To promote observance of these requirements and to keep the courts from any connivance in law-breaking, the Supreme Court declared again in the *Mallory* case of 1957, as it had declared before in the *McNabb* case of 1943, that confessions obtained from a suspect unlawfully held in the police station should not be admissible in federal prosecutions.

Metropolitan Police Chief Robert Murray has repeatedly complained that these requirements hamper crime investigation unduly by making it impossible to interrogate suspects effectively. He has asked for "a little leeway." This newspaper, which has been critical of the Police Chief on this score, now presents a proposal which it hopes will afford the police a measure of leeway for asking questions without trenching in any way upon the rights of defendants.

We propose that when the police want to question someone in connection with a crime, whether as a suspect or a material witness—and when that person will not answer questions voluntarily—the police go before a judge and ask for a subpoena requiring the person's appearance not at police headquarters but at the United States Courthouse. This is the procedure followed in bringing persons before a grand jury for questioning. The persons responding to the subpoena would appear before a District Court or a Municipal Court judge or a United States commissioner who would advise them as follows: (a) that they are not under arrest but summoned simply because the police believe they have information which might be helpful in the solution of a crime; (b) that as citizens they have a responsibility to assist in law enforcement but that under the Constitution they are not obliged to give any answers that might implicate them in a crime; (c) that they may have the advice and assistance of a lawyer and that the court will provide one for them if they do not wish to retain a lawyer of their own choice.

With these instructions, the subpoenaed persons would be sent to another room in the courthouse, where a police official investigating the crime would question them. They would be free to remain silent if they wished and to leave the courthouse at any time.

Admittedly, this would not give the police all the leeway Chief Murray would like. But it would, in our judgment, give them all the leeway the Constitution allows; and it would produce, if astutely utilized, a good deal of valuable information.

It should not be assumed that all subpoenaed persons by any means would avail themselves of the privilege against self-incrimination and refuse to answer questions. On the contrary, most of them would answer, more or less fully, in an effort to exculpate themselves. Their answers would, of course, be subject to check by the investigators. Those who demonstrated their innocence could be cleared and eliminated from further inquiry; those who lied would invite additional investigation and interrogation. Some would make admissions which could be used in evidence against them; the *McNabb-Mallory* rule would be no barrier to the use of confessions obtained under these circumstances.

We believe it is vital to this plan that the interrogation be conducted at a courthouse rather than at police headquarters in order to free subpoenaed persons from fear of coercion or prolonged detention. We think it no less vital that the judge or commissioner advise the subpoenaed persons of their rights fully and in plain, readily understandable language. And we think it most vital of all that the subpoenaed persons be furnished with a lawyer to counsel them and see to it that their rights are respected.

It is precisely at this stage in the investigation and prosecution of a crime that legal help is of the greatest importance. Although the provision of legal counsel at this stage is not now recognized as a constitutional requirement, we think elementary fairness dictates it as a balance or corollary to the subpoena power and to make sure that the interrogation is not coercive. Counsel ought to be available alike to rich and poor so that justice will be applied equally to all.

The restraints placed upon the police by this proposed procedure are restraints which are fundamental to freedom. They protect rights which the founders of the American Republic characterized in the Declaration of Independence as "unalienable." It is true that in some measure they diminish police efficiency. But efficiency alone can never be the sole criterion for police procedure. These are some of the restraints which make the essential distinction between a police state and a free society. These are some of the restraints which make it possible for Americans to boast that they live under a government of laws.

INQUISITORIAL JUSTICE

MARCH 6, 1966

A tentative draft of the American Law Institute's long-heralded Model Code of Pre-Arraignment Procedure has at last been made public. What it amounts to is nothing less than a proposal to abandon the American system of accusatorial justice and to embrace in its place at least the beginnings of the European system of inquisitorial justice. The European system is certainly not without merit. However, it is at variance with the Constitution of the United States and could not be adopted here without major amendments of that Constitution, and especially of its Bill of Rights.

The dominant theme of the ALI proposal is that police officers must be afforded opportunity to investigate a crime by interrogating a suspect during a period following arrest of the suspect and prior to his being taken before a magistrate and charged with a specific offense. To facilitate this kind of investigation, the ALI code would allow the police to arrest a suspect whenever they believed they had "reasonable cause" to do so but without requiring them to let a magistrate pass promptly on the validity of the arrest. The ALI code would also allow the police to detain the arrested person for a period of "preliminary screening" to last not more than four hours—longer in some situations—during which they could question him whether or not he had a lawyer present; and no lawyer would be provided for persons unable to hire one.

We think these procedures are constitutionally and morally wrong. First, they make possible arbitrary and capricious arrests, the very hallmark of a police state. It is true that they authorize arrests only when the police think they have "reasonable cause" to make them but they abandon that judicial check on police action which is indispensable to the protection of liberty. "History shows," as Mr. Justice Douglas has observed, "that the police acting on their own cannot be trusted."

Second, these procedures seem to us to fly directly into the face of what a unanimous Supreme Court said in the *Mallory* case. . . . .

Third, these procedures dangerously erode the constitutional privilege against self-incrimination by making it contingent upon an arrested person's knowledge of his rights and upon his resolution in asserting them under hostile conditions. It is true that the code provides for a police declaration of right to silence; but this is in no sense equivalent to a judge's explanation.

Fourth, these procedures wipe out the constitutional right to the assistance of counsel at the moment when such assistance can be most effective. Again, the code flies in the face of Supreme Court decisions. The court has said that "a Constitution which guarantees a defendant the aid of counsel at . . . trial could surely vouchsafe no less to an indicted defendant under interrogation by the police in a completely extrajudicial proceeding." And it has said in another case that "when the process shifts from investigatory to accusatory and its purpose is to elicit a confession—our adversary system begins to operate, and . . . the accused must be permitted to consult with his lawyer." If a rich man may obtain a lawyer, equal justice demands that a poor man be provided one.

America has no need to cheat men of their constitutional rights, or to take advantage of their ignorance and helplessness, in enforcement of its laws. America has no occasion to enthrone its police or to confer judicial powers upon them. . . . The Constitution of the United States is doubtless a difficult and restrictive document. But it has this virtue: it has kept America a free country.

RESTRAINING THE POLICE

JUNE 18, 1966

[On June 13, 1966, in *Miranda v. Arizona,* the Supreme Court barred the use of evidence of any statements stemming from the interrogation of persons in custody unless those persons had been told of their rights to remain silent and to have assistance of counsel and had been allowed to exercise those rights if they wished to do so.]

. . . The restraints imposed upon the police by the court have produced, as was expected, forecasts of calamity from policemen, prosecutors and assorted Cassandras. The executive director of the National District Attorneys' Association, for example, promptly announced that "fewer crimes will be solved, even fewer crimes will be prosecuted." And the new Police Commissioner of New York dolorously asserted that "we just won't be able to offer the district attorneys and the courts as much evidence." Then he reiterated once more that hackneyed nonsense: "How far and how long are the rights of the accused to be considered with little regard for the rights of the victim?" The rights proclaimed by the court are the constitutional rights of a free people!

There was more moderation and better sense from U.S. Attorney David G. Bress here in Washington. He had already taken steps, before the decision, to make counsel available to indigent persons under arrest. And he put the court's ruling in precise perspective: "The Supreme Court is saying that it is dedicated to the rights of the individual even if it means some cost to society. The rights of the individual have been held paramount."

How could it be otherwise in such a society as ours? The rights of the individual were held paramount when this Republic was founded. The Declaration of Independence laid it down as a fundamental proposition that governments are instituted among men precisely in order to secure these rights. And specification of them in a Bill of Rights was demanded before the Constitution could be ratified.

Let us assume, although it is by no means certain, that the rules fixed by the court for in-custody interrogation will make the work of the police more difficult. The same can be said of the rule that forbids the searching of a house without a warrant. It can be said, in an exact analogy, of the ban on any use of the thumbscrew.

Consider the thumbscrew. It is one of the most effective instruments of investigation ever invented. Compact, portable, inexpensive, easy to operate, it can produce confessions from even the most hardened of criminals. Why, then, renounce its assistance? The simple answer is that it is incompatible with the kind of society Americans desire to live in. So is the sweating of a confession from an indigent defendant ignorant of his rights and without the assistance of counsel promised to him by the Constitution.

What's all the bleating about, anyway? American cops are not about to throw in the sponge in their long conflict with the robbers. The country needs more policemen, better-paid, better-trained and better-equipped policemen. It needs more reliance on brain than brawn in solving crimes. It needs more emphasis on prevention. It needs painstaking, patient, expensive attention to the causes and sources of crime. But it really doesn't need to junk its Constitution and its freedom.

QUICK CONFESSION

JUNE 25, 1966

Those who think the Supreme Court was sentimental and unrealistic in curbing police interrogation of suspects ought to take a good look at the case of George W. Whitmore, Jr. Perhaps because he has been in the hands of the police before, Whitmore was a ready confessor. The New York police got confessions from him in three distinct crimes.

The first confession contributed to his conviction of attempted rape—a crime for which he is now serving a prison sentence. The victim in that case identified him. The second confession was to the atrocious Wylie-Hoffert murders of 1963. He repudiated this confession on the day he made it; nevertheless, he was indicted for the killings and probably would have been convicted had someone else not come along unexpectedly and claimed the discredit. "I am positive," an Assistant District Attorney said at the time, "that the police were the ones who gave Whitmore all the details of the killings that he recited to our office." And he added:

> If this had not been a celebrated case; if this case hadn't got the tremendous publicity; if this case was what we so-called professionals call a run-of-the-mill murder, Whitmore might well have been slipped into the electric chair and been killed for something he didn't do.

The other day Brooklyn District Attorney Aaron E. Koota announced that he would move for the dismissal of a murder indictment against Whitmore in still another case. A confession similarly elicited was the sole evidence—a confession, that is to say, obtained without advising the suspect of his right to remain silent and without giving him the assistance of a lawyer. Is the Supreme Court really so silly to be concerned about such confessions?

EXTRACTING THE TRUTH:
TEA LEAVES OR POLYGRAPH TESTS?*

Some highly classified information about negotiations with the Russians "leaked" or "oozed" to a newspaper recently—the Secretary of State wasn't quite sure which term to use—and so, apparently, the FBI was sent in to investigate the State Department among other agencies.

"Is there anything wrong with investigating a crime when it occurs?" the Secretary asked a news conference rhetorically. "I don't think anyone will be charged," he added, "but it looked like a crime had been committed. . . . I don't believe there was a crime but it looked on the surface like there might be."

So the FBI, a very modern, scientific investigative agency, moved into the department with some polygraph machines and subjected an undetermined number of the churls, potential double agents and other suspects who work there to lie-detector tests.

Fortunately for them, the Secretary said reassuringly, "We are going to make certain people are not intimidated."

Is there anything wrong, one is tempted to ask, with finding out whether a crime has been committed before investigating it with lie detectors?

It is somewhat disappointing to learn that so up-to-date an agency as the FBI is still using polygraphs. Amusing as these electrical slot machines may have seemed during the reign of the late Senator Joseph McCarthy, they are now outmoded. Secretary Rogers said as much as can possibly be said for them in a somewhat enigmatic observation: "It can be a very good instrumentality for showing innocence but it is not a very good instrument, in

---

*Article, the Washington *Post*, September 7, 1971.

my opinion, for showing guilt." Where does that leave us?

The more modern detection agencies have turned from the polygraph to the reading of tea leaves or the use of compurgation or reliance on some form of trial by ordeal in evaluating the trustworthiness of government employees.

Tea leaves are economical, readily available and easy to use for anybody with the slightest gift for divination. Where the lie detector, at best a cumbersome, costly, complicated instrument, really needs to have someone with a grade-school education or better to interpret it, tea leaves can be read by anyone. The tea leaves themselves, of course, cost almost nothing at all and can be used repeatedly—almost indefinitely—just by a fresh swirl of the teacup.

In reliability, the two tests are more or less on a par. Tea leaves, it must be admitted, do have one tiny defect. They can be a very good instrumentality for showing guilt but not a very good instrument for showing innocence. But at least that's an improvement.

Compurgation—the exculpation of an accused person by the oaths of persons who swear to his veracity—is perhaps useful only as an adjunct to the reading of tea leaves and has no more than ritualistic or corroborative value. Still, it's always fun to see who comes forward in such situations. In really questionable cases, it may be necessary to resort to examining the entrails of sheep— a tested and always interesting method of looking into the future.

Trial by ordeal, which used to be so much in vogue for testing reliability during the Middle Ages, has begun to come back into its own of late. It must be admitted, however, that it is often messy, troublesome and expensive.

One form of ordeal—and a very good one, too—is by fire. In this proceeding, an accused person walked barefoot across a bed of glowing coals, or carried a red-hot weight for a prescribed distance, or licked a white-hot iron spoon—being adjudged innocent if he came through the test unharmed. This, too, was a form of trial more satisfactory for determining guilt than for determining innocence.

Ordeal by water, which was extremely popular in Europe during the late Middle Ages, is probably better suited for State Department employees. This was the approved way of identifying witches—the medieval term for subversives.

In this form of ordeal a suspected witch was stripped naked and cross-bound, the right thumb to the left toe and the left thumb to the right toe, then cast into a pond or river. If the water received her—that is, if she sank—she was adjudged innocent and, one hopes, fished out and given mouth-to-mouth resuscitation. If the water rejected her—that is, if she floated—it was taken as proof positive that she was a witch.

In one respect only, the lie-detector test can be said to have a certain superiority over these more ancient forms of trial. It is so insulting, demeaning and humiliating that one is justified in assuming that anyone who would administer it or submit to it ought not to be allowed to represent the United States anywhere in the world. That much can be taken for granted.

EIGHT

◆

Essentials of

Individual Liberty

From the moment an arrested person first appears in court and the question of bail arises until a prison door clangs shut or an electric chair hums, the criminal law is full of situations in which the rights of individuals and notions of fairness or decency are pitted against efficiency in law enforcement and popular sentiment about how criminals should be handled. There is no general agreement and, indeed, much conflict about almost every step in the judicial process.

Alan Barth had occasion over the years to write about almost all these steps, insisting—as he always did—that individual rights came first when they had to be balanced against the wants or needs of law enforcement or public opinion. Most of the matters about which he wrote are still controversial, although the right of indigents to have government-appointed lawyers defend them in serious criminal cases—once a matter of strenuous debate—was settled definitively by the Supreme Court twenty years ago. Legislation is introduced almost every year to alter the present situation concerning bail and pre-trial detention of criminal suspects; the power of federal courts to review, through *habeas corpus*, convictions obtained in state courts is a constant irritant to many lawyers, judges and legislators; the press and the legal profession engage in a continuing struggle over pre-trial publicity and secret judicial proceedings; the problem of what to do with drug addicts has never been solved; debate over the insanity defense and the purpose of prison sentences—punishment or rehabilitation—goes on; the practical and philosophical ramifications of the death penalty come up in every discussion of criminal law.

Barth had strong feelings and deep beliefs on all these questions. They reflected his view that the quality (and quantity) of freedom in a country is measured by the respect it gives to individual rights and his belief that every human being, no matter how degraded, must have some inherent worth as a child of God.

FIXING BAIL

DECEMBER 23, 1960

Can an indigent person charged with crime be denied freedom pending trial—in circumstances under which a wealthy man would be released on bail—simply because he does not have enough property to pledge for his freedom? Justice Douglas wrestled with this problem in a case in which the Supreme Court recently granted *certiorari* and leave to proceed *in forma pauperis*. It is a problem which casts a heavy shadow on the American promise of equality before the law.

It would be unconstitutional to fix excessive bail to assure that a defendant will not gain his freedom. But what is excessive bail? What may seem small change to one defendant may be wholly beyond the resources of another. "In the case of an indigent defendant," Justice Douglas observed, "the fixing of bail in even a modest amount may have the practical effect of denying him release." And he went on to explain the effects of such a denial:

> The wrong done by denying release is not limited to the denial of freedom alone. That denial may have other consequences. In case of reversal, he will have served all or part of a sentence under an erroneous judgment. Imprisoned, a

man may have no opportunity to investigate his case, to cooperate with his counsel, to earn the money that is still necessary for the fullest use of his right to appeal.

Why should a money surety be required as a condition of release pending trial and why should the furnishing of such surety
be a livelihood for the corps of court hangers-on? The purpose of
bail is to insure a defendant's appearance in compliance with a
court order. That compliance can more equitably be assured by
sanctions other than a money forfeiture—for one thing, by punishment for non-compliance. Modern police forces are well able to
catch fugitives and bring them back to justice.

FAIR TRIALS FOR INDIGENTS

AUGUST 26, 1962

When a state prosecutes an indigent person for a crime, does it
have an obligation to furnish him a lawyer to help in his defense?
The Supreme Court is likely to give a definitive answer to the
question in the pending case of *Gideon v. Cochran,* in which it
has agreed to review a decision by the courts of Florida.

Since 1938 it has been recognized that an indigent defendant
has an absolute right under the Sixth Amendment to have counsel
assigned to him—in the federal courts. But a 1942 decision by a
divided Supreme Court in the case of *Betts v. Brady* held that the
Fourteenth Amendment does not require a state to assign counsel
to an indigent in a non-capital felony case unless substantial un-
fairness results from the absence of counsel. Several subsequent
Supreme Court decisions have indicated doubts about the wisdom
of *Betts v. Brady.* The pending case will afford an opportunity for
reconsideration.

In preparation for the case, the Attorney General of Florida has
sent out letters "inviting the attorneys general of all states to
submit *amicus* briefs" in support of his position that people too

poor to hire lawyers can fairly be left to defend themselves alone against serious felony charges. A notable response to this appeal has come from the Attorney General of Minnesota, Walter F. Mondale. He wrote:

> As chief law-enforcement officer of one of the 35 states which provide for the appointment of counsel for indigents in *all* felony cases, I am convinced that it is cheap—very cheap— at the price. I can assure you that such a requirement does not disrupt or otherwise adversely affect our work. . . . Since I firmly believe that any person charged with a felony should be accorded a right to be represented by counsel regardless of his financial condition, I would welcome the court's imposition of a requirement of appointment of counsel in all state felony prosecutions.

This is the attitude of a law-enforcement officer who gauges victory not by the number of convictions he obtains but by the advancement of justice. Failure to furnish counsel to an indigent defendant amounts to denial of the concept of equal justice under law; it means that his chances of winning an acquittal are not as good as those of a wealthier defendant. The most innocent of men may be incapable of defending himself effectively in a trial court without a lawyer to weigh the validity of the indictment, to cross-examine accusing witnesses, to present an orderly defense and to see to it that the jury is properly charged. And if this assistance is vital in a trial court, it is even more so in an appellate proceeding. . . .*

---

*The Supreme Court overturned *Betts v. Brady* in the case discussed in this editorial, establishing the constitutional requirement that indigents must be furnished with counsel in all felony prosecutions.

"HABEAS CORPUS"

AUGUST 6, 1955

Not long before the adjournment of Congress the House Judiciary Committee issued a favorable report on a bill introduced by Representative Celler the effect of which would be to limit the authority of federal judges to grant writs of *habeas corpus* based on state proceedings. The purpose of this proposal is evidently to eliminate a potential cause of federal-state friction and to ease the burden of federal courts obliged to pass on a considerable volume of *habeas corpus* petitions. The limitation would operate, however, to impair what stands as perhaps the most fundamental protection of individual freedom and impede the function of federal courts in protecting citizens against local injustice. *Habeas corpus* is too precious a right to be curtailed for considerations of convenience.

Testifying in opposition to the bill, Irving Ferman of the American Civil Liberties Union observed that the framers of the Constitution "took for granted that the Federal courts would always provide a ready forum for those seeking the writ which is the greatest safeguard to our personal liberty embodied in the common law." Experience has made it plain that there may be grave danger in denying an imprisoned individual access to the federal courts on a writ of *habeas corpus* simply because state courts have ruled against him. State courts are not always free from prejudice and discrimination. If applications for the writ are burdensome, they constitute a burden which needs to be borne in the interest of justice. From 1945 to 1952 some 3702 applications for *habeas corpus* were filed in the federal courts; of this number only sixty-seven applications were granted and a lesser number of petitioners were released from prison. But the jurisdiction and authority of the federal courts served, no doubt, to keep the state courts on guard against any discrimination or injustice. We think that the federal power ought to be retained intact as a deterrent to arbitrary or capricious conduct by state courts and as a guarantor of a fair trial to all accused persons.

ASSURING FAIR TRIAL

JUNE 5, 1957

The principle underlying the Supreme Court decision in the *Jencks* case is an elementary principle of fair play—that an accused person shall have every reasonable means of defending himself. The sole novelty of the decision lies in its application to confidential reports of the Federal Bureau of Investigation, hitherto considered sacrosanct. Indubitably, the decision raises problems for the FBI. But there seems no warrant whatever for Justice Clark's extravagant lament in a dissenting opinion that the court has afforded criminals "a Roman holiday for rummaging through confidential information as well as vital national secrets."

The court has not authorized rummaging of any sort so far as the FBI's files are concerned. In prosecuting Clinton E. Jencks for filing an allegedly false non-Communist affidavit, the government relied heavily on two witnesses, Harvey Matusow and J. W. Ford, former Communist Party members and undercover agents for the bureau. These men had made reports to the FBI. For the purpose of impeaching their credibility, the defense wanted to determine whether the contents of these reports were consistent with the testimony of the witnesses at the trial. All that the Supreme Court did was to declare that the defense "was entitled to an order directing the Government to produce for inspection all reports of Matusow and Ford in its possession, written and, when orally made, as recorded by the FBI, touching the events and activities as to which they testified at the trial." This is narrowly and precisely limited. It gives a defendant no more than he genuinely needs to defend himself effectively.

In some situations, no doubt, the government may feel that, in the interest of national security, confidential reports should not be disclosed. It may be necessary then to forgo prosecution. This is a choice which the government must face frequently—in deciding whether to produce undercover informants as witnesses in court; in deciding, as in the *Coplon* case, whether to make pilfered documents public; in deciding whether to make available to the defense other relevant material which it considers privileged. As Judge Learned Hand observed some years ago, "The Government must choose; either it must leave the transactions in the obscurity from which a trial will draw them, or it must expose them fully. Nor does it seem to us possible to draw any line between documents whose contents bear directly upon the criminal transactions, and those which may be only indirectly relevant."

It is less important to a free people that, in some instances, a criminal may escape punishment than that he should have an untrammeled opportunity for self-defense. The frenzied bills which some members of Congress have already introduced, in response to the Supreme Court decision, to protect the confidentiality of FBI reports tend to ignore the protection of individual rights which lie at the heart of the American system of justice. In the last analysis, the assurance of a fair trial is one of the first essentials to the security of the United States.

JUSTICE FOR CHILDREN

MAY 16, 1967

The nub of the lengthy and illuminating decision yesterday by the Supreme Court in the *Gault* case is, as Mr. Justice Fortas phrased it, that "under our Constitution, the condition of being a boy does not justify a kangaroo court." The ruling was imperatively needed. For under the benevolent pretext of acting as parents for the protection and reformation of wayward children, juvenile courts all over the country have been meting out severe punishments without according the children brought before them essential safeguards of due process.

In the *Gault* case, an Arizona Juvenile Court ordered a fifteen-year-old boy to be taken from his parents and committed as a juvenile delinquent to the State Industrial School "for the period of his minority (that is, until twenty-one) unless sooner discharged by due process of law." The boy's alleged offense was that he called a woman on the telephone and made lewd or indecent remarks to her. The penalty for this offense which would apply to an adult in Arizona is $5 to $50, or imprisonment for not more than two months.

It can hardly be doubted that, from the point of view of the boy and his family in this case, the decision of the Juvenile Court amounted to punishment. It entailed an unmistakable deprivation of liberty. Yet the decision was reached without any formal notification or specification of the charge against the boy, without allowing him the assistance of a lawyer, without giving him a chance to confront or cross-examine the woman who accused him and in total disregard of the privilege against self-incrimination. This seems a very strange sort of benevolence.

Children were surely meant to be included within the promise of equal justice for all. The elements of due process enumerated in the Bill of Rights . . . were not devised out of idle sentiment. They were adopted as means for the discovery of truth and for the assurance of justice. Their value for these purposes is in no sense diminished when children are brought to judgment. Some relaxation of formalities and of procedural rules is justified in juvenile courts, to be sure, when these can genuinely be said to work for the child's benefit. But they can never be justified to penalize him or to lessen his chances to defend himself against a charge.

No doubt the Supreme Court's decision in this case will make the work of juvenile courts more difficult, demanding and time-consuming. It will require expanded personnel and resources. But neither the current levels of juvenile delinquency nor the rate of recidivism among those in the custody of juvenile courts recommends the continuance of present practices. Justice for children is an indispensable attribute of a civilized society.

CLOSED COURTS AND
PRIVATE TRIALS

DECEMBER 7, 1971

Carmine J. Persico, charged with the crime of extortion in New York, waived his constitutional right to a public trial and asked that he be tried in a courtroom closed alike to the press and the public. State Supreme Court Justice Arthur Postel granted this request. A committee of newsmen appealed to the Appellate Division of the State Supreme Court, asking that the Persico trial be reopened and asserting that there is a public right as well as a private right to a public trial. Unhappily, in our judgment, the Appellate Division followed a 1954 ruling of New York's highest court and rejected this appeal.

It is easy to think of reasons which might lead Mr. Persico to prefer a private to a public trial. The charge against him is an ugly one; and adverse testimony concerning him, if published in the newspapers, might hurt his reputation. But this reasoning could lead many, if not most, criminal defendants, especially if they are guilty, to seek exclusion of the press and the public from their trials. The consequence of this might be to have the whole process of criminal prosecution carried on *in camera*.

We can think of nothing more pernicious for the administration of justice. Secrecy is the fertilizer of suspicion. Wherever it prevails, distrust becomes endemic. People who learn that a man has been convicted or acquitted in a trial from which the press and public were excluded wonder inevitably if justice was really done; they tend to suspect that a conviction was rigged, that an acquittal was fixed, that there may have been some collusion between the court on the one hand and the prosecution or the defense on the other. And this becomes particularly pertinent in a trial such as Persico's in which the defendant is alleged to be a major Mafia figure. . . .

The wording of the Sixth Amendment—that "the accused shall enjoy the right to a speedy and public trial"—lends a certain color, unfortunately, to the contention that the right belongs exclusively to the accused and can be waived by him at will. But, as a succession of California court decisions have recognized, the public also has a right—and a vital interest—in observing the course of justice and deciding for itself whether that course has been equitable and honorable. How else is it to judge the fairness of its laws? How else is it to weigh the caliber of its judges, many of them subject to popular election? How else is it to learn about the prevalence and gravity of crime? "Publicity," Jeremy Bentham once observed, "keeps the judge while trying under trial." Indolence, arrogance, partiality, callousness, sentimentality, vindictiveness on the part of judges can be exposed only by the presence of the press and public in their courtrooms. Bribery and underworld influence can be forfended only by publicity.

Moreover, there are other practical virtues to publicity. The reporting of trials promotes public understanding of the law. It operates to bring forward witnesses who may not otherwise have known about a prosecution. It serves to keep judge, jury and contending counsel on their best behavior. Precisely because the administration of justice is pre-eminently the public's business, it ought to be conducted in public.

BEDLAM AT COURT

JUNE 7, 1966

Guilty or not of bludgeoning his pregnant wife to death twelve years ago, Samuel H. Sheppard was convicted of this atrocious crime in a trial altogether incompatible with civilized standards of justice. It is a monstrous misfortune that the incongruity of this trial was not authoritatively recognized long ago. Dr. Sheppard has spent most of the intervening years in prison. Even worse than this, however, the proceeding has remained a reproach to American justice. The Supreme Court of the United States has now said a conviction obtained in such a way cannot stand and has sent the case back with instructions that Dr. Sheppard be released from custody unless the State of Ohio puts him to its charges again within a reasonable time.

The trial was a circus. "The fact is," Mr. Justice Clark said for the court, "that bedlam reigned at the courthouse during the trial, and newsmen took over practically the entire courtroom, hounding most of the participants in the trial, especially Sheppard." In simple truth, the conduct of the press in Cleveland—newspapers, radio and television alike—was abominable. Convinced of his guilt, the press denounced him as a fiend and declared him guilty day after day on front pages and in broadcasts before he ever came to trial. And throughout the course of the trial it published wild allegations about him which were never introduced in court, where they might have been subjected to denial and possible refutation.

Had the trial judge chosen to discipline the press for these excesses, a different—and extremely interesting—constitutional case might have arisen. But the trial judge, a candidate for reelection within a fortnight after the trial's commencement, did nothing even to curb the press or to protect the jury from its misbehavior. He might have granted a change of venue as the defense requested. He might have had the jury sequestered for the duration of the trial. He might have warned the jurors sternly against reading newspapers or listening to broadcasts about the case. He might, at the very least, have insulated the jury and the witnesses from the press in the courtroom itself, instead of letting them mingle at frequent recesses. He might have forbidden officers of the court to divulge impending testimony and evidence.

Whether such measures would have been fully effective is, of course, open to argument. Had they been taken, perhaps, as Justice Clark declared, "The news media would have soon learned to be content with the task of reporting the case as it unfolded in the courtroom—not pieced together from extra-judicial statements." But in Justice Clark's words, "the state trial judge did not fulfill his duty to protect Sheppard from the inherently prejudicial publicity which saturated the community and to control disruptive influences in the courtroom." The conviction, therefore, had to be reversed.

SICKNESS AND CRIME

JUNE 28, 1962

Drug addiction, like addiction to alcohol, is a disease more to be pitied than to be punished. Fortunately, it afflicts relatively few people in the United States; there are said to be some sixty thousand drug addicts in the country as compared with nearly half a million full-fledged alcoholics. But because the drug traffic is a peculiarly pernicious one and because the prohibitive price of illicit drugs often leads addicts into crime, the country has reacted to addiction with horror and has sought to stamp it out by police measures which are often careless of civil liberty and lacking in compassion.

An extreme example of this carelessness and callousness was apparent in the California law struck down as unconstitutional by the Supreme Court on Monday because it inflicted a cruel and unusual punishment. It made it a criminal offense for a person to "be addicted to the use of narcotics," and in the case of Lawrence Robinson, reviewed by the court, it was used to convict a man, although, as the court said, "he was not engaging in illegal or irregular conduct of any kind, and the police had no reason to believe he had done so in the past."

California has statutes which provide punishment for peddling, purchasing or even possessing narcotics and for anti-social or disorderly behavior resulting from their use; it also has laws providing for compulsory medical treatment, including confinement, of addicts in certain circumstances. But, as Mr. Justice Stewart suggested in his opinion for the court, to make addiction itself criminal is as unreasonable as it would be to "make it a criminal offense for a person to be mentally ill, or a leper, or to be afflicted with a venereal disease. Even a single day's imprisonment for such misfortunes would amount to 'cruel and unusual punishment.' " . . .

MENTAL ILLNESS AND CRIME

JUNE 6, 1954

In Samuel Butler's imaginary land called Erewhon, persons who contracted any sort of bodily illness were liable to fines, imprisonment or even, in severe cases, capital punishment. Those who committed what elsewhere would be called crimes, such as housebreaking or embezzlement, were accorded the sympathy of their families and friends and given the help of a "straightener," or healer—or what is currently called a psychiatrist. The Erewhonians were perhaps unduly harsh toward the physically ill. But they understood what the law in most enlightened Western countries has only just begun to realize—that there is a close correlation between anti-social conduct and mental illness.

A landmark step toward recognition of this correlation was taken last week by the Court of Appeals for the District of Columbia. Speaking for a unanimous panel, Judge David Bazelon undertook to inform and illuminate the ancient and obsolete rules governing criminal responsibility with some of the insights into mental processes afforded by modern psychiatry and psychology. This long-overdue modernization of one of the important standards of criminal justice reflects the highest credit upon Judge Bazelon and his colleagues, Judges Edgerton and Washington, and also upon Messrs. Abe Fortas and Abe Krash, appointed by the court to serve as counsel for the indigent appellant in the case, Monte Durham.

The bare facts of the Durham case reveal the shocking inadequacy of prevailing standards for the determination of criminal responsibility. When he was seventeen years old, Durham was discharged from the Navy after a psychiatric examination had shown that he suffered "from a profound personality disorder." Thereafter his record included a series of commitments to prison and to St. Elizabeth's Hospital, a suicide attempt, a parole violation, a lunacy inquisition in which he was found to be of unsound mind, a diagnosis that he suffered from "psychosis with psychopathic personality" and finally a release from St. Elizabeth's with a certification that he was "mentally competent to stand trial."

District Judge Holtzoff rejected a defense of insanity on the ground that it had not been established "that the defendant was of unsound mind . . . in the sense that he didn't know the difference between right and wrong or that even if he did, he was subject to an irresistible impulse by reason of the derangement of mind." These are the classic legal tests of insanity. The Court of Appeals ruled that Judge Holtzoff erred even by these crude tests. In remanding the case for a new trial, however, it set forth a different test to be adopted in place of the old, unsatisfactory criteria. Judge Bazelon's opinion declares:

> The science of psychiatry now recognizes that a man is an integrated personality and that reason, which is only one element in that personality, is not the sole determinant of his conduct. The right-wrong test, which considers knowledge or reason alone, is therefore an inadequate guide to mental responsibility for criminal behavior. . . . We find that the "irresistible impulse" test is also inadequate in that it gives no recognition to mental illness characterized by brooding and reflection and so relegates acts caused by such illness to the application of the inadequate right-wrong test. We conclude that a broader test should be adopted.

This new test, by the very reason of its superior subtlety, will no doubt present problems of application. "The question," said the Court of Appeals, "will be simply whether the accused acted because of a mental disorder, and not whether he displayed particular symptoms which medical science has long recognized do not necessarily, or even typically, accompany even the most serious mental disorder.'' This fusion of law and psychiatry will do much to enlighten justice, bring it into conformity with the moral tradition that men may not be blamed or punished for acts which were the products of mental disease or defects, and to infuse into the law some of the humanity without which it would be tyrannical.

MORALITY AND CRIME

AUGUST 28, 1960

The Municipal Court of Appeals rendered a service to common sense and common decency when it ruled the other day that a homosexual act is not a crime if performed in privacy between two consenting adults. Such an act is, of course, offensive to the morals and mores of Western civilization. But in attempting to deal with it as a crime, the police have been led into another form of immorality.

In making its ruling, the Court of Appeals reversed a conviction obtained by a common—and contemptible—police practice involving something very like provocation and entrapment. A policeman posing as a derelict from out of town made contact with a man suspected of homosexual tendencies, asked the man if he could stay overnight in his home and then, shortly after arriving there, arrested the man for making homosexual advances. There is no better word for this than disgusting.

The court chose not to upset the conviction on the ground of entrapment. . . . Instead, it simply ruled that the law forbidding indecent acts in the District of Columbia "was not designed or intended to apply to an act committed in privacy in the presence of a single and consenting person." This is eminently sensible.

Homosexuality is an expression of emotional impulses congenital or psychoneurotic in origin. Homosexual advances made to a minor or to any unwilling person inflict an injury which obviously must be punishable by law. But it is futile to seek to punish men for a relationship carried on in private and without injury to others. Moreover, the attempt to punish it almost inevitably leads to the type of police practice condemned by the court. The problem of homosexuality in such non-violent and non-public manifestations is in any event one that can be dealt with more wisely and more effectively by the clergy and the psychiatrists than by the police.

THE LIMITS OF PUNISHMENT

AUGUST 9, 1969

Punishment is the easiest way to deal with criminals. You stash them away, like so much surplus humanity, behind bars, confident that, while they are there at least, they won't commit the same offenses and hopeful that others, warned by their suffering, will avoid engaging in similar misconduct. The only trouble is that it doesn't seem to curtail crime. The criminals out of jail seem to learn nothing from the experience of the criminals inside; and, judging from the rate of recidivism, the criminals inside seem to learn even less.

None of this carries much weight, however, with those who regard punishment as the sovereign remedy for social ills. The less it works, the more they believe in it—or, at any rate, the more of it they believe in. Their instant response to a rising crime rate is to increase penalties. In his recent recommendations for changes in the District Criminal Code, for example, Attorney General Mitchell has proposed that persons convicted of an offense for the second time may be given a sentence half again as great as the maximum sentence for a first conviction of the same offense; that a person convicted three or more times may be sentenced to three times the maximum punishment for a first conviction; and that a person convicted of a felony who has been previously convicted of two or more felonies may be sentenced to imprisonment for an indeterminate number of years up to life. The logic of this seems to lie in multiplying what has been of no avail in the first place.

Punishment of itself has never had very much deterrent effect on crime. In an earlier age, men branded convicts with hot irons, cut off their hands, slit their noses or broke them on the wheel; yet crime continued unabated in the slums of great cities. There are contemporary judges who strive to emulate these horrors of the past by imposing ferocious sentences today. In Danville, Virginia, just last week, for example, a twenty-year-old youth was sentenced to twenty-five years in the Virginia penitentiary after pleading guilty to a charge of possession of marijuana. The "judge" mercifully suspended five years of the sentence, adding to it a fine of $500.

What can such a sentence do to a young man who has broken the law except to confirm him in lawlessness? In all probability, he will leave prison embittered, disgraced, an enemy of society. Try to imagine what twenty years in prison—or ten years, for that matter—must mean to a youth of twenty. It must mean, literally, the abandonment of all hope.

Punishment has its educative uses, no doubt, for children— provided it is administered with understanding and with love and with the expectation of forgiveness and redemption. But criminals are not children; they are adults warped in childhood or made indifferent to the laws because they have no stake in maintaining them. And the patent concern, as well as the moral obligation, of the community must be to help and heal them when it can and to give hope and opportunity to the desperate.

It is easy, of course, to dismiss this as idealism. But redemption is more productive than retribution; rehabilitation is less costly than recidivism. Idealism, if the term is to be used as a taunt, means adherence to ideas after experience has proven their inefficacy. Until society can extirpate the poverty, ignorance, squalor, injustice and human wretchedness which are the real causes of crime, it must, of course, confine its criminals to keep them from committing more crimes. But is it not sentimental folly to let that confinement be an end in itself—to let that confinement destroy rather than re-create? Is it idealistic, or is it merely pragmatic and sensible to think of prisons which will serve genuinely as hospitals for the socially sick and as schools for the maleducated—to think of the warped in terms of help instead of in terms of punishment?

VENGEANCE AND THE LAW

DECEMBER 23, 1969

Christmas Day was to be the last day on earth for Marie Hill, a black girl convicted a year ago, when she was seventeen years old, for the killing of a white grocer in the course of a robbery in Rocky Mount, North Carolina. A couple of weeks ago, the Supreme Court of North Carolina upheld the conviction, automatically setting the date for her execution in the state's gas chamber for December 26. But the Chief Justice of North Carolina, in a sudden surge of Christianity, has ordered a delay in the execution to let her appeal her death sentence to the Supreme Court of the United States.

The crime of which she has been found guilty is a monstrous one. The nature of the evidence which led the jury to its verdict is unknown to us; no doubt it was compelling, or the courts would not have affirmed the conviction. It is worth noting, however, that the girl maintains she was not in Rocky Mount on the day of the killing. At any rate, Marie Hill is now eighteen years old—an age at which, for most girls, life is just beginning to unfold itself in terms of usefulness and love and hope and the re-creation of life.

Can society fairly say of Marie Hill—or of any eighteen-year-old—that she is beyond redemption, that her life is so devoid of any possibility for usefulness as to be without value, deserving to be snuffed out deliberately by the fumes from a cyanide pellet released in a sealed chamber while a few chosen onlookers observe the final throes of her asphyxiation? Is the community where she grew to young womanhood wholly free from responsibility for the influences and education that shaped her? Are the older, luckier men and women who judged Marie Hill really justified in taking her life for the taking of a life?

For this is precisely what North Carolina proposes to do to Marie Hill at eighteen, unless the Supreme Court of the United States finds some basis for intervention. Her execution will be an act of vengeance under law. There will be pious rhetoric, of course, about its utility as a deterrent to other warped, ill-educated, perhaps embittered seventeen-year-olds trying to pick up some easy money in a culture where money seems to be the symbol of virtue and the key to high repute. But nobody seriously believes that the obscure extermination of Marie Hill will be heeded by other heedless, hopped-up youngsters with guns readily available to make them feel mighty.

Would you like to watch the execution of Marie Hill? Maybe you can wangle a pass from the North Carolina authorities. Executions used to be considered great fun; they were attended by huge throngs when they were seriously thought to have deterrent value. But a more enlightened age came to feel squeamish about them and felt that the public ought not to be exposed to anything so barbarous. All official executions are now carried out in secret.

In England, the source of so many American institutions and, indeed, of the whole American legal system, the House of Commons last week voted to end capital punishment except for such rare offenses as treason, piracy and arson in the royal dockyards and arsenals. For five years England has lived under a suspension of the death sentence without any evidence whatever to suggest that the suspension increased murder or other crimes for which capital punishment had previously been meted out. Public opinion appeared to be opposed to abolition of the death penalty; but Parliament was overwhelmingly moved by conscience and a sense of civilization.

"I think," said the Lord Chancellor, "that human beings who are not infallible ought not to choose a form of punishment which is irreparable." An even more exalted authority spoke to the same subject long, long ago: "Vengeance is mine; I will repay, saith the Lord." Is it not time for America to take one more lesson from England—and one more lesson from that greatest of teachers whose birth mankind now reverently observes?

REVERENCE FOR LIFE

APRIL 19, 1962

The firing squads have been busy of late in the Soviet Union. They have been snuffing out the lives of Soviet citizens condemned to death not for treason, murder or other atrocious crimes of violence but for what are commonly known as economic offenses. According to the New York *Herald Tribune,* twenty-four persons have been sentenced to die for such offenses—and sentenced under a law passed after the commission of the offenses, an *ex post facto* law.

The evolution of capital punishment in the Soviet Union is interesting. As the movement to modify or abolish the death penalty has gained ground in the Western world, capital punishment has been finding increasing acceptance in Russia. This is the more remarkable when one recalls the Soviet disposition in the earlier days of the revolution to stigmatize capital punishment as a capitalistic barbarity and to promise its complete abandonment in the Socialist Utopia. Stalin abolished the death sentence in 1947, but restored it in 1950 for traitors, spies and those seeking to undermine the state, a fairly comprehensive category as he defined it.

Anyone perplexed by the paradox of numerous Soviet executions reported despite Soviet abhorrence of the death penalty should bear in mind that the executions were largely "administrative" executions; that is, they were ordered by Stalin, not by courts as a punishment fixed by law. Although this did not make those who were executed any less dead, it made the law seem less punitive.

The desire to avoid the death penalty as a matter of law found expression rather wistfully in a speech to the Supreme Soviet on the draft criminal code in 1958:

> The Soviet state is still compelled to retain such a severe measure of punishment as the death penalty. But the possibilities for applying it are greatly restricted in the draft. It can be permitted in peacetime only in the case of commission of such grave crimes as treason to the homeland, espionage, subversion, a terrorist act, premeditated murder committed under aggravating circumstances, and banditry.

In the course of the past year, however, seven additional crimes have been made punishable by death: making and passing counterfeit money, currency speculation, pilfering state or public property in large amounts, certain categories of rape, assault on administrators of labor camps or terrorization of prisoners by hardened criminals, attempts on the life of policemen or citizen-volunteers, and giving or extorting bribes "under specially aggravating circumstances."

Now it is interesting, is it not, that in capitalist countries like the United States, which are denounced by the Soviets as grossly materialistic and overly concerned with matters of property, there is no thought of administering the death penalty for such money crimes as counterfeiting, speculation, embezzlement and bribery? The capitalist countries exhibit a measure of contempt for human life, it is true, by imposing a kind of retributive jungle justice which exacts a life for a life in connection with aggravated crimes against the person and against the security of the state. But it has remained, in modern times at least, for Communist Russia to take away life as a punishment for taking property.

THE LAW IS THE LAW

APRIL 16, 1967

Cyanide gas fumes ended the life of a murderer in California's San Quentin prison Wednesday evening as the Governor of the state sat in his office close to a direct-line telephone to the prison. Governor Reagan did not use his power to stay the execution. "The law is the law," he said, "and must be upheld." One can hardly help wondering, then, what use there was in the law's allowing him discretion to abate its awful operation—or why he chose to remain in his office until the awful ritual of taking a human life was completed.

The execution was witnessed by fifty-eight persons. It would be interesting to know their individual reactions. Did they, or did some of them, exult at this demonstration of the law's majesty? Did others among them think of the miserable sinner who died in their presence as a fellow-traveler to the grave whose fate, but for the grace of God, might have been their own? And did this fleeting consideration of God's grace lead one or two at least to reflect upon the arrogance entailed in destroying a human being endowed with life by a common Creator?

The fifty-eight spectators must have pondered a little on the purpose of the performance. Its main purpose, as we understand it, was to deter others from committing murder. How many of the fifty-eight spectators were actually deterred by their gruesome experience is hard to tell. Perhaps most of them would never have murdered anybody anyway. It is not easy to understand, moreover, how the sight of someone being killed by the state would serve to teach the lesson that killing is abhorrent.

Assuming, however, that an execution has deterrent value, it seems a pity to restrict its benefits to a chosen handful in a prison death chamber. California is planning to kill another convict in the same prison next Tuesday, having some sixty condemned men on the waiting list for its gas chamber. Would Tuesday's execution not have much more deterrent value if it could be carried out, say, in the Rose Bowl and televised on one or more of the national networks so that as many people as possible could see it and learn that killing is morally wrong? Why keep an educational experience like this behind closed doors? Are they ashamed of it or something?

NINE

Controlling Crime

Anyone who writes about the impact of the Bill of Rights on the criminal law is inevitably drawn into the unending debate about crime—what causes it, how can it be controlled, whether it can be eliminated. Alan Barth wrote often on these questions. In his view, crime—the kind of violent crime that terrifies ordinary citizens, anyway—was largely the product of an environment and a society that thrust some citizens aside and left them uneducated, unskilled and with a belief that the law-abiding community around them had shut them out. This followed ineluctably from his belief in the inherent worth of every person. Thus, the causes and the cures for crime were not, in Barth's view, to be found in the courts or in the get-tough, lock-'em-up theory of punishment. Urban renewal, about which he wrote occasionally, and education, about which he wrote often, were central to his solutions to the crime problem. Training and a second chance were his medicine for those who commit crime.

THE NEW MIGRANTS*

. . . According to the Statistical Abstract of the United States, in the twenty years between the 1940 census and the 1960 census the urban population of this country rose from 74 million to 125 million. The rural population during the same interval dropped from 57 million to 54 million. In percentage terms, the country was 56.5 per cent urban in 1940, 70 per cent urban in 1960.

The Statistical Abstract offers a comparison between 1940 and 1960 as to the number of persons employed in agricultural and in non-agricultural pursuits. There were about 9 million persons working on farms in 1940, as compared with 43 million in trade and industry. By 1960 the number of farm workers had dropped to 4 million, while the non-agricultural workers had increased to 64 million. . . .

Plainly, there has been a great migration—a migration comparable to the dramatic movement of people from Europe to America around the turn of the century. Just as men and women came in great numbers from the old world to the new, seeking freedom and economic opportunity, so Americans moved from the countryside to the city and the town for the same purposes.

In the nineteenth century and the early years of the twentieth century there was plenty of work for the immigrants, however uneducated and unskilled they may have been. But migrants now face a quite different situation. American industry has jobs only for those schooled enough and skilled enough to perform them. Those who cannot read or write the English language and who lack training in a trade need not apply.

Moreover, contemporary cities lack the devices which fifty years ago did so much to help the immigrants adapt to their new envi-

*From a speech on May 31, 1967, to the Yale Law School Association, in Washington, D.C.

ronment. The melting pot worked in those days, in part because there were Americanization schools and night schools and immigrant-aid societies and settlement houses to make it work. But for the contemporary migrants there is little assistance and even less welcome.

The melting pot is not now a reality. As of old, the migrants are crowded into ghettos. But the ghettos are meaner and uglier and more imprisoning because so many of the new migrants are black in color and wholly unequipped to compete for jobs in an industrial economy.

The terrible truth is that we have turned the decaying inner portions of all our great cities into cages where embittered, frustrated concentrations of poor people are huddled—despised, rejected, surrounded by affluent white Americans and locked into their despair by their color, their ill health, their lack of education and, above all, by the pervasive fear of them felt by all their fellow-countrymen responsible for their ruin.

The whole country is in a state of something like panic about these caged, disinherited and desperate Americans. Panic, as I understand the term, is an unreasoning fear of what you do not understand and do not know how to combat. It is aggravated in America today by a profound sense of guilt and shame—by a troubled awareness on the part of the comfortable that they are really responsible for these urban cages that contain, but do not confine, deadly forms of pestilence—deadly threats to their comfort and security.

The two most common preoccupations of Americans these days—so far as domestic affairs are concerned—are the crime wave and the fear of mob violence—usually referred to in that gingerly euphemism, "the long, hot summer ahead."

You can get some notion of the extent of the panic from the recent exhortation by the National Rifle Association to its 800,000 members to arm themselves and to form armed civilian posses in order to provide "a potential community stabilizer" against urban rioting.

It does not require great scholarship in sociology to recognize the basic causes of crime and violence in the United States today.

The National Crime Commission identified them plainly; and President Johnson quoted and endorsed its identification in his message on crime to the Congress:

> There is no doubt whatever that the most significant action, by far, that can be taken against crime is action designed to eliminate slums and ghettos, to improve education, to provide jobs, to make sure that every American is given the opportunities and the freedoms that will enable him to assume his responsibilities. . . .

I spent most of last week attending the annual Michigan State University Institute on Police and Community Relations. There were about 325 participants in the institute, two-thirds of them sent by police departments in cities all over the country, one-third of them engaged in various aspects of community-relations work.

The police were predominantly white. The community-relations workers were mostly Negro. Between them there was a gulf which discussion seemed to broaden rather than to bridge.

The police, for their part, seemed doggedly defensive. Some of them felt unappreciated, even persecuted. They were extremely resistant to the idea of civilian complaint-review boards to judge charges of police misconduct. They complained that the courts have not been definite enough in laying down the rules for arrest, search and interrogation of suspects. They felt that they were being called upon to do the work not alone of policemen but of teachers, parents and psychiatrists.

Some of the spokesmen for minority groups in the communities felt, on the other hand, that the police were not *their* police, the laws not *their* laws. Socrates said in one of the Dialogues . . . that "justice is the interest of the stronger." It was dismaying to me to learn how strongly some of the people in the slums have come to feel that the function of the police is not to protect *them* but to protect the white community *from* them.

For these people, the great promise of equal justice under law has come to read: unequal law under a system of justice.

When you couple this alienation with hopelessness and with a sense that they have no real stake in the maintenance of law and order, you have the perfect critical mix for crime, violence and anarchy.

The harsh, terrible truth is that today our schools are not educating the children of the slums, our police are not controlling them and our prisons and correctional institutions are not rehabilitating them when they get into trouble. . . .

THE SYMPTOMS AND THE
SOURCES OF CRIME

AUGUST 18, 1970

Your personal chance, as an individual, of becoming a direct victim of crime in the United States is now a little more than twice as great as it was ten years ago. The likelihood that you will be murdered has gone up by 44 per cent. The likelihood that you will be robbed has gone up by 146.1 per cent. The likelihood that your car will be stolen has gone up by 137.8 per cent. These are not figures pulled out of a hat; they are pulled out of the latest issues of the FBI's Uniform Crime Reports. Even if you are not a direct victim of crime, the cost of all this criminality in terms of money, in terms of your sense of personal security, in terms of your enjoyment of life, is altogether beyond reckoning.

The most striking fact about the crime review is that the crime rate—not the absolute number of crimes alone but the rate of crime per 100,000 inhabitants of the country—has gone up steadily, almost without a break, year after year after year. There must be something radically wrong with the way we are tackling the crime problem. Great strides have been made in the techniques of law enforcement. As the director of the FBI puts it, "Advanced technologies have been adapted to police management and operations. . . . Computer and communications technologies have been applied to the problems and are playing a major role in improving law enforcement performance.'' Yet these technologies are not generally available to the police forces that have to protect public safety at night in the streets of our cities. As Mayor John Lindsay of New York told the American Bar Association last week, "Despite all the experts and all the advice and all the commissions, there is still too little reform and too much pretense. Waging an effective war on crime, the Violence Commission warned, would cost an additional six billion dollars.''

We have learned a great deal about penal reform, too, and the rehabilitation of men turned outlaw. But again, instead of applying what we have learned in an effort to redeem offenders and give them a stake in society, we choose, in the name of a philosophy called "toughness," to rob them of all hope by the imposition of ferocious sentences to prisons which only corrupt and destroy them. Mayor Lindsay observed realistically enough that "the criminal offender usually does his time in a prison that is a school for crime. He is finally released with nothing more than a free bus ride back to the slum he came from. It is almost assured that he will return to a life against the law.'

Finally, we deal with criminal offenders, as the Chief Justice said so eloquently in his address to the Bar Association, through a system of "cracker barrel" courts the inadequacies and intricacies of which tend to mock the quality of justice. In short, we have chosen to cope with crime through a rhetoric which neither frightens the criminal nor reassures the law-abiding citizen, and with gimmicks and constitutional short-cuts like "no-knock" police raids and preventive detention and indiscriminate bugging—gimmicks that cost relatively little money and are paid for only through the sacrifice of privacy and personal liberty.

Police forces, courts, prisons deal, of course, only with the symptoms, the manifestations, of crime. They do not touch its sources. The sources of crime are indeed complex, as the superb 1967 report of the President's Crime Commission made plain. But some of them at least are known. The squalor, hopelessness and brutality of city slums breed criminals inexorably—and breed them faster than the best of all possible police forces can arrest them or the best of all courts can sentence them or the best of all penal systems can rehabilitate them.

Ultimately, relying on police and courts and prisons to control crime is like relying on mosquito netting and citronella to control malaria while ignoring the stagnant pools of water where the malaria-bearing mosquitoes are bred. While the mosquitoes abound, there has to be protection against them, of course. But eradication of the conditions that create them must be of no less concern. It is an improvident sort of economy that deals with consequences only and ignores causes.

Curiously, however, those who would focus attention upon the sources *as well* as the symptoms of crime are often scoffed at as "bleeding hearts" and "do-gooders" by persons who suppose that "toughness," for all its unbroken record of failure in the past, will somehow make crime disappear. The usual rationale for disregarding the sources of crime while grappling with its symptoms is that the "sources" constitute a long-term problem, while the "symptoms" can be dealt with instanter. The real point is that the two are inseparable.

A unified attack on crime—an attack that genuinely dealt with its realities, symptoms and sources alike—would undoubtedly cost a great deal of money, perhaps as much money as winning a small war; and nowadays the expenditure of large sums of money, except for military purposes, is commonly looked upon as uneconomical or even sentimental by those who would like to get rid of crime on the cheap. But would the cost of urban renewal really be as great as the cost of the 14,590 murders and the 297,580 robberies and the 1,959,800 burglaries that the FBI reported in the United States in 1969? Is it really sentimental to spend money for the re-creation of a country where you can walk with your wife in safety night or day?

THE WAR ON CRIME

SEPTEMBER II, 1969

An attack on crime, akin in magnitude and determination to the launching of a major campaign in the course of a war, is more than ever a domestic imperative. The need for such an attack, mobilizing all the resources at the community's command, has long been evident. But despite the sounding of an alarm by President Johnson and an equally insistent call by President Nixon, the necessary nationwide sense of urgency simply isn't evident except perhaps in the trenches, where outnumbered, under-equipped police forces battle on against impossible odds. In the command posts, however—in Congress, in the federal bureaucracies, in many statehouses and city halls—the war is still being waged, in the main, rhetorically; the needed resources are not being mobilized on anything like the necessary scale.

The inadequacy of the effort is nowhere more evident, or more deplorable, than in the District of Columbia, not only because this is the capital of the United States but because violent crime in the streets has grown here to appalling proportions. The official police disclosure that 714 armed robberies occurred in this city during the month of August gives a grim foundation to the fear that has become an epidemic in the community. Washington is a city under siege. It must be liberated.

"What is needed," Congressman Brock Adams said in a most distinguished speech last week to a meeting here of the International Association of Chiefs of Police, "is a total commitment of resources—energy, finances, and manpower—toward the eradication of fear, control of crime, and restoration of domestic peace." But the Congressman is not content to attack crime with the crude, cheap weapons of demagogy—slurs on the Supreme Court, contempt for civil liberty and for the rights of privacy, sheer sloganeering. "Fighting for human rights," Mr. Adams observed wisely in defense of his libertarian colleagues, "is not inconsistent with fighting crime." Indeed, it is not. Respect for human rights is the indispensable condition of a respect for law.

Some of the sensational proposals in the Justice Department's crime bill—wiretapping, for example, or the wresting of confessions from ignorant suspects—have little to commend them save theatricality. They are expressions of panic. One might as sensibly suggest combating crime by declaring a state of martial law or imposing a permanent curfew on the community. Such remedies entail prohibitive social costs.

Mr. Adams' approach is more pragmatic. He begins with advocacy of an enlarged, more mobile, better-educated and better-paid police force for the District—and with a willingness to face and foot the bill for such a force. Congress, as he observes, has not been entirely inactive on this subject. It passed comprehensive anti-crime bills in 1967 and 1968 providing assistance to local law-enforcement agencies. But it takes time to recruit and train police professionals. The process needs the utmost acceleration now. Visible police officers unmistakably deter crime.

But this isn't the only answer by any means. "No matter how many police officers we have and no matter how many arrests are made," Mr. Adams went on to say, "criminals will not be deterred unless speedy justice is dispensed." This is why the proposed court reorganization and expansion now pending in the House is of such vital importance. The District Court of General Sessions acknowledged recently that it had more than 1500 defendants awaiting trial in July. The U.S. District Court here has more than 1700 criminal cases pending. It is an appalling fact—an appalling reproach to the conscience of the community—that the average time between indictment and disposition of a case in the District Court, as Mr. Adams has pointed out, is 254 days, and twice as much in the Court of General Sessions. If time for the completion of an appeal in criminal cases is added to this, the average span of a criminal proceeding comes to almost two years.

This is a travesty on justice. There is no good reason or justification for such delay. It is unknown in the criminal courts of England. It can be abated in part by increased personnel throughout the judicial system here—not on the bench alone but in the U.S. Attorney's office, in the defense services available to indigent defendants, in the marshal's staff—and, perhaps above all, in the parole, probation, counseling and correctional forces.

The whole correctional system is in disrepair—antiquated, overloaded, operating to corrupt rather than to cure the offenders consigned to it. "Holding tanks," Brock Adams calls the city's jails. What kind of supervision and guidance can the seventeen probation officers of the Court of General Sessions give the offenders assigned to them when they carry a caseload of 122 probationers apiece?

In the costly correction of these dramatic defects—and not in assigning policemen to sit for hours on end monitoring telephone conversations at random on the chance of picking up something juicy—lies the real hope of an effective attack on crime. Justice delayed is triply destructive. It breeds a sense of helplessness and hopelessness in beleaguered citizens. It breeds cynicism and disheartenment in conscientious police officers who see the offenders they risked their lives to arrest set free by lags and loopholes in the law; see them intimidating witnesses; see them continuing to prey on the community. It breeds contempt and derision in criminals, especially in young punks, who see the forces of law and order frustrated and demoralized. The very heart and center of a realistic attack on crime must be a determination to make the law take its course swiftly and sternly—and with the goal not of sterile retribution but of redemption.

When all this is done—and it all must be done to meet the realities of a condition caused by persistent neglect—it remains essential to remember that such measures deal only with the consequences, not with the causes, of crime. These causes—slums, inadequate schools, squalor, human wretchedness, poverty—will continue, until they are ameliorated, to breed criminals faster than cops can catch them, faster than courts can condemn them. The cost of ignoring these causes is far greater, in terms of money and public safety and human happiness, than the cost of conquering them.

CAN CRIMINALS BE REHABILITATED?

JUNE 8, 1971

Chief Justice Warren E. Burger has referred to contemporary prisons as "non-correcting correctional institutions." Two stark statistics document the observation. One, supplied by the Chief Justice himself, is that two-thirds of the two hundred thousand inmates of federal and state prisons are "alumni" of other prisons. The other, supplied by an associate administrator of the Law Enforcement Assistance Administration, is that about eighty per cent of all felonies are committed by repeaters—that is, by persons who, in one way or another, were processed through the correctional system and came out uncorrected. . . .

What are the roots of this futility? It is possible that criminals are not corrigible—that they suffer either from some innate quirk which makes them incapable of conforming with the laws of society or that they have been so corrupted in youth by the squalor and immorality of their early environments and the inadequacies of their schooling as to leave them hopelessly warped and impaired. But there is no reason to believe that either of these possibilities is true for more than a minor fraction of the more than two hundred thousand Americans now in prison. It is a fact that they are overwhelmingly uneducated and unskilled. But this is not to say that they are uneducable or unredeemable. And the inescapable truth is that on their redemption depends, to a very great extent, the safety of society. . . .

Three things, it seems to us, are necessary to rehabilitate a person—young or old—who has turned to crime. One is to give him some sense of ethical values—which is to say, really, some belief in the humaneness of society and of its willingness to accept him as a member if he can abide by its reasonable rules. Second is to teach him a means of gaining a livelihood by honest work, a trade of some sort related to his own capacities and aptitudes and yet useful and marketable in the community. And

268

third is to assure him a genuine second chance—which means to see to it that he finds a decent job, forgiveness for his past errors and a fair measure of acceptance in the community. The last is very difficult yet inseparable from rehabilitation. Giving a man a second chance means taking a chance on his ability to accept it. . . .

POLICE SLEEPINESS:
SIGN OF ALIENATION*

It was enterprising if somewhat heartless of the New York *Times* to make a study recently of the nighttime habits of New York's Finest. "Night after night, in obscure corners all over New York City," the newspaper reported, "policemen on foot and policemen in patrol cars disappear into their 'coops.' " The *Times* bolstered this accusation with a photograph of three patrol cars gathered in a Brooklyn park with patrolmen allegedly fast asleep inside.

"Cooping" is police slang for sleeping on duty. It is said to be extremely widespread and extremely common in the small hours between 2 a.m. and 6 a.m. Some patrolmen, according to the *Times*, carry pillows and alarm clocks under their coats when they go on duty to make sure their rest is comfortable and that they do not oversleep.

The practice is by no means confined to New York. In Washington it is referred to as "huddling," and in some places it is called "going down." It is well known to the administrative authorities of police departments; but what they don't know is how to cope with it. Maybe it reflects inefficient use of available manpower. But current crime statistics do not lend encouragement to

*Article, the Washington *Post*, December 26, 1968.

the idea that policemen are unneeded on the streets of American cities in the early hours of the morning.

It seems much more likely that "cooping" reflects a growing alienation between the police and the public they serve. That alienation has expressed itself of late in a number of other ways— in threatened police strikes, in police resistance to civilian control and civilian review boards, in police opposition to restraints on their use of firearms. Policemen asleep on duty are at once a reproach and a taunt to the community.

On the community's side, alienation from the police has found expression in reports vehemently critical of police conduct—the recently published Walker Report called *Rights in Conflict,* for example, dealing with the confrontation of police and demonstrators in Chicago during the Democratic National Convention.

The public makes extravagant demands on its policemen. It expects every cop to know enough law to keep on the right side of the Constitution in any emergency; it wants him to know enough sociology and psychology to deal sympathetically with the poor and the young and the misbegotten; it wants him to be able to handle crowds, to deliver a baby on a moment's notice, to soothe a would-be suicide, to help an old lady across a street and to face thugs or madmen with aplomb and intrepidity. A policeman must be Superman and Clark Kent at the same time, equal to anything yet always modest, self-effacing and good-natured. For these qualities he is paid rather less than a football player and accorded status only slightly above that of a sanitation worker.

And on top of this a policeman may not unreasonably suspect that a goodly part of the public secretly wants him to rough up demonstrators and wrest confessions from criminals while the public looks the other way and enjoys the luxury of extolling civil liberty and condemning police brutality.

In simple truth, a large part of the public today wants the police to "get tough" with criminals; and a lot of policemen are sulking because the courts won't let that toughness take the form of cutting constitutional corners. The courts, in consequence, are taking a bad beating from both sides.

But history affords not the slightest indication that the courts could remedy the situation by relaxing their standards of due process or even by imposing the most savage sentences imaginable upon convicted felons. That exceptionally astute student of police problems, Professor James Q. Wilson of Harvard University, remarked recently: "Now that 'crime in the streets' has become a major issue it is probably too much to expect that public officials, sensitive to this popular concern, will be much inclined to encourage police administrators to do better those things the police *can* do (maintaining order) and to look elsewhere (primarily to the correctional agencies) for help in doing those things that the police cannot do (reducing the incidence of these crimes committed by repeaters)."

There is a great deal that the country can do, and ought to do, to help the police combat crime. But as is so often the case with social illness, the real remedies are costly and time-consuming.

We could raise the current standard—which, anyway, is rarely reached in practice—of 2.5 police officers per 1000 population and double it. We could step up recruiting quite easily by paying policemen something a mite closer to what we pay Congressmen. We could professionalize the police by recruiting college graduates and giving them real training. We could give them vastly improved equipment for mobility and communication. We could light city streets more brightly. We could diminish the ease with which persons tempted toward crime are now able to obtain the gun often needed to yield to the temptation.

We could do a lot to help the courts, too, if we could just bring ourselves to stop reviling them and remember that they are the bulwarks of our civilization. We could increase the number of judges, prosecutors, marshals, probation officers, youth counselors and others needed to make justice swift and curative rather than corrupting.

But these remedies are commonly dismissed with scorn as suitable, perhaps, for the long term but not for the immediate present. And so, decade after decade, they are forgotten in favor of a "toughness" which serves only to create more criminals.

There is the wisdom of experience in the ancient adage: an ounce of prevention is worth a pound of punishment.

TEN

Disarmament at Home

There was no topic about which Alan Barth felt more strongly, or wrote more often, than gun control. Singlehandedly, he turned the Washington *Post*'s editorial page into the nation's leading crusader for strict limitations on the possession and use of hand-guns. Never a month went by, except when he was on leave, that the *Post* did not speak to the subject; it sometimes spoke even in his absence because his colleagues shared his view. On two oc-casions, first in 1965 and again in 1968, his zeal led the *Post* to mount a sustained barrage. In 1965 it published gun-control edi-torials on seventy-seven consecutive days, an effort which strained even Barth's ability to find something new or bright to write each day. In 1968, after the assassinations of Robert F. Kennedy and Martin Luther King, Barth wrote a gun-control editorial almost every day for six months. These helped spur President Johnson into seeking the first comprehensive federal gun-control law—a law that Barth thought helped some, but not much.

PERSONALLY SPEAKING*

NEW YORK CITY—I have been putting together a rather ghoulish collection of clippings. They tell very similar stories and they all have in common the fact that they leave unanswered the same perplexing question.

I'll give you a couple of samples. First, one from the [Beaumont] *Enterprise* of February 5, which starts as follows: "Firing as he ran from bed to bed in the crowded wards of the Tewksbury State infirmary, a giant inmate today killed three fellow patients and critically wounded two others with a mail order pistol." The Associated Press story then goes on to relate that the murderer "had saved his tobacco money month by month to buy the pistol from a New York mail order house."

And here is the lead on a New York *Herald Tribune* story of February 8: "Frank Brossart, 59 years old, of 413 East Seventeenth street, was arrested and placed in the psychopathic ward of Bellevue hospital last night after he had endangered the lives of eight persons in the hospital by shooting them with a .38 caliber revolver."

You will note in this latter story that the reporter who wrote it was meticulous in finding out the age and the exact address of the genial Mr. Brossart and even went to the trouble of learning the caliber of the firearm with which he went on his little bender. This is certainly very careful reporting; but nowhere in the report is there any mention of whence or how Mr. Brossart came into possession of the revolver. That item seemed to be of no importance.

In the first story, to be sure, the Associated Press man ascertained that the pistol was purchased from "a New York mail order

*Column, the Beaumont (Texas) *Sunday Journal*, March 6, 1938. Reprinted with permission.

house." Yes, but what mail-order house? That remains undisclosed.

It does not seem to me, however, to be irrelevant to this story. If this lunatic in Tewksbury State infirmary had killed three human beings by putting potassium cyanide in their coffee, there would have been great interest in discovering the source of the cyanide. Whoever supplied it would be held as an accessory to the crime. And quite properly. Cyanide being a lethal poison, it is against the law to dispense it without proper medical authorization. But a revolver, which is a lethal weapon, can be sold over the counter, or even by mail, to any malcontent imbecile who happens to feel like popping it off in the direction of his fellow-men.

And nobody thinks of bringing criminal charges against the manufacturer of that revolver or against the mail-order house or retail store which rang up a profit on the cash register for selling an instrument which cost the lives of several quite innocent individuals.

What use has any law-abiding citizen for a revolver? For hunting he uses a rifle or a shotgun. But if he keeps or carries a revolver, it is only on the pretext that he needs it to defend himself against unlawful persons who have revolvers in their possession. And it is really of very doubtful value in defense because it tempts criminals to shoot first and overlook the formality of asking him to stick up his hands. You don't very often read in the papers about burglars who are shot or captured by armed householders. Not nearly as often as you read about youngsters who discovered Daddy's pistol in a bureau drawer and pulled the trigger on the assumption that it wasn't loaded.

The *World-Telegram* of this evening has a jaunty headline on page one, reading: " 'HE WAS MEAN, SO I SHOT HIM,' DOCTOR QUOTES MRS. RYAN." Well, Mrs. Ryan will probably plead temporary insanity—perhaps quite truthfully—and be found not guilty. But if there hadn't happened to be a gun lying around handy just when she went temporarily insane, Mr. Ryan would be alive today and Mrs. Ryan would no doubt manage to cope with his manners in some more temperate fashion.

There is no need to shrug shoulders and say nothing can be done about it. Something very effective can be done about it if we want to clamp down firmly on the right of firearm manufacturers to make money by selling an article which can be used only for suicide or homicide. As we clamp down, for example, on the right of chemical manufacturers to make money out of the indiscriminate sale of poisons or narcotics.

Of course, there would remain a bootleg problem in pistols, just as in dope. But at least we wouldn't have the law giving its sanction to this crazy kind of merchandising; and if we made the sale of pistols without proper and stringent authorization illegal, we'd win a good deal more than half the battle. It would be far more useful to tackle this evil at its source than merely to forbid the carrying or possession of revolvers.

There is a federal law called the Harrison anti-narcotic act which provides that every physician who prescribes any of the cocaine or opium derivatives must obtain a license and be registered with the federal narcotics bureau; every such prescription he writes must be turned in to the bureau with the name of the patient to whom he has given it. Is this an invasion of the doctor's and druggist's liberty? If it is, it's one that makes thoroughly good sense.

The same kind of restriction and responsibility could be put upon the makers and dispensers of pistols. Just bear in mind that a shot in the arm is not nearly so dangerous as a shot through the heart.

CONCEALED WEAPONS

FEBRUARY 17, 1951

State civil-defense directors have been implored by Major General M. A. Edson (retired), now president of the National Rifle Association and himself director of public safety for the State of Vermont, "to eliminate any reference to privately owned firearms from your civil defense questionnaire." Acknowledging that, at first glance, it might seem a good idea for any civil-defense director to know who owns guns in his state, General Edson warns that, nevertheless, any attempt to find out would play right into the hands of fifth columnists. "The accepted fifth column technique," the general was quoted in Friday's Washington *Post,* "calls for raids on the homes of citizens who possess firearms." Dear, dear!

On the same page of the same newspaper on the same day appeared a story about a young housewife in Brooklyn who, having been erroneously informed that her husband, a bomber pilot, had died of combat wounds in Korea, attempted to end her own life by means of a .25-caliber Belgian pistol which happened to be lying handy around the house. A letter to the editor on the opposite page (same newspaper, same day) complained that "unless something is done in an organized way to prohibit shooting in the Great Falls area, it must be considered unsafe for use as a park and recreational area." On another page (same day, same newspaper) there was a story about a Marine recruit who shot his wife to death as the police smashed a locked bedroom door in a vain attempt to save her.

So it goes (in any newspaper, any day). The menace of the fifth column may be grave indeed. Perhaps they already have plans to raid the homes of all known members of the National Rifle Association. Pending the revolution, however, registration and licensing of firearms may serve the useful purpose of keeping them, to some extent, out of the hands of criminals, homicidal maniacs, children and—who knows—even the fifth column.

RIGHT TO BEAR ARMS

APRIL 17, 1965

Gunsters are much given to arguing that the Second Amendment confers on them an absolute immunity against any attempt to protect the general welfare by controlling the distribution of deadly weapons. They are quite mistaken. The Supreme Court said in 1894 that the restraint of the Second Amendment applied only to Congress; it said in 1897 that an Act of Congress which prohibits the carrying of concealed weapons does not violate this Amendment; and it said in 1939 that Congress could prohibit the possession of arms which had no "reasonable relationship to the preservation or efficiency of a well-regulated militia."

At the time the Second Amendment was adopted, the court observed, men called for military service were expected to appear bearing arms supplied by themselves and of the kind in common use at the time. Several changes have taken place since then. Men called for military service are given arms by the national government now. And these arms are of a complex character, not very useful for private citizens in private life. Conversely, the arms commonly held by private citizens could hardly be considered decisive weapons for modern warfare. The pistol, for example, while admirably designed for robbing liquor stores, committing suicide, avenging personal slights, settling family quarrels or transforming disconsolate wives into merry widows, has no more than limited utility for repelling missile attacks or even for coping with guerrilla warfare in the jungle of Vietnam.

We think the efficiency of the militia will not be affected in any way by rigorous gun-control legislation; but the safety and welfare of the average American will be immensely enhanced.

A PARTING SHOT

APRIL 28, 1965

For seventy-seven consecutive days—eleven full weeks—this [editorial] page has carried an editorial about guns. It has done so because of a belief that the almost uncontrolled distribution and availability of firearms in the United States presents a senseless peril to public safety and because of a strong desire to bring this peril to public notice. This kind of effort to arouse public opinion constitutes, we think, one of the first functions of a free press.

The stream of editorials has produced, in unprecedented volume, a responding stream of letters to the editor—most of them critical of the editorials, many of them insensately angry. Some of the editorials were meant to be informative—to document the danger and to describe what seemed to us appropriate legislative remedies. Some were frankly meant to be provocative—to arouse a sense of outrage by recounting tragedies reported as commonplace in the news pages every day. Some were meant to rebut the standard arguments of the National Rifle Association and other opponents of the President's recommendations for firearms control. Some were meant to be sardonic or shocking—and seemed, perhaps, no more than smart-aleck.

Since we propose now to declare a moratorium, or temporary cease-fire, on the subject, it seems opportune to recapitulate our reasons for wanting effective firearms control and to restate the kinds of control we deem effective. Guns are indubitably dangerous. About five thousand homicides and more than eight thousand suicides are committed through the use of guns every year in the United States. Many of these killings could have, and perhaps would have, been accomplished by other means; but guns made them easy.

To begin with, guns contribute to crime. Possession of them emboldens many to undertake assaults or robberies; and it leads to many fatalities which might not have resulted if these crimes had been undertaken with less lethal weapons. In a three-year period, according to FBI Director J. Edgar Hoover, 168 law-enforcement officers were murdered in the performance of their official duties. Firearms were used in 162 of these killings, with revolvers and automatic pistols accounting for 131 of the deaths and rifles and shotguns for 31; knives, clubs and other weapons were responsible for the remaining 6.

Even more tragic, in a way, is the death toll from guns used by those not intending to commit crime—the killing of children by demented parents, the killing of wives and husbands and lovers and relatives and neighbors in pointless quarrels, the killing of youngsters by other youngsters who did not know the gun was loaded, or by sheer accident or carelessness, the killing, altogether at random, of innocents who happened to be at hand when some drunk or fool was skylarking with a gun. Not a day passes in any major American city without some such tragedy.

For these reasons, we want to prevent, or at least diminish, the possession and easy acquisition of guns by criminals, drunkards, juveniles, drug addicts and the mentally ill. We are convinced that this can be done—to the vast betterment of the general welfare—without preventing the legitimate enjoyment of firearms for hunting, collecting, target-shooting and, where necessary, self-defense by responsible, law-abiding, qualified adults.

Nationally, we urge adoption of . . . bills . . . [that] would rigidly limit the importation of guns—mainly cast-off military weapons—from abroad; prohibit mail-order sales of firearms to individuals by limiting firearms shipments in interstate commerce to shipments between licensed importers, manufacturers and dealers; and help states to control the firearms traffic within their borders by requiring that any gun purchaser be a *bona fide* resident of the state in which the gun is purchased.

Locally, we urge the registration of all firearms; the limitation of ownership to persons over twenty-one years of age who have not been convicted of a crime, who have not been adjudged mentally incompetent and who have demonstrated by test a knowledge of the rules of safety for handling firearms. In addition, because pistols are peculiarly dangerous and peculiarly susceptible to employment in the commission of crime, we urge that the possession of a pistol be narrowly limited to *bona fide* collectors, to target-shooters whose use of them will be carefully controlled by regulation, and to persons who, in isolated places and special situations, are adjudged, in accordance with fixed standards, to have a genuine need of them for self-protection.

There is nothing in these proposals, we think, which infringes on the constitutional right to keep and bear arms as that right is related to the maintenance of a well-regulated militia. There is nothing in these proposals which interferes with participation by responsible adults in the great and popular sports of hunting and target-shooting, or in the hobby of gun collection. The frontier is gone in the United States. Americans today live increasingly in crowded urban centers where the indiscriminate possession of guns has become a deadly danger.

In a country where four Presidents have been assassinated by gunfire and where guns exact a terrible toll in death and tragedy every year, sportsmen can fairly be asked to incur minor inconvenience for the sake of the general welfare. It is time for America to come of age. Disarmament needs to begin at home.

. . . AND TAKE AWAY THE GUNS

JUNE 7, 1968

The shooting of Robert F. Kennedy and five other innocent persons in Los Angeles was merely the most sensational of numberless shootings that took place in the United States on Tuesday night. Here in Washington, at a Georgetown hamburger shop, two young Marine lieutenants, twenty and twenty-one years old, were shot dead and a third officer and a young woman were wounded by gunfire at almost the same moment that the tragedy occurred in Los Angeles.

The United States can put a stop to this senseless slaughter— or at least very greatly lessen it. Congress has it within its power to do this simply and effectively, as every other civilized country has done it—by bringing the sordid traffic in guns under control. There were, as President Johnson said yesterday, more than five thousand homicides by firearms in this country during 1967—not to speak of suicides and accidental shootings which brought the year's death toll from guns up to about eighteen thousand. Gun homicides are fewer than fifty a year in England or in Japan.

Thanks to the insensate obstructionism of the National Rifle Association, the gun-control provisions of the current omnibus crime bill are piddling and ineffectual. It is time now to deal with the gun peril in this country definitely, on its own merits and in a distinct piece of legislation, not squeezed casually into a hodge-podge measure of doubtful constitutionality. We applaud most warmly the President's appeal to Congress "to enact a strong and effective gun control law, governing the full range of lethal weapons." But control must go beyond the purchase of firearms. It must govern possession as well.

Regarding pistols and revolvers, the control should be just as rigid as possible. No one ought to be allowed to possess one of these weapons, designed only for the killing or maiming of human beings, unless he is a member of the military, a law-enforcement officer or an individual whose peculiar occupation and circumstances require him, in the judgment of the police, to possess a handgun for self-protection.

In short, private sale of these weapons should be ended. Everyone now possessing a pistol or revolver should be required to turn it in to police authorities by a fixed date—with just compensation, of course. Licensed shooting galleries and clubs may be allowed to keep such guns under stringent controls for target-shooting purposes. But unlicensed possession of one of these weapons by anyone should be subject to severe penalties.

Possession of sporting rifles and shotguns should be limited strictly to law-abiding, responsible adults; and every one of these weapons should be registered, along with all sales of ammunition for them. Regulations should be formulated also for the responsible handling of these firearms, requiring that they be kept unloaded and disassembled except when being employed at appropriate places for target-shooting or hunting. Better still, perhaps, they should be kept, as in Japan, at gun clubs where they can be obtained by their owners when actually needed for sport.

These measures will not forbid legitimate and reasonable use of guns for lawful purposes. They will, however, make it extremely difficult for criminals, lunatics, children and assassins to acquire guns. And they will reduce the tragic incidence of shootings by infuriated or intoxicated or careless individuals who happen to find a gun handy when they lose control of their minds or their tempers.

The frontier has passed from American life. Americans now live in much too close proximity to each other to leave guns lying around at random for their mutual destruction. The one redeeming benefit that could flow from the Kennedy tragedy in Los Angeles is effective action to save the lives of his fellow-Americans. Common sense and a decent respect for the sanctity of human life command the President and Congress to deal with this peril now.

DISARMING CRIMINALS

OCTOBER 26, 1968

"Today," said President Johnson in a White House ceremony on Tuesday at the signing of the gun-control bill, "we begin to disarm the criminal, and the careless and the insane." This is a somewhat optimistic and ebullient view of the legislation. By putting a stop to the mail-order merchandising of firearms, the new law may fairly be said to make it more difficult than it has been in the past for the criminal, the careless and the insane to purchase guns. Unfortunately, however, it does not disarm anybody.

There are, as the President observed, "over 160 million guns in this country—more firearms than families." And, as he went on to point out, "if guns are to be kept out of the hands of the criminals, out of the hands of the insane and out of the hands of the irresponsible, then we just must have licensing. If the criminal with a gun is to be tracked down quickly, then we must have registration in this country.''

The President ardently sought licensing and registration from Congress. He presented compelling arguments and statistics to show that these would promote law enforcement and public safety without interfering with the legitimate use of firearms by law-abiding and responsible citizens. And he was supported in this position, as public-opinion polls made plain, by an overwhelming majority of the American people. But these safeguards, he remarked with absolute justification, were blocked by "the voices of a powerful gun lobby that has prevailed for the moment in an election year.''

Let us say something simple, obvious and straightforward about guns. They are undoubtedly necessary for certain forms of sport. They are also necessary for certain forms of crime. It is virtually impossible for anyone to hold up a bank without a firearm. It is difficult for anyone to hold up a liquor store or a grocery store or a gas station or to burglarize a home or to terrorize a group of law-abiding citizens unless he possesses one of these indispensable crime tools. The President is incontrovertibly right in saying that the key to effective crime control remains effective gun control.

Now, it is an inescapable fact that licensing is the simplest device by which guns can be made readily available to responsible, law-abiding citizens and at the same time kept away from irresponsible and criminal persons. Licensing is the best way to separate the fit from the unfit. And registration is the most practical means of tracing the ownership of a gun used in the commission of a crime.

So long as the gun lobby resists registration and licensing, it aids and abets crime. And it bears, inevitably, a heavy measure of responsibility for the twenty thousand human lives that will be extinguished by gunfire in the United States in the year ahead. The American people are just not going to put up much longer with so much blind, reckless and selfish pandering to a narrow special interest—and at so heavy a social cost. The completion of effective gun control lies ahead as an imperative for the public welfare. Disarmament of the criminal, the careless and the insane must become a reality.

HANDGUNS AND HOUSEHOLDERS

JANUARY 9, 1971

Like so many other committees and commissions which have looked at the crime problem in America objectively and realistically, the National Commission on Reform of Federal Criminal Laws has recommended . . . that all firearms be registered and that private ownership of handguns be outlawed. This is not a sentimental or idealistic recommendation and it entails no limitation of essential liberty. It is designed simply to protect liberty, and indeed life, by restricting possession of the weapon most frequently used for crime and for killing.

One can say with confidence right now, at the very beginning of 1971, that before the next New Year's Eve rolls around at least nine thousand persons will be murdered by gunfire in the United States; at least twelve thousand will use a bullet to put an end to their own lives; and at least a hundred thousand robberies will be committed with the aid of a gun. These are the stark facts that prompted the commission's recommendation that handguns be made contraband and restricted to police officers and the military.

It is true, of course, as the gun lobbyists are so quick to assert, that the mere passage of a law forbidding private possession of pistols would not of itself induce every criminal to surrender his crime tools. The law, like every other law, would be more faithfully observed by the law-abiding than by the lawless. Such a law would, however, begin the process of curbing the spread of pistols, first, by authorizing confiscation upon discovery; second, by making mere possession punishable; third, by diminishing the easy availability of pistols in bureau drawers and bedside tables where children, drunks, angry spouses and other irresponsibles can get at them; fourth, by forbidding the sale of such weapons by gun merchants.

Would this diminish killing in the United States? We think it undoubtedly would. It would make it more difficult—and increasingly so as time went on—for criminals to obtain handguns, and it would make pistols less accessible for the kind of killing so carelessly called "accidental." One ought always to remember that most gun fatalities in the United States occur within families or in a relationship where the killer and his victim are known to each other, and where, presumably, the killer is sorry after he has done his killing.

Would the recommended outlawing of handguns entail a major deprivation or injustice to law-abiding Americans? We think not. It would, admittedly, entail an inconvenience for persons who like to shoot pistols at targets. Their sport is an entirely legitimate one and could be carried out by keeping their pistols safely locked up at an NRA gun club or some licensed shooting range. Responsible citizens ought to be willing to undergo that much inconvenience for the sake of the general welfare.

But what about the people who think of themselves as armed protectors of their homes? These would be, perhaps, the principal beneficiaries of the proposed law. They might well be saved by it from gunning down a member of the family or a neighbor mistaken for a prowler in the dark; and their own lives might be saved from the fatal consequence of a gun duel with some vicious gunman.

What it all boils down to is a recognition that the United States is no longer a frontier society and that pistols as playtoys are not tolerable in crowded urban communities. Getting handguns out of circulation will certainly not be accomplished quickly or easily. But it is high time to begin.

BETTER DISTRIBUTION
FOR BIG SHOOTOUT?*

Domestic disarmament having plainly failed, it must now be the responsibility of sportsmen to see to it that everybody is armed equally and evenly for the great shootout that lies ahead. Sportsmanship is deeply ingrained in Americans. It is not too much, indeed, to say that it is as American as the six-shooter. Should we then aim, so to speak, at equality of opportunity for every sportsman?

In the spirit of just that aim, the Rev. Douglas Moore, leader of the Black United Front, remarked the other day in discussing the activities of the Pioneer Gun Hunting Club of Cedar Heights, a group of predominantly black sportsmen, the BUF is simply utilizing the "good American principle" of using guns "for sporting purposes."

"We follow the rules of the National Rifle Association," the kindly clergyman declared, adding casually that his group plans to compete soon in national shooting competitions sponsored by the NRA. He managed to give his remarks particular point by saying that, instead of demonstrating against Cambodia and the Kent slayings, BUF members were "in the woods" practicing at an undisclosed shooting range.

Well and good, so far as it goes. This approach can be counted upon to achieve a perfect parity between black and white contingents in the community. But there are other elements that remain the victims of intolerable discrimination.

Take students, for example. It was mortifying, if that is not too strong a term, to see students shot down recently at Kent State University and at Jackson, Mississippi, without a chance to shoot

*Article, the Washington *Post*, May 31, 1970.

286

back at their assailants. What happened at those places was a mockery of fair play.

Obviously, students need to be armed for self-defense. But when this imbalance has been righted, what about construction workers and other "hard hats" in New York and other cities? Surely fairness dictates that they be granted some means of asserting their point of view effectively.

Ordinary householders, as several members of the local clergy have made indisputably clear, have an imperative need for sporting weapons in order to mow down any police officers who may, by mischance, enter their homes in pursuance of the no-knock provision of the crime bill which Congress seems about to enact. It would hardly be fair to let the law take effect until the citizenry has had a reasonable chance to stock up on guns and ammunition.

Whether the arming of these groups will serve to make available an adequate supply of firearms for the settlement of marital spats, domestic altercations and neighborly differences of opinion remains to be seen.

The experience on this score has so far been most encouraging. Usually when a youngster wants to show a pistol to his baby brother, he can find one, loaded, in a family bureau drawer or night table. And ample equipment seems to be available for those who like a round of Russian Roulette.

A special problem exists, it must be acknowledged, in connection with differences of opinion between wives and husbands. Too frequently, when one spouse is displeased with another, there is only a single sporting weapon in the house with which to settle the dispute. Perhaps it would be desirable for some enterprising firearms manufacturer to put on the market a gift package—a sort of His-and-Hers combination—containing a pair of pistols of the sort that used to be so much in vogue for dueling. The NRA could sponsor such a special combination in the name of true sportsmanship. It would, when you come to think about it, make an ideal wedding gift.

Perhaps, however, there is no need for uneasiness about home armament. Alan L. Otten reported recently in the *Wall Street Journal* that "fully half of all gun killings occur within the family,

80 per cent among family or friends." And he added encouragingly that "by 1968, there were an estimated 24 million handguns in civilian hands, with another 2.5 million being manufactured or imported each year."

The NRA says, and very forcefully, too, that any attempt to limit the possession of guns, or even to keep track of who has them by some system of licensing or registration, would run directly athwart the spirit of true sportsmanship. So that approach to the problem, as you can readily see, is out.

The aim, therefore, must be to make possession universal so that it can be completely equitable. And when that has been achieved, it would be desirable, we think, to develop some chivalrous, and genuinely American, code for shooting one another. The NRA can be helpful in this connection.

Would it not be possible to have tournaments, as it were, in which all sorts of dissident groups could shoot it out under orderly conditions, say on the Ellipse, or with adversaries ranged on either side of the Reflecting Pool? There could be a return to something like the knightly jousting of the Middle Ages—although, of course, with deadlier weapons than those cumbersome, old-fashioned lances. We could have regular carnage carnivals, say semi-annually—all carried out under rules and regulations prescribed by the NRA in the highest traditions of American sportsmanship.

Grandstands could be erected and tickets sold for attendance at these sporting events so that the more timorous citizens who did not want to participate themselves could share in the fun. Undoubtedly, this would serve to diminish some of the irregular slaughter which takes place so pointlessly, nobody really enjoying it. And out of the resolution of differences achieved through these tournaments could come a new American consensus shared by all the survivors. Provided there are any survivors.

ELEVEN

A Sentinel for Freedom

While Alan Barth was, first and foremost, a civil-libertarian, he was also by profession a newspaperman. Unlike many of his colleagues, however, he did not blindly defend the operations of the American press. He believed that the press, like the government, had responsibilities—quite different ones, to be sure—that grew from a heritage too often forgotten.

Thus, Barth criticized the press sharply during the McCarthy era for reporting, without evaluation, almost all the charges made by almost all the Communist-hunters; he thought the press had a duty not to report such "facts" without making an independent effort to determine if they were true or, at the very least, telling its audience that such charges were only unverified and undocumented allegations. Barth held the press responsible, then and later, for what he perceived to be a decline in respect for civil liberties because of its failure to convey to its audience the idea that limitations on the rights of any one citizen are limitations on the rights of all citizens.

At the same time, Barth defended the right of the press to do whatever it chose, completely free from any outside control. He believed that restrictions, even those imposed by organizations of journalists, on what it could publish were a greater threat in the long run to the American system of government than anything the press itself might do through irresponsibility, recklessness or malice. This flowed from his basic belief that democracy works and freedom and liberty survive only in societies where channels of communication are totally open and free.

Barth's view of the job of the press as an institution was the same as his view of his own obligation as part of it: to bring truth to readers, to put current events into their proper historical context, to entertain and amuse as well as to inform, to fight hard—on its editorial pages—for the causes in which it believed, and above all to be responsible not to the government but to the people and to the heritage given it by those who wrote the First Amendment and by those who fought for freedom and liberty long before the American government was founded.

THE PRESS AS CENSOR
OF GOVERNMENT*

. . . The press in the United States is, in many respects, the most privileged of American institutions. Although newspapers are big business enterprises operated for private profit, and although they are, in some degree, subsidized by the government through the grant of second-class-mail benefits, the Constitution shields them from any form of official interference or regulation.

Moreover, this privileged position is no mere legalism or abstraction. It has been strengthened by time and buttressed by popular reverence. Freedom of the press is an American shibboleth. And although not everyone who uses it knows precisely what it means, most Americans would fight for it and, perhaps, even die for it.

*From the Lucius W. Nieman lecture on February 22, 1962, at the Marquette University College of Journalism, Milwaukee, Wisconsin. The text was published in *Vital Speeches*, March 15, 1962, and abridged in the *Progressive*, June 1962.

It has long been a settled matter in American life that newspapers are entitled to cuss the government out as lustily and as unreasonably as they please; but few officials of the government have the hardihood to cuss out the newspapers, and none of them dares to suggest that newspapers be called to account in any way for their supposed misconduct.

The men who established the American Republic sought censorship of government by the press rather than censorship of the press by the government. This concept of the press was expressed by Americans even before they became a nation. The first Continental Congress referred to liberty of the press as a means "whereby oppressive officers are shamed or intimidated into more honorable or just modes of conducting affairs."

Thomas Jefferson spoke of the press explicitly as a censor of the government. "No government ought to be without censors," he wrote in a letter to George Washington in 1792, "and while the press is free, no one will." And as late as 1823, although he had been mercilessly maligned by the Federalist journals of his day, he was still able to write to a French correspondent, "This formidable censor of the public functionaries, by arraigning them at the tribunal of public opinion, produces reform peaceably, which must otherwise be done by revolution."

Certainly the founders of the American Republic desired a relationship between press and government just as they desired a relationship between church and government, different from that existing in the England from which they declared their independence. No other conclusion can comport with the bracketing of the two in the same unequivocal language of the First Amendment.

In England, by the time of the American Revolution, the press was already free from prior restraint in the form of licensing, or direct censorship. It remained, however, subject to the formidable restraint of severe punishment for publication of any matter that might be deemed seditious or subversive. This amounted to an extremely effective form of censorship. As the late Professor Zechariah Chafee put it drily, "A death penalty for writing about socialism would be as effective suppression as a censorship."

And he cited the observation made in 1799 by Madison, who drafted the First Amendment, that it embodied "the essential difference between the British Government and the American Constitution."

Nothing expresses more clearly the essential difference between a totalitarian society and a free society than the relationship in each of the press to the government. Among the totalitarians, the press, like every other institution, is an instrumentality of the state; it is used to propagate support for official policies and to promote official doctrines. In a free society, however, the function of the press is, rather, to oppose the government, to scrutinize its activities and to keep its authority within appropriate bounds.

That extraordinary analyst of the American psyche, Alexis de Tocqueville, observed that "the more we consider the independence of the press in its principal consequences, the more we are convinced that it is the chief, and so to speak, the constitutive element of freedom in the modern world. A nation which is determined to remain free is therefore right in demanding the unrestrained exercise of this independence."

The key word here is "independence." To the founders of the Republic, freedom of the press meant a simple thing—independence of the government. For they desired a press which would operate as a tribune of the people, championing their liberties, and as a censor of the government, challenging its powers.

Now, a press which enjoys such independence of the government is, almost by definition, in some degree irresponsible. And no one ought to be surprised if it behaves at times altogether irresponsibly. A measure of irresponsibility was the price which had to be paid—and which the Founders were quite prepared to pay—for the independence without which the press could not discharge its vital function.

A great deal has been said in a great many lectures by a great many eloquent lecturers concerning the irresponsibility of American newspapers. I do not propose to add to that indictment. . . . On the contrary, I mean to raise a rather different question for your consideration. I want to ask—and not altogether rhetorically by any means—whether the press in the United States today has not become excessively *responsible,* whether it has not, in fact, to an alarming degree, become a mouthpiece and partner of the government, rather than a censor.

A free press—that is, a press free from governmental regulation or control—serves as a censor of the government in two ways. First, it is supposed to give the people of a democratic society the information about the world they live in and about what their government is doing without which they cannot possibly, in any real sense, be self-governing. This is, of course, the business of the news pages.

Second, a free press is supposed to speak out in defense of the rights and liberties of the people whenever these are threatened— even in the name of national security—and to give warning of any extension of governmental power beyond the perimeters fixed for it by the Constitution. It is supposed, in short, to speak for the people and against the government. This is, of course, the business of the editorial pages.

Now, let me at this point enter a general disclaimer. I am well aware that generalizations about the American press are apt—nay, are almost certain—to be misleading. There are some 1700-odd dailies in the United States—almost every single one of them odd, as a matter of fact—and no two are exactly alike. They have done their jobs with varying degrees of skill and courage and conscience under varied circumstances and in accordance with the various views of their editors and publishers. Some have been conspicuous for gallantry in the face of popular hostility; some have been conspicuous only for their orthodoxy and their docile following of the crowd. Some have been noble at one time and ignoble at another—and I am conscious, of course, that the distinction between the two must be a matter of individual judgment and point of view.

But it is a reasonable generalization, I think—at least I shall offer it for your consideration and criticism—that American newspapers are not now doing as much as they could do, and must do if democracy is to survive, to give the American public an understanding of the complex circumstances and developments concerning which they have to make fateful decisions as to national policy and action.

I think the failure can be discerned to begin with in a widespread tendency to subordinate what is important to what is sensational in the news—to give readers entertainment in preference to facts, to give them stories that titillate their curiosity rather than stories that challenge their intellects. In a good many cities, when you pick up the daily paper you get an impression that the entire local populace has been engaged for the preceding twenty-four hours in an orgy of sex, crime and violence. This often makes interesting reading; and in many newspapers it is reported with remarkable vividness and journalistic craftsmanship.

Needless to say, I am not presenting this as an illustration of excessive responsibility on the part of the press. I am aware that it is a staple part of the charge that newspapers are often irresponsible. Neither do I intend to suggest that sex, crime and violence should go unreported. They are a part of the pattern of life about which the community needs to know. The probable consequence of concealing them would be panic—or at the very least an encouragement of the conditions which propagate them.

No, they need to be reported, all right; and the only question in connection with them is a question of emphasis in relation to other kinds of news. Many a time, in traveling around the country, I have picked up a strange newspaper in a strange city—and found myself almost completely cut off from news I wanted and needed to know of the larger world. It is disconcerting, for example, to read a wire story from Washington telling that the Supreme Court has decided a major case by a five-to-four division and then discover that this is *all* the story is going to tell about the decision; there is nothing to let one know which Justices were in the majority, nor what they said in their opinion, nor what views were expressed by the dissenters. How can readers form for themselves any intelligent judgment about the decision on the basis of such incomplete and inadequate reporting?

It is not true, I am pretty sure, that readers in small cities are less interested than readers in big cities in what is happening in

Algeria or in Berlin or in the Congo. And if they *are* less interested, is this not almost inescapably the fault of the newspapers serving them? At any rate, they have just as much need to be informed as their big-city fellow-citizens; and they have at least as large a part to play in shaping national policy respecting those events. They need not only hard news about these events but they need also interpretive and informed comment about them. If newspapers are to fulfill their function of enabling and equipping a people to be self-governing, they must tell the people about what is going on in the world in a way that will make the world's developments understandable and real.

The common excuse for failure to do this is a shoddy excuse— the same shoddy excuse that is given by radio and television for pandering to the lowest common denominator of public taste. The excuse is that the public would rather read about local rape, mayhem and scandal. Perhaps it would. But if the public taste is so debased, the newspapers can scarcely escape a measure of blame for the debasement. It is sometimes said that readers get the newspapers they deserve; but I think it more accurate to say that newspapers get the readers they deserve.

At any rate, the obligation of the press to cultivate an informed citizenry is not diminished by the difficulty of doing so. If newspapers are to continue to enjoy their privileged position, they must justify it by a recognition of *noblesse oblige*. And if they want to preserve freedom of the press, they had better foster a public opinion which comprehends and appreciates the blessings of liberty.

Let me turn now to the area in which I think that the press, out of a desire to be responsible, has become too largely a partner and apologist for the government rather than a censor and critic. This is the area which concerns the news of political controversy and national security.

The area is peculiarly difficult for the public to understand, for it involves today technical and scientific matters which are wholly a mystery to most ordinary laymen and also because it is of necessity, at least to some extent, shrouded in secrecy.

Everyone acknowledges that some secrecy on the part of the

government is indispensable to national security. But what everyone tends to forget is that secrecy, no matter how necessary it may be, is inevitably at odds with freedom. This basic truth has been put better than I know how to put it by my favorite editor—who happens by a fortunate coincidence to be the editor I work for. J. R. Wiggins, who has long led the American Society of Newspaper Editors in its fight for freedom of information, stated the situation simply in his book of a few years ago, *Freedom or Secrecy:*

> To diminish the people's information about government is to diminish the people's participation in government. The consequences of secrecy are not less because the reasons for secrecy are more. The ill effects are the same whether the reasons for secrecy are good or bad. The arguments for more secrecy may be good arguments which, in a world that is menaced by Communist imperialism, we cannot altogether refute. They are, nevertheless, arguments for less freedom.

It may be contended, in other words, that it is desirable, or even necessary, to have a Central Intelligence Agency which takes upon itself to launch a little invasion here, engineer a putsch there or install a puppet dictator in some other part of the solar system; but it is obvious that people who have authorized an agency to act in this way—and in complete secrecy, without any kind of accounting whatever—have relinquished a large measure of control over their own destinies.

I am not now trying to attack or to defend this kind of secret activity by government. I am trying simply to suggest to you that a press which allows it to go on without exposing it is a press which has become much more an accomplice or partner of the government than a censor.

Again, let me acknowledge that there are some mighty persuasive arguments to support journalistic cooperation with the government for the sake of national security. Nevertheless, however "responsible" such cooperation may be, it is a far cry indeed from the kind of check on governmental conduct which the press was originally supposed to provide.

Whatever the justification, I think it fair to say that newspapers and newspapermen are generally less inquisitive, less probing, less insistent upon being told what's going on than they used to be. And they are much more "responsible" than they used to be—in days when competition spurred a large degree of irresponsibility—about telling all they know. There is no doubt that the motivation behind this self-restraint—this "responsibility"—is patriotic. But one can reasonably ask whether it furthers the function for which the press was given its extraordinary grant of freedom from governmental control.

There is always a danger, moreover, that self-restraint will lead unconsciously into lethargy or indifference. When secrecy is tolerated at all, it may well be used to mask selfish as well as patriotic purposes. What is to be said, for instance, about the discovery a couple of weeks ago—a discovery made not by a newspaper but by Senator John J. Williams of Delaware—that the federal government bought millions of pounds of feathers during the Korean war to build up a giant stockpile—bought inferior feathers at vastly superior prices and at a time when representatives of most of the companies selling feathers to the United States were on the advisory board on feather-purchasing policies?

I'll tell you what Senator Williams said about it: "I was told that it would be a great disservice to national security to tell me how many feathers we have in the stockpile. I suppose they think Nikita S. Khrushchev could win the cold war if he found out how many feathers we had in the stockpile. . . . Are they expecting us to engage in a pillow fight over Berlin?"

Secrecy and security are not necessarily synonymous. Indeed, there is a good deal of evidence to suggest that they are opposites. "Everything secret degenerates," Lord Acton once wrote. . . . "Nothing is safe that does not show it can bear discussion and publicity."

Let me turn now to the aspect of the relationship between government and press which concerns me most of all and seems to me most significant. I want to talk briefly about the role of the editorial page. It is this department of the newspaper for which the First Amendment's guarantee of freedom has most meaning. And it is pre-eminently this department which is supposed to discharge the newspaper's function of censoring the government.

The editorial page, once the heart and soul of the American newspaper, has fallen in many instances into disuse. Almost every newspaper continues to publish an editorial page. Too often, however, it has become a mere vestigial appendage—an adornment perpetuated long after its purpose has been forgotten, as men continue to wear on the sleeves of their jackets buttons which have become altogether devoid of utility. Too often the editorial page is a newspaper's least-read feature—perhaps because too often it has ceased to be a censor and become a part of the official establishment.

This is especially true today, it seems to me, in foreign affairs. The most remarkable thing about American editorial comment on the U-2 incident, on the Cuban invasion, on the impasse at Berlin, on Laos and Vietnam and the Congo, is its essential uniformity. There are, to be sure, a few discordant, strident voices; every profession has its reprobates, of course. But nowadays criticism of the government seems like politics, to stop at the water's edge. In other words, there is no real debate on the matters that mean life or death to the nation.

In a crisis, the press rallies to the support of the government. Patriotically, it recognizes that criticism of official policy might be taken by enemies of the United States as evidence of internal dissension and division. So there is a closing of the editorial ranks. This "responsibility" is very commendable, in a way. But it deprives the country of the kind of conflict of opinion by which the national policies of a democratic people are supposed to be hammered out. It deprives the government of the stimulating and therapeutic influence of criticism. It deprives the people of that censorship of official action for which the press was made independent of the government.

On the domestic side, editorial pages can be credited, if you like, with a good deal of vigor and bite in criticizing the more conventional forms of corruption in government. There has been some useful exposure and censure of the kind of corruption that takes the form of venality.

The record of the press is not so praiseworthy of late, however, in regard to a kind of corruption deeper and more dangerous than venality—a corruption of basic American values and an encroachment of governmental power upon traditional civil liberties of a sort that the authors of the Bill of Rights would have considered intolerable and which they relied on a free press to prevent.

In appraising the press as a guardian of individual liberty—as a censor of the government—one may fairly ask what it has done to arrest the institutionalization of a Federal Employee Security program which relies for its condemnation of American citizens on hearsay information from faceless informers. That program was instituted in 1947 as an emergency measure to deal with what was supposed to be a crisis. And now, fifteen years later, it remains in full force, in all its essentials as repugnant as when it began to every American tradition of fairness and respect for individual dignity; and now no one even questions the need for it or the wisdom of it or the basic un-Americanism of its operation.

No more than a few newspapers have cried out against the often arrogant and arbitrary and cruel behavior of certain congressional investigating committees. They have let these committees—the House Committee on Un-American Activities in particular—thrust their inquisitorial noses into areas of American life traditionally considered immune from governmental control—universities, churches, labor unions, the press itself—without any apparent understanding of how recklessly these committees were expanding the reach and power of the government.

I submit to you that nowhere in the United States has the press been muzzled by the government or had conformity forced upon it. It has simply, out of a sense of patriotism, or "responsibility," silenced itself and supported the powers that be. I think that American newspapers are in little danger of having freedom of the press taken away from them. But many of them are in serious danger, I think, of losing their freedom through disuse, through atrophy.

Atrophy of the editorial page, let me add, is most common in the smaller cities where monopoly situations prevail. It has its most unfortunate effect in a tendency to avoid local controversy out of a fear of alienating or antagonizing any segment of the community. Yet it is precisely in regard to local matters that editorial pages are capable of the greatest expertness and the greatest impact on community life.

It has long been extremely fashionable among American editorial writers to deplore the trend toward centralization of authority in the federal government; yet those most prone to view this trend with alarm rarely press with much vigor for the solution of local problems at the local level. They are usually content to look above and beyond these to more remote national and international issues, about which their opinions are less likely to evoke resentment among their readers. The decline of the editorial page, so often noted with so much lamentation by so many journalists, can fairly be said to have taken place in direct ratio to a decline in attention to those affairs which lie at the heart of the community which a newspaper is supposed to serve.

. . . I have, quite consciously, made some rather sweeping assertions. . . . I am well aware that there are significant and honorable exceptions to the conformity I have deplored, maverick newspapers which adhere to an old-fashioned concept of the role of the press. It is my own great good fortune to work for one of them. I hope there will be more such newspapers, expressing a diversity of views, even at the cost of some degree of irresponsibility. And I am mindful of a shrewd if slightly cynical remark made long ago by Denis Brogan that no nation could possibly afford to have more than one really responsible newspaper.

The men who established the American Republic were not sentimentalists. They were, in the true sense of the term, idealists—but idealists of the most practical sort. They provided for freedom of the press because they knew that the best government is government which is incessantly subjected to critical scrutiny, and because they understood what we tend so largely to forget today, that the eternal vigilance so commonly said to be the price of liberty is vigilance against duly constituted authority.

A press which serves faithfully and fearlessly as a censor of the government is a source of great national strength. Perhaps, indeed, it will afford to the free world precisely that margin of superiority requisite to its survival in the long struggle it faces against totalitarianism.

When he was defending Thomas Paine against a libel charge in a British court long ago, Thomas Erskine said: "In this manner, power has reckoned in every age; government *in its own* estimation, has been at all times a system of perfection; but a free press has examined and detected its errors, and the people have from time to time reformed them. This freedom has alone made our government what it is! This freedom alone can preserve it!"

A MORAL CHALLENGE
TO THE PRESS*

. . . Walt Whitman, you remember, said that "the American compact is altogether with individuals."

And the Americans who wrote the Declaration of Independence regarded it as self-evident that men are endowed by their Creator with certain unalienable rights, and that it is in order to secure these rights that governments are instituted among men. . . .

Now, it is precisely this traditional regard for the dignity of the individual which, in my view, is undergoing a dangerous corruption today. And the press has been to some extent, I fear, an agent—perhaps an unwitting and unwilling agent, but nonetheless an agent—of that corruption. . . .

The breakdown in respect for individual rights is revealed most strikingly in the conduct of certain congressional investigating

*From an address on May 20, 1952, at the University of Colorado, Boulder, Colorado. The text was published in the *Colorado Quarterly,* Autumn 1952, and abridged in *Nieman Reports,* July 1952. Reprinted with permission.

committees and in the abuse by certain members of Congress of
the privilege of congressional immunity. And it is precisely in this
connection, I think, that the problem affects the press most intimately. For the inescapable fact of the matter is that all of us in
the field of journalism are being used, unwittingly and involun-
tarily, as instruments for the execution of punishment by publicity—as instruments of punishment for offenses which Congress
has no constitutional power to declare criminal or to make punishable by law.

Moreover, we are being used to inflict this kind of punishment
without any semblance of a trial, without any determination as to
whether the victims are guilty or innocent. We are used sometimes, indeed, when we know that the punishment is altogether
unjust.

When we publish in headlines that Senator McCarthy has spewed
out wild charges of treason or espionage against a career Foreign
Service officer or an economic adviser to the President or a university professor having no connection whatever with the government—we do the Senator's dirty work for him and we inflict on
his victim an irreparable injury. The fact is that we do this often
when there is not the slightest corroboration of the Senator's
charges—often, indeed, when we know them to be altogether
absurd.

This comes, I think, very close to irresponsibility. And the
injury resulting to innocent individuals is perhaps the least serious
cost involved. This kind of journalism makes the press a partner
in a corruption of the democratic process. It imposes on the whole
society a kind of intellectual reign of terror, suppressing speech
quite as effectively as any formal censorship. As Senator Margaret
Chase Smith observed a couple of years ago in a protest against
Senator McCarthy's name-calling tactics, "Freedom of speech is
not what it used to be in America. It has been so abused by some
that it is not exercised by others."

American newspapers pride themselves on being impervious to
the tricks of press-agentry. They have learned to detect the contrived handout, the planted story, the trial balloon. Yet they have
found themselves in recent years sucked in as the purveyors of

gossip, and in some cases malicious falsehood, put out in the guise of news—simply because it has been uttered on the floor of Congress or under the auspices, and the protection, of a congressional committee.

I am not talking now about those newspapers that seek to do no more than circulate scandal. I am talking about newspapers that are trying conscientiously to give their readers a proportioned and honest view of the world around them. These newspapers— the best elements of American journalism—are being cynically manipulated and exploited to advance purposes which they abhor.

They are being hoist, it seems to me, by their own tradition of objectivity. That tradition is responsible, of course, for making the American press the most accurate and reliable in the world. But it is also responsible, I am afraid, for imposing serious handicaps on the press in dealing with some of the realities of contemporary politics.

The tradition of objectivity has kept us in particular, I think, from conveying to our readers any full awareness of the degree to which the vital investigating function of Congress has been warped and twisted into a system for punishing individuals for holding opinions which the investigators happen to dislike. It has kept us, for example, from giving the American public anything like a fair and focused picture of the procedures of the McCarran Internal Security Subcommittee—the most flagrant contemporary form of the *auto-da-fé*.

The McCarran Subcommittee has made a practice of throwing the protective arm of congressional immunity round the shoulders of any ex-Communist who wants to point an accusing finger at someone he dislikes. Yet distinguished scholars like Owen Lattimore and John Fairbank are treated like common criminals when they come before this group and dare to defend themselves.

The tradition of objectivity has led the press to treat with perfectly straight faces, as though they were entitled to equal weight and credibility, on the one hand the dredged-up reminiscences of professional witnesses—of the ex-Communists gifted with what someone has aptly called "recuperative memory"—and, on the other hand, the denials of their victims, who have been guilty in most instances of nothing worse than having expressed doubts as to the divinity of Chiang Kai-shek.

I listened for some days to the proceedings of the McCarran Subcommittee in connection with Owen Lattimore. They seemed to me to resemble a medieval inquisition into heresy—or a variation on the bear-baiting which used to be considered such great sport a few centuries ago. It was as though the counsel and members of the subcommittee had succeeded in chaining some helpless creature to a stake and were deliberately goading and tormenting it. It seemed to me an ugly performance, a sadistic performance. And I was not alone in this impression among the newspapermen who were there. But there was no way, within the techniques of detached and objective reporting, to make news stories about the hearings convey to readers this sense of what was going on. I was able, I hope, to do it in some degree in editorials. But the news reports, in my judgment, missed the essence of the story.

You may defend or excuse this or that item in my bill of particulars as being made necessary by the circumstances of our times. Taken together, however, it cannot be denied, I think, that they demonstrate a monstrous corruption of the fundamental premise of our society.

Why is this corruption tolerated? It is tolerated because it is supposed by many sincere and patriotic people that the sacrifice of individual rights will make the nation more secure. Here, I believe, is the most tragic fallacy of our time. Here is the most mischievous concoction of political patent medicine ever swallowed by the American people. . . .

You know, there is a prevalent myth that totalitarian governments are somehow much more efficient than governments that depend upon the voluntary consent of the governed. It is true enough, of course, that a dictatorship can move more swiftly in certain situations than a democracy. But this may mean only that it can more swiftly translate into disaster the errors of the dictator.

Free speech and a free press provide an antidote for error. They give a free people the means of correcting their mistakes and replacing incompetent officials. The totalitarians lack any such self-regulating mechanism. And the lack is likely, in the end, to be a fatal one—as it proved to be in the case of Adolf Hitler's thousand-year Reich.

Freedom of speech is, in addition, a stabilizing influence. It makes for enduring government because it provides an orderly outlet for discontent. Thought that is silenced is always rebellious. Like any force that is confined, it tends to become explosive. But exposed to reason and counter-argument, it can go only as far as its merits will carry it.

The men who wrote the Constitution understood another basic point which we are tending to forget today—that tolerance of diversity is the only way to gain real and lasting national unity. National unity grows not out of uniformity but out of resolved conflict. It grows out of general participation in the shaping of public policy, out of granting to everyone a chance to be heard and to win acceptance if he can for his opinion. And this means, obviously, tolerance of opinions which the majority may consider distasteful, even of opinions which the majority may consider disloyal. . . .

All that I am trying to tell you . . . was expressed not long ago . . . by one of the great Americans of our time, Judge Learned Hand. He was speaking extemporaneously at a reception, just after he had announced his retirement from the federal bench, and this is what he had to say:

My friends, our future is precarious. . . . I like to hope—although I agree that we can have no certainty, still I like to hope—that we have a good chance, a splendid fighting chance and much assurance of victory; but on one condition: that we do not go to pieces internally. It is there, I think, that you and I may be able to help. Because, my friends, will you not agree that any society which begins to be doubtful of itself; in which one man looks at another and says: "He may be a traitor,"—in which that spirit has disappeared which says: "I will not accept that, I will not believe that—I will demand proof. I will not say of my brother that he may be a traitor, but I will say, 'Produce what you have. I will judge it fairly, and if he is, he shall pay the penalty; but I will not take it on rumor; I will not take it on hearsay. I will remember that what has brought us up from savagery is a loyalty to truth, and truth cannot emerge unless it is subjected to the utmost scrutiny,' ''—will you not agree that a society which has lost sight of that cannot survive?

Here, I think, is the great moral challenge to the American press—and, indeed, to all free men: to maintain loyalty to the truth, to maintain loyalty to free institutions, to maintain loyalty to freedom as a basic human value, and, above all, to keep alive in our minds and hearts the tolerance of diversity and the mutual trust that have been the genius of American life. These are what have created in America a genuine and enduring Union; they are what have kept that Union, until now, secure and free.

RELATION OF MEDIA TO
CHICAGO EVENTS*

Events make news. The reverse, perhaps unfortunately, is no less true: news makes events. It was Bishop Berkeley, was it not, who conjectured that when a tree fell in the forest with no one to hear its fall, it made no sound? It must be acknowledged that, in fact, the tree fell nonetheless. Just so, an event unreported may make little stir. But this is not to say that it did not occur. And, conversely, the chronicling of an event gives it impact; and that impact is in pretty direct ratio to the number of persons who witness it or read about it.

There is no doubt that this was in the minds of those who wrote the recently released staff report to the Violence Commission on

*Article, the Washington *Post*, December 8, 1968.

the rioting in Chicago last summer. "Perhaps the most influential contributing factor to the strength of dissent," they declared, "was the existence of communications media of all kinds. There is no question that the protesters in Chicago, as elsewhere, 'played to the cameras' or that they often did it very effectively and, this, too, had been learned in earlier protests. What 'the whole world was watching,' after all, was not a confrontation but the picture of a confrontation, to some extent directed by a generation that had grown up with television and learned to use it.''

The public's perception of any event, obviously, depends on the point of view from which the news media show it; and it depends on what the media choose to show. A photograph of a youth with blood streaming down the side of his face creates one impression; a photograph of a lone policeman valiantly resisting the onslaught of a mob creates another. And then, to begin with, of course, disorder makes news; order is a commonplace.

Well, then, how fair, how objective, were the news media in reporting the Democratic National Convention, or at least the disturbances that coincided with it in Chicago? The staff report takes note of a few "staged" incidents—or, more accurately, allegedly "staged" incidents. There can be no question that such "staging" is indefensible. No TV reporter would attempt to justify it, any more than a newspaper reporter would attempt to justify the invention of a story, an outrage also allegedly committed.

A more subtle and more serious problem arises. News media, in a sense, set the stage for the Chicago confrontation; and perhaps, indeed, they were to some extent manipulated into doing so in a fashion favorable to the demonstrators. They published in advance what the report called "an elaborate array of potential threats to the city and to the delegates." Because the Chicago authorities took these stories seriously, they prepared for Armageddon. And it may well be that this had much to do with bringing about the violence that so malevolently marred the convention.

Perhaps if the news media had ignored the Democratic convention or had, at least, ignored the conflict in the streets of Chicago, there would have been no conflict or less of it. There are many who would like to think so. For years they have gone about saying that Joe McCarthy never would have amounted to anything if the press hadn't built him up, that Stokely Carmichael would never have been heard of if he hadn't been heard of, that most of the unpleasant people in the news would not have been in the news if the news media had not considered them newsworthy. There is much truth in all this, to be sure.

The press could have ignored Senator Joseph McCarthy as a mountebank when he stood before a Republican rally about eighteen years ago and said he held in his hand the names of eighteen or fifty-two or eighty-one Communists then employed in the State Department. It could, if it had been able to act collectively, have kept this preposterous assertion from reaching the American people.

But would the American people feel quite comfortable if the press decided, say, that a contemporary Senator McCarthy's criticisms of the State Department were not worth reporting? The press works that way in totalitarian societies.

The painful truth is that the press must make evaluations of this kind all the time and that it is far from infallible in making them.

It would have been considerably more comfortable to leave the Chicago rioting unreported. "Out of 300 newsmen assigned to cover the parks and streets of Chicago during convention week," the staff report observes, "more than 60 (about 20 per cent) were involved in incidents resulting in injury to themselves, damage to their equipment or their arrest." Without their performance, the world would never have known what happened in Chicago—if it had happened. Maybe they ought to be given a passing grade— say, B +—at least for effort.

NEWSMEN AS WITNESSES

AUGUST 13, 1970

. . . During the past year or so, federal prosecutors have taken to issuing subpoenas to newsmen and their employers with a kind of reckless abandon that seems to us full of peril for the freedom of the press. Newsmen who are forced to turn informer in the name of law enforcement, forced to tell in public what they were told in confidence and forced in addition, perhaps, to divulge the sources of their information, are likely to be heavily handicapped in the gathering of news. And the burden of that handicap is certain to be borne by the readers who depend upon them for information. . . .

This newspaper is convinced . . . as we have said in an *amicus* brief . . . that "The First Amendment grants to newsmen a constitutional privilege, absolute and unqualified, to refuse in all circumstances, without penalty, to divulge to anyone any information or source, confidential or otherwise, which they obtain in the course of their professional newsgathering activities."

Undoubtedly, such an absolute privilege may entail a loss under some circumstances to law enforcement and the administration of justice. The same may be said about exercise of the Fifth Amendment privilege against self-incrimination, about the privilege generally extended to communications between husbands and wives, lawyers and clients, doctors and patients, priests and penitents, and about the exclusion of evidence obtained unlawfully. All these are sometimes used as justification for withholding from a grand jury or a court information which might be of very considerable value. But the community has deemed the cost to justice a price worth paying for the vital social values conserved by the granting of the privilege.

A privileged status for newsmen in the discharge of their professional duties serves even more important social values. For, as Supreme Court Justice Frank Murphy said twenty-odd years ago, "A free press lies at the heart of our democracy and its preservation is essential to the survival of liberty. Any inroad made upon the constitutional protection of a free press tends to undermine the freedom of all men to print and to read the truth."

If newsmen began to act as informers or as investigative agents of the government, invaluable sources of information would cease to trust them. The free flow of news has not dried up before now for two reasons. One is that prosecutors and policemen have generally respected the special situation of newsmen, have acted as though the First Amendment privilege was a fact. The other reason is that newsmen have traditionally accepted fine or imprisonment rather than disclose confidential sources of information when prosecutors have tried to breach the privilege. Whenever newsmen have thus defied constituted authority, the public has tended to honor rather than to condemn them, as though this martyrdom were a sort of *noblesse oblige* of their calling. But it is at once foolish and unfair to impose such punishment on persons serving the public interest. Besides, news sources may not always rely on the willingness of newsmen to go to prison.

The preservation of a free press should not depend upon the caprice of government officials or upon the readiness of individual newsmen to sacrifice themselves for the sake of their sources. Rather, the responsibility for preserving a freely functioning press should be assumed by the government, and particularly by the courts, as guardians of a Constitution which guaranteed an independent press because such a press was deemed indispensable to a free and self-governing society.

PRESS FREEDOM IN DAYTONA

OCTOBER 15, 1971

The editor of the Daytona Beach *News-Journal* in Florida, Herbert M. Davidson, is currently embroiled in a controversy which goes close to the roots of press freedom and responsibility. The Mayor of Daytona Beach, Richard Kane, a candidate for re-election, felt aggrieved by a column in the newspaper written by its political editor and demanded space for a column of his own in reply. When his demand was rejected, he invoked a Florida statute which makes it a misdemeanor for a newspaper to refuse to publish a response to an attack.

"We will not be intimidated," said Editor Davidson. "We have the right not to publish irrelevant, ill-tempered and vituperative material offered by candidates who wish to use the *News-Journal* as a whipping boy . . . to further their candidacies." As for the merits of this rather stinging criticism of the Mayor's column, we offer no opinion, having had no opportunity to read it. But we will defend to the death (or as near to death as our constitutional scruples against capital punishment will permit us to go) Mr. Davidson's right to decide for the newspaper he edits what columns to publish and what columns to reject. That is what Mr. Davidson is hired to do.

The Florida law invoked by the Mayor was enacted a good many years ago when it was not so clearly understood as it is today that the Fourteenth Amendment made the First Amendment applicable to the states as well as to the federal government. We should suppose it to be very nearly self-evident that a law telling an editor what he must publish would constitute an abridgment of the freedom of the press. The very core and essence of press freedom is an editor's independence—and especially independence from any sort of government coercion—to determine the content of a newspaper for which he is responsible.

There are contemporary proposals, not unlike the Florida law, propounded by conscientious persons and designed to assure readers a "right" of reply to news articles and editorial comment. But this is a "right" only in a rhetorical, not in a constitutional, sense of the word. It could not be constitutionally guaranteed without diluting and, in effect, destroying that responsibility for the content of a publication which is the inescapable correlative of freedom to publish.

Undoubtedly, newspapers have an *obligation* to publish views critical of their own. They have an obligation also to report the news accurately, comment on it fairly and serve the public interest unflinchingly. But these are not obligations enforceable by public authority. They are what are called, perhaps disparagingly, "moral" obligations—a term applied to things one ought to do but cannot actually be required to do.

THE CONSTITUTIONAL QUESTION
REMAINS UNSOLVED*

The Supreme Court's settlement of the government's suit in connection with the publication of the Pentagon Papers seems to have given no one any great satisfaction. The government did not get the injunction it sought. The newspapers did not get the explicit reaffirmation of press freedom they hoped for. And the court itself seemed to feel that it had been pressured into conducting the case, as the Chief Justice put it, "in unseemly haste."

The great constitutional question remains unresolved. No one can say now with any more certainty than before whether prior restraint of publication is, under all circumstances, constitutionally impermissible, or whether, as Mr. Justice Marshall saw the issue, it would violate "the concept of separation of powers for this court to use its power of contempt to prevent behavior that Congress had specifically declined to prohibit."

So we are left in confusion about the way the court might respond to a future case involving prior restraint. And because there is a lot less doubt about the Nixon administration's thinking on the subject, we are also left with at least the possibility that with one or two changes in its makeup—changes which could well occur within the time remaining in Mr. Nixon's first term— the present court's ambiguity may be resolved the next time around

*Article, the Washington *Post,* July 18, 1971.

in favor of some very real limitations on the constitutional guarantees of freedom of the press. The possibility seems all the more real when you consider the unique nature of the material in the *Times/Post* case, involving as it did some seven thousand pages of classified documents of widely varying sensitivity; given the incredible bulk and complexity of the documents and the time pressures at work, it is not entirely surprising that the Pentagon Papers presented this court with a difficult test case; almost any future case involving prior restraint is likely to present those Justices who seemed most ambivalent on the subject with an easier choice.

And yet it would be a mistake to conclude from all this that the choice is foreordained or that we are necessarily headed toward an era of court repression against the press. Ironically, the court has moved in quite the opposite direction in recent decisions, assuring the press virtually complete freedom from civil suits for libel in connection with information published in good faith. Libel laws represent an effort by the state to prevent the publication of falsehoods injurious to the reputation of an individual citizen. Censorship, on the other hand, represents an effort by the state to prevent the publication of material which incumbent state officials think would be injurious to the state's safety. It seems self-evident that the second area is of much greater importance to a free press and to the public's right to know what its government is doing— but the constitutional principles involved in both areas are not unrelated.

Only a month ago the Supreme Court dealt—for the third time in less than a decade—with the libel problem. In 1964 the court ruled that a public official could collect damages for libel from a newspaper only if a false and defamatory statement about him was published with "knowledge that it was false or with reckless disregard of whether it was false or not." A few years later the same standard was applied to "public figures" who were not office-holders. And last month the court declared that the standard must be applied also to a "private individual."

Writing the principal opinion for the court, Mr. Justice Brennan said: "We honor the commitment to robust debate on public issues which is embodied in the First Amendment, by extending constitutional protection to all discussion and communication involving matters of public and general concern. . . ." The rationale for this commitment is that self-censorship by newspapers and broadcasters growing out of a fear of libel suits for innocent error might keep them from fulfilling their essential function, the function of providing the public with the information essential to self-government. Justice Brennan quoted James Madison's great plea:

> Among those principles deemed sacred in America, among those sacred rights considered as forming the bulwark of their liberty . . . there is no one of which the importance is more deeply impressed on the public mind than the liberty of the press. That this *liberty* is often carried to excess; that it has sometimes degenerated into *licentiousness,* is seen and lamented, *but the remedy has not yet been discovered. Perhaps it is an evil inseparable from the good with which it is allied; perhaps it is a shoot which cannot be stripped from the stalk without wounding vitally the plant from which it is torn. However desirable those measures might be which might correct without enslaving the press, they have never yet been devised in America.*

So the press enjoys a very large measure of freedom—perhaps even more than it actually needs—respecting injuries which it might inflict upon individuals. But regarding censorship—the prior restraint of publication out of fear that it may do damage to the national security as perceived by government—the court has spoken with a far less certain trumpet. All it could say in terms of a decision on the government's suit to impose prior restraint on the publication of the Pentagon Papers was that the government had not met the "heavy burden of showing justification for the enforcement of such a restraint." This was, of course, a victory for freedom of the press in that it permitted publication to go forward. But there was no very resounding ring to it.

In the most recent of his libel opinions, Mr. Justice Brennan was joined by the Chief Justice and Mr. Justice Blackmun. But neither of these loose constructionists was able to go along with

Justice Brennan's clear assertion concerning the Pentagon Papers that "the First Amendment stands as an absolute bar to the imposition of judicial restraints in circumstances of the kind presented by these cases."

"In this case," said the Chief Justice, "the imperative of a free and unfettered press comes into collision with another imperative, the effective functioning of a complex modern government, and specifically the effective exercise of certain constitutional powers of the executive." That may be good law but it is hardly what you can call strict constructionism. It leaves a lot of discretion to the judge.

Freedom to publish without fear of censorship, or government control, is even more important than freedom to publish without fear of libel litigation. A suit for libel, at worst, entails the payment of money damages, which may or may not be ruinous to a newspaper. But a restraint on publication effectively curtails the public's knowledge. There are risks, serious risks, in freedom of the press, in leaving publishers perfectly free to determine what to publish. But the theory of the First Amendment—a theory which worked well for this country throughout its history—is that the risks inherent in a free press are not so great as the risks inherent in letting the government determine what the public should learn.

A FREE AND IRRESPONSIBLE PRESS*

. . . My title . . . is taken, with a little poetic license, from that admirable and extremely useful study published just thirty years ago by the Commission on Freedom of the Press. It was called *A Free and Responsible Press*. It found a great deal of fault, as,

*From a speech on March 30, 1977, at the Graduate School of Industrial Administration, Carnegie-Mellon University, Pittsburgh, Pennsylvania.

indeed, it ought to have done, with the performance of the press in the United States. It looked with thoroughly justified dismay at the diminution of diversity in newspapers and the growth of monopoly in newspaper ownership. It concluded that "the press must know that its faults and errors have ceased to be private vagaries and have become public dangers. Its inadequacies menace the balance of public opinion. It has lost the common and ancient liberty to be deficient in its function or to offer half truth for the whole."

The essential constructive recommendation of the commission was that the press examine itself, that it engage in self-criticism, that it embrace a spartan measure of self-discipline, that it forgo its excesses, overcome its shortcomings and behave, to put it very simply, more responsibly. For, warned the commission, "there is a point beyond which failure to realize the moral right will entail encroachment by the state upon the existing legal right."

There is nothing in this with which I can say that I disagree. The concentration of press ownership in this country has continued without abatement. Indeed, its pace has accelerated, and the narrowing control of communication has been exacerbated by monopoly ownership, in some communities, of television as well as newspapers. The reporting of news has become, in many situations, the making and shaping of news. Intrusions of the press into personal privacy and into the conduct of criminal prosecutions have sometimes done wanton injury to individuals. And it is demonstrably true that public impatience and annoyance with the press may indeed lead the public to throw out the baby with the bathwater—to impair press freedom for the sake of gaining press responsibility.

Nevertheless, I find myself greatly troubled by the idea that a "free" press must, of necessity, be a "responsible" press. Although it is a platitude of American politics that freedom and responsibility are indissolubly linked, the two are, in my opinion, essentially incompatible—at least so far as expression is concerned. . . .

I believe I know well enough what is meant by a free press—at least in the sense in which that term was used by the men who wrote the Constitution of the United States. By a free press they meant simply a press that was immune from government regulation or control. The Commission on Freedom of the Press recognized this, too. "The aim of those who sponsored the First Amendment," it declared, "was to prevent the government from interfering with expression." That is a simple and understandable idea. It is, in point of fact, an indispensable condition of any political system based on government by the people. For only a public that knows a great deal about what its government is doing— including a great deal that its government might like to conceal from it—can be in any realistic sense self-governing. . . .

In the very last opinion he wrote as a Justice of the Supreme Court, Hugo Black set forth with his customary clarity and precision the nature of this peculiar and necessary function which a free press was intended to fulfill. I can do no better than to quote him:

> In the First Amendment the Founding Fathers gave the free press the protection it must have to fulfill its essential role in our democracy. The press was to serve the governed, not the governors. The Government's power to censor the press was abolished so that the press would remain forever free to censure the Government. The press was protected so that it could bare the secrets of government and inform the people.

Justice Black was writing in that opinion about the publication of the Pentagon Papers. The government of the United States, in a frantic attempt to prevent publication of the Pentagon Papers, had gone into court asserting that publication would do irreparable injury to the security of the nation. And, in point of fact, publication of the Pentagon Papers over the government's protest was widely denounced as journalism of the most irresponsible kind. Justice Black, however, added this observation in his opinion: "In my view, far from deserving condemnation for their courageous reporting, the New York *Times,* the Washington *Post,* and other newspapers should be commended for serving the purpose that the Founding Fathers saw so clearly. In revealing the workings of government that led to the Vietnam War, the newspapers nobly did precisely that which the founders hoped and trusted they would do.''

Now, although I have, as I say, a clear idea of what is meant by a free press, I have no idea at all of what is meant by a responsible press. I am heartily in favor of press responsibility, of course—as I am heartily in favor of virtue, truthfulness and honor. But I suspect that these attributes are indefinable and depend largely upon the eye of the beholder. Even men and women so wise and learned as we who are gathered in this room this afternoon would almost certainly have sharp differences of opinion as to whether the publication of this or that piece of information called ''news'' should be deemed responsible or irresponsible.

I have sat in many news and editorial conferences and have seen editors of great judgment, experience and probity quarrel bitterly over whether certain stories should or should not be published. I entirely agree, of course, that every editor ought to strive to the limits of his ability to be as truthful, fair and ''responsible'' as it may be given him to be. But I think at the same time that the imposition of any standards of ''responsibility''—whether by government, by societies of newspaper editors, by publishers' associations, by unions of journalists or by so-called press councils— is fraught with the gravest peril to freedom of the press. Let me try to say as simply as I can why I take that view.

First, I think it is self-evident that the imposition or enforcement of any standards of responsibility whatever by the government would constitute a gross violation of the First Amendment. And the imposition or enforcement of standards by any non-governmental association or board or colloquium of chosen judges or sages would be just about equally onerous. The imposition of standards means the extirpation of eccentricity. It operates to eliminate the rebel. And in the search for truth, rebels and eccentrics are indispensable.

Second, responsibility would become, almost inescapably, synonymous with conformity. Responsible conduct would be conduct considered becoming by the majority—and more than that by people in power, what is commonly called ''the establishment.''

People in power rarely relish seeing apple carts upset. What we used to call "muckraking" and what is now known under the more euphemistic rubric of "investigative reporting" is usually looked upon by the members of the establishment as somewhat undignified and a little bit vulgar—in short, as irresponsible. The result tends to be a dampening of the ardor which might lead hungry and ambitious reporters to expose corruption, injustice or exploitation on the part of government or of powerful business corporations. Standards of responsibility operate to reinforce the natural timorousness and conventionality of the owners of the press.

One other point should be made in this connection. Newspapers (or broadcasters) who do not themselves get exclusive stories that are ferreted out by the enterprising reporters of other newspapers rarely applaud this kind of enterprise. They are much more disposed to regard the publication of news they missed as the very definition of irresponsibility.

Let us look at just a few of the recent instances of journalistic exposure which served to give the American people some significant facts of life about which they had been entirely ignorant—and about which those in power preferred to keep them that way. The House of Representatives last year voted to suppress a report by one of its own committees regarding the widespread electronic surveillance of political dissidents and non-conformists by the Central Intelligence Agency. But Daniel Schorr, one of the ablest and most energetic of television reporters, got hold of a copy of the report and made it available for publication so that interested Americans could learn about what an agency of the government was doing in the name of gathering intelligence. Mr. Schorr's enterprise was not only widely denounced in and out of Congress as shockingly irresponsible, but in addition he was taken off the air by his own network.

Just a short while ago the Washington *Post* uncovered the rather interesting fact that the CIA had been keeping the King of Jordan on a sort of retainer for about twenty years, handing over to him each month—secretly and under the table, of course—a thick wad of dollars furnished, although without their knowledge, by American taxpayers. Granted that the publication of this information was embarrassing to King Hussein and also, without doubt, to the CIA and the United States government. Granted, too, that the timing of that publication—just as Secretary of State Cyrus Vance arrived in Jordan for consultations with King Hussein—was somewhat unfortunate. Nevertheless, the results were hardly catastrophic. Hussein did not abdicate; the American government was not toppled. And the American people, who are supposed to be their own bosses in matters of this kind, had a chance to consider whether they really wanted a CIA which would spend their money in this way.

But the publication of this titillating bit of news was roundly scored as "irresponsible" by great numbers of opinion-leaders in this country—and among them, it has been reported by the Associated Press, the President of the United States himself. Should the people of this country really be kept in the dark about a matter of this kind?

One more illustration. A couple of weeks ago, the District of Columbia was held in thrall for a period by a group of Hanafi Moslem terrorists who took more than a hundred hostages and threatened to cut their heads off one by one. The development of this crisis was reported, naturally, in detail by newspapers and broadcast stations. But there were those who argued vociferously that it would have been better had the media remained mute. Even so thoughtful and libertarian an observer as U.N. Ambassador Andrew Young was heard to remark that the press coverage of this crisis put dangerous ideas into the heads of other fanatics, and that the solution might be to restrict the press by law in its coverage of violent crimes.

Can you imagine what the state of mind would have been in Washington if the people of that community had come to feel they were not getting a full account from their newspapers and broadcast stations of what was happening in that terrible crisis? The town would have been rife with rumors of unspeakable atrocities. The danger of rioting and vigilantism and racial strife would have been very great. Not the least of the functions of a free press is to impose on the people of a community a sense of responsibility by giving them confidence that they know what is going on.

There is not the slightest doubt that if the press is granted full freedom, it will sometimes abuse it. It will sometimes stultify its freedom by publishing lewd and lascivious material pandering to prurient interests—as, for instance, in the case of that genteel and fastidious publication called *Hustler*. It will sometimes publish information regarding criminal prosecutions that make the conduct of a fair trial more difficult. It will sometimes pry into the privacy of individuals and publish stories that inflict wanton injury. It will sometimes publish official secrets of the government.

Let me say something briefly at this point about government secrets. There are many matters, it must be recognized, that governments—even the governments of democracies—ought and must keep secret. No reasonable person suggests that the President of the United States is not entitled to talk with his Cabinet or his assistants or his ambassadors in private; and naturally there are many government enterprises, including, obviously, military matters and diplomatic negotiations, that should be carefully guarded.

But the responsibility for guarding them is a government responsibility. It is not a responsibility of the press. Nor should the press be considered in any sense a partner or agent of the government in discharging this responsibility. It is only after the government has lost control of its secrets—after they have been leaked or have otherwise ceased to be secrets—that the possibility arises of their being published by the press. Once that has happened, the basic obligation of the press is not to the government but rather to the people living under the government. That basic obligation is to tell the people what the government is doing so that the people may judge the government—may be, in a true sense, self-governing.

What it comes down to, in the end, is simply this: press responsibility is very desirable indeed—provided, of course, that it reflects my idea of what is responsible. You, for your part, to be sure, may prefer your idea of what is responsible. Ah, but where are we to find arbiters so wise as thee and me? Whom can we trust to exercise such discretion? And, indeed, is not the granting of authority to define responsibility the very antithesis of freedom? In short, is it not simply a mask for censorship?

Freedom of the press, like freedom of speech, is always risky. Grant it, and you can be sure that a great deal of folly as well as wisdom will be uttered. That, if you please, is the price of liberty.

The founders of the American Republic were well aware of the risks inherent in assuring to the press a complete freedom from government control. They were prepared to run those risks for the sake of the benefits they believed freedom of the press would confer. James Madison, the leading spirit in the preparation of the First Amendment, expressed this sense of comparative values most aptly:

> Some degree of abuse is inseparable from the proper use of everything, and in no instance is this more true than in that of the press. It has accordingly been decided by the practice of the states, that it is better to leave a few of its noxious branches to their luxuriant growth, than, by pruning them away, to injure the vigor of those yielding the proper fruits. And can the wisdom of this policy be doubted by any who reflect that to the press alone, chequered as it is with abuses, the world is indebted for all the triumphs which have been gained by reason and humanity over error and oppression; who reflect that to the same beneficent source the United States owe much of the lights which conducted them to the ranks of a free and independent nation, and which have improved their political system into a shape so auspicious to their happiness?

If you want a watchdog to warn you of intruders, you must put up with a certain amount of mistaken barking. Now and then he will sound off because a stray dog seems to be invading his territory or because he sees a cat or a squirrel or is outraged by a postman. And that kind of barking can, of course, be a nuisance. But if you muzzle him and leash him and teach him to be decorous, you will find that he doesn't do the job for which you got him in the first place. Some extraneous barking is the price you must pay for his service as a watchdog. A free press is the watchdog of society. . . .

I think this country is in greater danger today from excessive press responsibility than from excessive irresponsibility. With a very few exceptions, the press employs a standard of responsibility that is no more than a gloss for complacency and conformity—for letting well enough alone and for leaving the establishment undisturbed. Indeed, "responsibility" has become no more than a code word for respectability.

What do we want of a free press in this country? We want a press free enough to be able to tell us when authorities acting in the name of national security have us under secret surveillance and are tapping our telephones and reading our mail. We want a press free enough to search out venality and tell us when public officials are lining their own pockets out of public funds. We want a press free enough to probe beneath the surface of events and to report the hidden currents running there, to give us the information necessary to determine what social needs have gone unanswered, what unrests and discontents menace the good order of society, what adaptations we must make to changing circumstances in our national life. We want, in short, a press free enough to serve as a sentinel for freedom. Only a wholly independent, somewhat obstreperous and slightly irresponsible press can do all this—or even any part of it.

BIBLIOGRAPHY

Alan Barth's papers are in the Manuscripts and Archives section of the Yale University Library. Collected there are correspondence files, the typewritten text of many speeches and articles, some biographical and personal items, clippings of some of his articles for the Beaumont (Texas) *Enterprise-Journal* and for the *Guild Reporter,* and clippings (or photocopies) of most of the articles and editorials he wrote for the Washington *Post.*

Barth wrote five books:

The Loyalty of Free Men. Viking Press, 1951.
Government by Investigation. Viking Press, 1955.
The Price of Liberty. Viking Press, 1961.
The Heritage of Liberty. McGraw-Hill, 1965.
Prophets with Honor. Alfred A. Knopf, 1974.

He contributed to these books:

Years of the Modern: An American Appraisal. Ed. by John W. Chase. Longmans, Green, 1949.
The Good Samaritan and the Law. Ed. by James M. Ratcliffe. Anchor Books, 1966.
Rights in Conflict. Report of the Twentieth Century Fund Task Force on Justice, Publicity, and the First Amendment. McGraw-Hill, 1976.

Bibliography

Among the pamphlets he wrote were:

When Congress Investigates. Public Affairs Pamphlet No. 227. The Public Affairs Committee, Inc., 1955.
American Issues Forum, a Study Guide for Courses by Newspaper, No. 1. Ed. by Michael E. Parrish and Helen S. Hawkins. Publisher's Inc., 1975.

Barth's magazine articles include:

"Only the Cows Are Contented." *The Nation*, January 1, 1938.
"Financing the Fifth Column." *The New Republic*, December 2, 1940.
"Millions for Defense." *Public Opinion Quarterly*, Fall 1941.
"Lend-Lease Works Both Ways." *The Nation*, August 7, 1943.
"Television Comes of Age." *The Nation*, July 29, 1944.
"Washington at Work." *Transatlantic*, August 1944.
"F.D.R. as a Politician." *Harper's*, February 1945.
"The 'Discovery' of Buchenwald." *The Nation*, May 5, 1945.
"Truman: a Trial Balance." *The Nation*, May 19, 1945.
"FM and Freedom of the Air." *American Mercury*, July 1945.
"Fuel, Food and Freedom." *The Nation*, August 11, 1945.
"Oil Beneath the Waters." *The Nation*, November 3, 1945.
"Strategic Bombing—an Autopsy." *The Nation*, November 24, 1945.
"The Decline of the Editorial Page." *American Mercury*, May 1946.
"Rule or Ruin in Germany." *The New Republic*, June 24, 1946.
"Position of the Press in a Free Society." *The Annals of the American Academy of Political and Social Science*, March 1947.
"Outlawing Mass Murder." *The Nation*, February 14, 1948.
"The Loyalty of Free Men." *Bulletin* of the American Association of University Professors, Spring 1951.
"The High Cost of Security." *The Reporter*, July 24, 1951.
"A Moral Challenge to the Press." *Nieman Reports*, July 1952.
"The Democrats and FEPC." *The Reporter*, August 5, 1952.
"A Moral Challenge to the Press." *The Colorado Quarterly*, Autumn 1952.
"The Heat of the Headlines." *Nieman Reports*, April 1953.
"Congress on the Campus." *The Nation*, April 18, 1953.
"Universities and Political Authority." *Bulletin* of the American Association of University Professors, Spring 1953.
"Universities and Political Authority." *The Education Digest*, November 1953.
"How Good Is an FBI Report?" *Harper's*, March 1954.
"How Good Is an FBI Report?" *U.S. News and World Report*, April 16, 1954.
"Growing Abuse of an Ancient Power." *The Reporter*, March 24, 1955.
"Common Sense About Security." *The New Republic*, June 23, 1956.
"The Supreme Court's June 17 Opinions." *The New Republic*, July 1, 1957.

Bibliography

"Trial by Jury—the Southern Argument." *The New Republic,* July 15, 1957.

"The Censor of the Government." *Journalism Review,* Spring 1958.

"Why Handle Criminals with Kid Gloves?" *Harper's,* September 1959.

"Exiles in the Capital." *The Reporter,* February 4, 1960.

"Report on the Rampaging Right." *The New York Times Magazine,* November 26, 1961.

"The Press as Censor of Government." *Vital Speeches,* March 15, 1962.

"Freedom and the Press." *The Progressive,* June 1962.

"Needed: Irresponsibility." *Nieman Reports,* March 1963.

"The Levellers and Civil Liberties." *Civil Liberties,* March 1964.

"The Vital Function of a Free Press." *Nieman Reports,* September 1964.

"Civil Liberty and Individual Responsibility." *Vital Speeches,* December 15, 1964.

"Homage to Alexander Meiklejohn." *Rights,* February 1965.

"Lawless Lawmen." *The New Republic,* July 30, 1966.

"We Need a Firearms-Control Law—Now!" *Reader's Digest,* January 1967.

"Protest, Dissent and Violence." *Maryland Libraries,* Summer 1969.

"Robert G. McCloskey, 1916–1969." *Nieman Reports,* December 1969.

"The Function of a Free Press." *Bulletin,* International House of Japan, Inc., October 1971.

"Mr. Justice Black's Legacy." *The Bill of Rights Journal,* December 1971.

A NOTE ABOUT THE AUTHOR

Alan Barth was born in New York City in 1906 and was graduated from Yale University. He was a reporter for the Beaumont (Texas) *Enterprise* and worked for the Department of the Treasury before joining the editorial board of the Washington *Post* in 1943. He was a Nieman Fellow in 1948 and won awards for his editorial writing from the Sidney Hillman Foundation, Sigma Delta Chi, the American Newspaper Guild and many other organizations. He retired from the *Post* in 1972 and died in 1979.

A NOTE ABOUT THE EDITOR

James E. Clayton was a staff member of the Washington *Post* from 1956 to 1982. He was on the editorial board for thirteen of those years.

A NOTE ON THE TYPE

The text of this book was set in a computer version of
Times Roman, designed by Stanley Morison for *The Times*
(London) and first introduced by that newspaper in 1932.

Among typographers and designers of the twentieth
century, Stanley Morison was a strong forming influence
as typographical adviser to the English Monotype Cor-
poration, as a director of two distinguished English publishing houses, and as a writer of sensibility, erudition,
and keen practical sense.

Composed by Centennial Graphics,
Ephrata, Pennsylvania
Printed and bound by The Haddon Craftsmen, Inc.,
Scranton, Pennsylvania